Shale Barrel Politics: Energy and Legislative Leadership

ERIC M. USLANER

STANFORD UNIVERSITY PRESS

Stanford, California 1989

Stanford University Press
Stanford, California

©1989 by the Board of Trustees of the
Leland Stanford Junior University
Printed in the United States of America

CIP data appear at the end of the book

To Debbie, Bo, and future Uslaners

I do not want to stand here like the old sage and indicate that I have been around long enough to understand everything that goes on around here. I have not. But I have learned one thing in 19 years of public office . . . and that is politicians do not like to look too far into the future. We are very defensive and very reactive. We do not want to look beyond the next election, because if we try to plan 5 or 10 or 15 years down the road, how does that get us credit and votes at the next election?

Sen. Jake Garn (R–Utah) in the debate to abolish the Synthetic Fuels Corporation, Oct. 31, 1985 (*Congressional Record,* daily ed., 99th Cong., 1st sess., p. S14539).

The reverse Houdini consists of a politician tying himself in knots and then going before the public and saying, "Gee, I wish I could help you, but I can't because I'm tied up in knots." This concept is frequently embodied in legislative rules that contain various devices by which it can be made to appear that many legislators are being restrained by someone from doing something that they have absolutely no interest in doing.

Rep. Barney Frank (D–Mass.), "A Rhetorical Quadriad for the Busy Politician," Washington *Post*, May 9, 1985, p. A19.

Preface

S I N C E   T H E oil shocks of the 1970's, petroleum prices have stabilized, indeed even fallen, and the Organization of Petroleum Exporting Countries (OPEC) no longer controls the fate of Western economies. Indeed, OPEC now seems to be torn, not over how much money to extort from the West and the Third World, but over how to reach an accord on *maintaining* price levels. Looking back at resource constraint politics may therefore appear to be little more than an interesting history lesson. Yet even if this were the case, the lesson can be very instructive: How can a society cope with increasing tensions that threaten to disrupt politics as we have known it for the better part of the twentieth century? The energy crises brought out the worst in our political tradition and it is imperative that we learn from them lest our politics degenerate into the name-calling, and even violence, that we witnessed on the gasoline lines of the 1970's.

The prospect may prove to be all too realistic, especially in the event of another energy crisis. Many observers believe that such a crisis is inevitable, perhaps not next year but within a decade. The declining prices of 1986 may well have set the stage for greater American dependence on foreign sources amidst increasing consumption and declining domestic production. If we cannot anticipate developments in energy markets, we can at least understand what befell us during the last two crises so that we can think more clearly about energy and in particular energy politics while supplies are still plentiful. The story of natural gas shortages in the 1980's, the subject of Chapter 5, should remind us that exogenous shocks are not strictly necessary for a politics of nastiness and an economics of resource scarcity.

The lessons we must learn, as suggested by the quotations preceding this Preface, are (1) that the politics of resource scarcity are not conducive to long-range policy formation, and (2) that legislative myopia must be traced to the preferences of members and their constituents and not to the institutional structure of Congress. This means that a quick fix for our *political* energy problems is not likely to be attainable. We cannot achieve a better energy policy simply by restructuring our legislative institutions. The battle to change jurisdictions will fail for the same reason that we cannot achieve policy coordination: legislators are myopic. But so are their constituents, whom they represent on highly salient issues quite well.

I began thinking seriously about the energy issue shortly before the 1979 energy crisis and had an opportunity to witness energy politics firsthand in 1979–80 when I served as a consultant to the Select Committee on Committees of the House of Representatives, generally called the Patterson Committee after its chair, Rep. Jerry Patterson (D–Calif.). The Select Committee (see Chapter 6) had a more circumscribed task than previous reform efforts had had. Its primary focus was the establishment of an Energy Committee in the House of Representatives. In working on that project I was perhaps too enamored of the prospects for structural reform, as well as the likelihood of achieving it. It seemed to me at the time that the more limited goal of the Patterson Committee should lead it to success. Energy was also the issue of the hour, and reasonable men and women could hardly disagree that the goal of greater coordination on energy policy was desirable. I was dumbstruck when we lost by a greater than three-to-one margin.

In putting the pieces of that debacle together, I came to realize, first, that the reason we were no more successful than previous reform efforts was that the scope of the energy issue was so very broad and that the issue cut across so many different interests, and second, that legislators opposed jurisdictional reforms for the same reasons they did not like the substantive energy proposals. My work on the Select Committee led me to develop the framework offered in this book. I am grateful to staff director Don Radler for providing me with the opportunity to work with the Select Committee. Paul Rundquist and Walter Oleszek of the Congressional Research Service, on detail to the Patterson Committee, helped me understand the background of its internal politics, while Betty Abrams, Lou Alexander, and Felix Krayeski of the staff eased my path in traversing the ins and outs of Capitol Hill.

Since that time, I have been, in Dick Fenno's phrase, "soaking and poking" in the literature of energy and its economics and politics. Until recently, this effort consisted mostly of soaking. Having overcome my own energy crisis, I returned full steam to this project in the spring of 1984. In the meantime, I had drafted many papers and also spent a year as a Fulbright Professor of American Studies and Political Science at the Hebrew University of Jerusalem, where some of the ideas took shape and even initial written forms. I am indebted to Dan Krauskopf of the United States–Israel Educational Foundation for making that year so pleasurable, to Christine Rimon of the American Cultural Center in Jerusalem for providing access to American newspapers, magazines, and journals during my year abroad, and to the Departments of American Studies and Political Science for secretarial assistance and overall support and good cheer.

The Everett McKinley Dirksen Congressional Leadership Research Center provided me with a small grant to permit time off to conduct research for this project, as did the General Research Board of the University of Maryland—College Park and the College of Behavioral and Social Sciences. The Graduate School of the University of Maryland provided funds to present papers based on this research in such diverse forums as Ottawa, Rio de Janeiro, and Exeter. The University of Maryland Computer Science Center provided the resources to conduct the data analyses in Chapters 5 and 7. The data in Chapter 7 were provided by the Inter-University Consortium for Political and Social Research, which is not responsible for any interpretations herein. The Canadian Embassy also provided small grants to develop a curriculum related to Canadian politics and to develop some of the research reported in Chapter 7. The director of the Embassy's academic programs, Dr. Norman London, provided much support and encouragement for this project.

Portions of this manuscript have been previously published or presented at professional meetings. A much earlier version of Chapter 7 appeared in Manfred J. Holler, ed., *Coalitions and Collective Action* (Wurzburg and Vienna: Physica-Verlag, 1984). More recent versions formed the subject of a lecture I gave at McGill University in April 1986, as well as "Energy Politics in the United States and Canada," *Energy Policy*, 15 (Oct., 1987), "Energy Policy and Political Parties in Canada and the United States," in Martin Lubin, ed., *Public Policy: Canada and the United States* (Westport, Conn.: Greenwood Press, 1988), and "Looking Forward and Looking Backward: Prospective and Retrospective Voting in the 1980 Federal Elections in Canada," *British Journal of Political Science*, 19 (Apr., 1989). A related paper, "Energy, Issue Agendas, and Policy Typologies," appeared in R. Kenneth Godwin and Helen Ingram, eds., *Public Policy and the Natural Environment* (New York: JAI Press, 1985). A paper, "Shale Barrel Politics," that ultimately formed the basis for Chapters 2 and 3, was presented at a conference of the Atlantic Council on Canadian and American Energy Policies in Ottawa, Ontario, in 1981 and, in considerably revised form, at the Annual Meeting of the American Politics Group of the United Kingdom at Exeter in 1985. A version of Chapter 5 was presented at the 1985 Annual Meeting of the American Political Science Association, and some new analysis since then (also reported in Chapter 5) appeared in "Is Energy Voting Ideological?," *The Energy Journal*, 10 (Jan., 1989). An earlier draft of Chapter 6 was presented at the Conference on Congressional Leadership: The State of the Art, sponsored by the Everett McKinley Dirksen Congressional Leadership Research Center in Washington, D.C., in 1980.

John E. Chubb, M. Margaret Conway, Charles Stewart III, Peter Van Doren, and especially Karol Soltan each read at least 100 percent of this manuscript and greatly affected its shape and refined its arguments. Joe A. Oppenheimer and Stephen L. Elkin read portions of the manuscript and generously gave of their time in a seemingly never-ending quest to force me to get the theoretical arguments right. Many others read one or more chapters and offered criticisms and various forms of encouragement and discouragement. I list them alphabetically, so as not to implicate any more than they might wish: George Boutin, Naomi Chazan, Harold D. Clarke, Roger H. Davidson, Charles F. Doran, John Ferejohn, R. Kenneth Godwin, Robert Goodin, Manfred J. Holler, Lawrence Hunter, Patrick James, Malcolm E. Jewell, Charles O. Jones, James H. Kuklinski, Terry Levesque, Martin Lubin, Michael J. Malbin, Michael Munger, Pietro Nivola, Mancur Olson, Jon Pammett, William H. Panning, Clifford Russell, Martin Sampson, Filippo Sabetti, and Glen Toner. All have given me good advice. I might have been better off had I taken all of it.

In preparing this manuscript, I have benefited from many very able research assistants. In particular, Terry Shea did the dirty work for the content analysis in Chapter 4, while Rodger Payne assisted with the computer analyses in Chapters 5 and 7. John Gates, David Cross, Michael Mumper, Cindy Kite, Steven Hill, Gregory Rost, and Regina von Sweringen helped sort through both literature and data bases. Jim Horney and Dennis McGrath helped out at earlier stages of the project. Denise DeLima, Carol Bellamy, and Judy Staples very ably and even more cheerfully typed the various drafts of this manuscript. Working with Grant Barnes and John Feneron at Stanford University Press has been a most pleasant experience.

While this is a book about energy politics, it is more than that. It focuses on the conditions for cooperation and conflict in a legislative body. Thus, in comparing the traditional universalistic politics of the pork barrel with a very different and disconcerting type of politics on resource scarcity issues, we see a type of morality play. Thus I have chosen to introduce each chapter with one or two quotations from two important morality plays. The first, whose title emphasizes cooperation, is Ben Jonson's *Everyman in His Humour*. The other suggests the degeneration of conflictual politics into atomized behavior, which typifies contemporary resource scarcity issues including energy: Jonson's *Everyman Out of His Humour*.

This book may leave the reader with a feeling that the politics of noncooperation extends beyond the energy issue. In Chapter 8 I briefly examine the prospects for a Congress in which a lack of cooperation predominates. Rather than extend this analysis in detail, I shall deal with it in another research project well under way that derives from this one. A book on the decline of comity in Congress is in progress.

My late parents, Abe and Irene Uslaner, gave me the drive and the means to pursue an academic career, and to them I shall always be more than grateful. Our springer spaniel, Bo, was well behaved enough not to disturb my writing more than he felt absolutely necessary. Much of the time he curled up first under my typewriter and then under my personal computer and expressed quiet contentment with my progress. My greatest debt is to my wife Debbie for always, or almost always, being in her humor so that I could keep mine and bring this project to a conclusion.

College Park, Maryland Eric M. Uslaner

Contents

SHALE BARREL POLITICS

Drawing by Joe Mirachi; © 1979 The New Yorker Magazine, Inc.

Everyman Loses His Humor
on the Gas Lines

There is no taste in this philosophy;
'Tis like a potion that a man should drink,
But turns his stomach with the sight of it.
I am no such pillied cynic to believe
That beggary is the only happiness . . .

(Everyman Out of His Humour, I.i, p. 296)

D URING THE acute petroleum shortages in 1973–74 and 1979–80, tempers flared throughout the United States. The long waits on gas lines, sometimes stretching for several miles, led to incidents in which angry motorists fired pistols at those who failed to wait their proper turn. Texans, believing that price controls had been foisted on them by Snow Belt residents, displayed bumper stickers proclaiming, "Let the bastards freeze in the dark" (Landsberg, 1980, p. 81). Fearing the wrath of their constituents, legislators in the Congress refused to vote for an emergency gasoline rationing plan because they thought that any plan would be unfair to their districts. They similarly rejected a tax on gasoline designed to reduce consumption. As one member of Congress stated, "We won't get reelected if we do that" (quoted in Drew, 1975, p. 56).

In 1973 the supply of petroleum to the United States was drastically reduced as the Arab-dominated Organization of Petroleum Exporting Countries (OPEC) stopped shipments to the United States and other Western nations for their support of Israel in the Yom Kippur War. In 1979 the radical Shiite Moslem regime in Iran, one of America's major oil suppliers, initiated a second boycott of petroleum products to the "Great Satan," the United States. Decades of cheap imported oil came to an end in 1973. Even as the boycotts were called off (in 1973) or slowly became ineffective (in 1979–80), petroleum prices skyrocketed. Prior to 1974 energy costs were rising at a slower rate than inflation. From 1974 to 1978 energy price increases were slightly higher than inflation, and thereafter they far outpaced increments in the Consumer Price Index (see Darmstadter, 1983, p. 19). Energy thus rose to the top of the nation's agenda. There was agreement on the need to do something, but few people could find any acceptable solution. Goodwin (1981b, p. 679) has argued that the Congress has shown a "preference for inaction" on the energy issue. Why this is so is the subject of this book.

Why does Congress perform so poorly on energy policy (or at least the most critical aspects of it), but quite well on some other issues, especially public works? Does the answer lie in some inherent weaknesses of Congress or in poor leadership either from within or from the executive branch? I suggest not. Congressional responses to the energy crisis reflect very well the cleavages on this issue in the country. There is no coherence in Congressional energy policy formation because the legislators receive no clear signals from their constituents about what they should do. On the other hand, what Representatives and Senators should *not* do is made abundantly clear. In a world of reelection-seeking legislators, it should hardly be surprising that little gets done on contentious issues.

Energy is different from most (though not all) other issues. On few other issues are feelings both so intense and so intertwined with other domains. It is the very distinctiveness of the energy issue that makes it an excellent case study in the development of a framework for analyzing the politics of cooperation and noncooperation in legislative institutions. Especially in the U.S. Congress, cooperation is the rule. By cooperation I mean simply the willingness of at least a majority (and possibly a significant majority) to agree to enact legislation, a familiar collective action problem. Theories of legislative life detail an elaborate system of "folkways" to which members adhere so that each can benefit from a regime based on comity and reciprocity (Matthews, 1960). Such folkways are widely shared and, as I shall argue below, often lead to the formation of coalitions of the whole. Even when such universalistic coalitions do not result, the conventions they are based on permit less inclusive blocs to enact legislation. Legislators recognize that members of today's minority may be included in tomorrow's majority. A live-and-let-live philosophy prevails. This is "everyman in his humor," the norm and the basis of the first of Ben Jonson's morality plays.

The politics of noncooperation, a war of each against all, is the exception. No bloc can form a majority coalition. Such a structure of preferences is hardly unusual. What is distinctive about the politics of noncooperation is that legislators are not willing to bargain to achieve some majority-supported outcome. Members feel so strongly about the policy outcomes that they prefer no decision to any of the possible compromises. Stalemate ensues. Extreme cases point to a pathology that threatens the entire body politic. This is why it is so important to recognize the pattern of politics on energy in the 1970's and early 1980's (especially prior to the oil and gas glut of the mid-1980's that heralded a return, albeit likely to be fleeting, to pre-embargo normalcy). Politicians did not know how to handle an issue of scarcity since they were used to dealing with abundance. This is "everyman out of his humor," the more disturbing of Jonson's morality plays.

The framework I shall offer in this book is couched in terms of energy, but its applicability is much more wide-ranging. The framework is designed to outline how scarcity leads to cross-cutting cleavages that in turn lead to policy stalemate. As a pathology, noncooperation can, much as a cancer, spread throughout the body politic and threaten comity and policy formation on other substantive policy issues—as it did in the 1980's on agriculture, mining, industries facing severe foreign competition, indeed the entire budget as deficits grew beyond control, and, perversely, even the effects of the oil glut on producing states. Much of the politics of the mid-1980's can be understood in terms of scarcity issues, in particular the decline of comity in Congress. But this is too large a tale to be told in this book. The story of energy politics is interesting enough in itself to set the stage for the larger story.

Energy in the 1970's

Prior to the 1970's the emphasis on energy policy was how to produce more fuels at ever-lower prices. U.S. energy use had doubled every 20 to 25 years for over 100 years. Furthermore, consumers of electricity were paying only 20 percent of the 1940 price in 1973; consumption was growing at a rate of 4.5 percent a year between 1965 and 1973 (Kash and Rycroft, 1984, p. 8). Energy policy was predicated on the belief that supplies of fuels were virtually unlimited and that cheap energy, like cheap food, was a U.S. birthright (see Katz, 1984, p. 5). It troubled few people that the United States consumed 30 percent of the world's energy production. To be sure, there were periodic calls to realize that the world, and particularly the United States, was running out of oil. However, when the United States first became a net importer of oil in 1947 and when domestic production peaked in 1970 and then began to decline, few took notice. The real price of imported oil continued to decline (Katz, 1984, pp. 3, 12–13; Stobaugh and Yergin, 1983, p. 3). Suddenly, everything changed in 1973: the price of imported oil jumped from $3.00 a barrel to $12.00. The rate of increase leveled off slightly for a few years thereafter, but tripled again following the Iranian cutoff in 1979. These price shocks had great redistributive effects: unemployment increased, as did the value of U.S. proved oil and gas reserves—by almost $2 trillion over the course of the two supply interruptions (Stobaugh and Yergin, 1983, p. 7).

These dramatic spikes in energy costs inevitably had far-reaching effects. Everyone needs energy for heating, air conditioning, and cooking. Farmers need energy to grow food, truckers to haul it. Plastics derive from petroleum. As supplies become tight, auto sales decline and pleasure travel is reduced, threatening the economic well-being of large cities with automobile plants and small ones that depend heavily on tourism. Energy costs affect the capacity of manufacturers to compete in the world market, changing the balance of trade in ways more complex than the simple payment of high prices to oil exporters. Energy is also intertwined with questions of national security. The West, including the United States, could be paralyzed by a coordinated boycott by the producers.

Because the scope of the energy issue is so broad, the politics of fuels in the 1970's was marked by a call for a "comprehensive energy policy." The government should step in to resolve the chaos either because the market could not do so or because the market was itself responsible for the mess. What is a comprehensive energy policy? Few proponents have outlined all the components of such an approach, but it seems clear that a wide-ranging policy would (1) provide for a secure and adequate supply of energy at a cost people are willing to pay, (2) either propose a particular course of energy development for a favored fuel that is in abundant supply or suggest how an optimal mix might be obtained, (3) guarantee the protection of the environment and public health, and (4) establish a mechanism for sheltering not only the United States but also its allies from further supply interruptions. Throughout the decade following the first embargo, a plethora of studies proposing such policies were published (see esp. Schurr et al., 1979; Landsberg et al., 1979; Stobaugh and Yergin, 1983). Yet little progress was made toward achieving the goal of energy independence and security. The immediate governmental response to the price shocks of 1973 was to impose price controls on oil and natural gas. The controls were initially imposed as part of the Nixon administration's overall economic stabilization program, designed to control inflation, two years before the Yom Kippur War. The price restraints on oil lasted until the newly elected Ronald Reagan lifted them in his Presidential inaugural address in January 1981. The natural gas regulatory regime was amended in 1978, although some controls were still in effect in the 1980's. The second oil crisis provided ample evidence, as detailed in Chapter 5, that price controls alone would not suffice to resolve the nation's energy problems.

There were efforts throughout the Nixon and Ford administrations to adopt comprehensive energy policies, but they failed. Jimmy

Carter pressed harder for such a policy in 1977–78 and almost succeeded (see Chapter 2). In 1979–80 another major initiative focusing
on synthetic fuels was made and appeared headed for success when
the Congress overwhelmingly passed legislation that included the
largest expenditure in U.S. history for a nondefense program. The
early optimism faded as it became apparent that few people had
adequately thought through the economic or environmental consequences of this new technology (see Chapter 4).

Why was there such pressure for a national energy policy? The
United States has no national agriculture policy, no transportation
policy, no health policy, no water policy, not even a clearly defined
strategy to fight inflation or unemployment. What makes energy different? Or is energy so unique? Before we understand the politics of
energy, we must comprehend the pressures that confront legislators
on this issue. The story of energy politics is one of many interests, but
so is that of agriculture and economic policy generally. The difference
is that energy is in acute shortage, or at least is perceived to be so, and
that the conflicts over energy issues do not fall into neat segments. It is
the classic war of each against all.

Institutional Structure and Public Policy

To see why energy politics is distinctive, we must consider a series
of interrelated arguments that present the opposite thesis: There is
nothing special about the politics (or economics) of energy; and the
failure of Congress to enact a comprehensive energy policy is simply a
consequence of the legislature's decentralization, which makes policy
enactment difficult across a wide array of issue areas. When Congress
does succeed in enacting legislation, this "success" can be traced to
mechanisms of institutional design that "induce" legislators to cooperate with each other.

The larger question that this perspective leads to is whether institutional structures or preferences are the critical determinants of policy
formation in a democratic society. This issue has become quite prominent in recent years. It has formed the basis of debates over whether
the structure of electoral laws or changes in mass behavior led to the decline in party-based voting in the late nineteenth century (Rusk, 1970;
Converse, 1972; Burnham, 1974), whether the Democratic party reforms of 1972 led to the proliferation of primary elections and the
splintering of the party or were responses to larger political forces
within the society (Cavala, 1974; Reiter, 1985), the extent to which
committees can set the agenda in legislative bodies such as the Con-

gress by controlling the amendment procedures (Shepsle and Weingast, 1984; McKelvey and Ordeshook, 1984; Wilson, 1986), and the
importance of both the Parliamentary form of government and the
electoral systems in shaping the regional basis of conflict in Canadian
politics (Cairns, 1968; Richards and Pratt, 1979; Chapter 7 below).

Institutionalists stress the importance of institutional design; electoral laws, party rules, the structure of committee systems, and the
like determine which coalitions are formed, shape voting choices, and
restrict the range of outcomes possible in legislative bodies. Furthermore, many of them view institutional structures as autonomous actors
in structuring policy choices (Shepsle, 1986). On the other side, the
most extreme statement of the macropolitical perspective is Riker's
(1980, p. 445) contention that "institutions are probably best seen as
congealed tastes."

I argue that the macropolitical thesis is correct in maintaining that
institutions are endogenous to preferences. However, it is definitely
not the case that structures can be changed at will as preference patterns shift. Rather, there are degrees of endogeneity. The most malleable of institutions are rules for consideration of legislation. Institutionalists (see esp. Shepsle, 1986; Shepsle and Weingast, 1987, 1984,
1981; Wilson, 1986) argue that these constraints play large roles in
shaping legislative outcomes. Yet there is a growing body of literature,
both empirical (Krehbiel, 1987) and experimental (McKelvey and Ordeshook, 1984; Salant and Goodstein, 1987), that demonstrates how
preferences can overwhelm these institutional barriers. In the face of
strongly held preferences it may not matter in which order the various alternatives are considered. Decisions to impose an order may be
subject to votes by the full legislative chamber. Rules of procedure
may amount to little more than strategies by committee leaders for
inducing their most favored outcomes. Like all strategies, they may be
unsuccessful.

At the other extreme we have constitutions. Unlike rules of procedure, they are not very malleable. Constitutions establish both national institutions and restrictions on what these institutions may do.
To change any of these "basic laws" it is usually necessary to garner an
extraordinary majority. Thus changes in "tastes" or preferences over
legislative outcomes are not likely to lead to constitutional reform.
While constitutions have great staying power, they are hardly divorced from public sentiments. The institutions of a society are endogenous not to "mere preferences" but to a more deep-seated set of
values that we often call "norms" or "conventions" (Hardin, 1982).
Such norms shape the development of preferences over policy pref-

erences, although we know little about precisely how these linkages are established (but see Sniderman with Hagen, 1985). What endogeneity means in this context is that constitutions are not to be taken as given. The separation of powers in the United States reflects an underlying distrust of majoritarian government. Similarly, as I shall argue in Chapter 7, the Westminster system in Canada reflects a greater acceptance of that nation's British heritage, while the strong federalist overlay points to the country's weak sense of nationhood. To be sure, there is often little difference between constitutional and statutory dictates, both of which may not always determine policy outcomes in the society. However, the former are almost always more difficult to change than the latter, and for present purposes that is what matters most.

At one extreme, then, institutional structures are extremely pliable. Rules for the consideration of legislation on the floor of the House of Representatives, for example, must be seen as strategies to advance particular policy proposals. Committee systems are also marked by policy predispositions rather than simply subject jurisdictions. They thus attract membership from those legislators who share this partiality. In contrast to constitutional reform, which has always been viewed with considerable skepticism, legislative reform proposals have played a large role on the Congressional agenda for much of the past forty years (Sundquist, 1986, ch. 1; Uslaner, 1987). Changes in legislative structure mirror the rise of new issues or new patterns of cleavages on old issues. On the other hand, alterations in constitutional design usually signify something considerably more important than changes in policy preferences. Rather, they point to larger shifts in underlying values. Yet their lesser malleability does not mean that such institutions float in a political free space.

The importance of this insight can be found by examining intermediate cases (see Table 1.1). Less pliable than constitutions, but surely more than just strategies, are statutes establishing regulatory bodies or rules for electoral competition. Macropolitical theorists argue that these institutional structures do shape coalitions and policy decisions, but that they are not autonomous actors. It is not accidental that some states adopted ballots that provided for straight-party voting while others did not (Burnham, 1974). What varies is the degree of malleability, not the extent of endogeneity. However, the degree of malleability is directly tied to *how* institutions are endogenous. Does structure represent policy preferences or more deeply seated norms?

The debate between institutionalists and macropolitical theorists is important to an understanding of energy politics for at least three

TABLE 1.1

Malleability and Endogeneity of Institutional Structures

Institutional structure	Degree of malleability	Level of endogeneity
Constitutional provisions	Very low	Norms
Statutes establishing institutions/electoral laws	↑	↑
Substantive laws	│	│
Congressional committee system	│	│
Party rules for nominating conventions	│	↓
Rules/orders of procedures in voting bodies	↓ Very high	Preferences over outcomes

reasons. First, some institutionalists present a theory of cooperation in legislative bodies (see esp. Shepsle, 1986). Since my framework is intended to do the same thing, it is important to consider alternative perspectives. Second, the argument that institutional structures determine coalitional structures and legislative outcomes *and* that these structures are autonomous suggests that policy failures can be remedied by appropriate reform efforts. The macropolitical perspective, on the other hand, maintains just the opposite: we must realize that the very same forces that inhibit successful policy formation on a particular issue will fight reform efforts with just as much, if not more, vigor and success. The debate, then, is not only over what determines legislative outcomes, but also over the prospects for changing policies that one does not like.

Third, and perhaps most critical, is the question of *how* preferences matter, not just whether they matter. Institutionalist arguments are remarkably content-free. They are general theories of cooperative behavior. Yet the coalitions in legislative decision-making vary by issue area (Clausen, 1973). Some issue areas, notably the distributive politics of the pork barrel, are marked by successful coalition building, while others, especially energy, are not (see Chapter 2). If the institutionalist perspective is found wanting, then the justification for a macropolitical approach is that it can fill in the gaps. An emphasis on preferences focuses our attention on how the configuration of values differs across issues areas. I argue that the energy issue is marked by cross-cutting cleavages that inhibit cooperation, rather than an ideological conflict that can be resolved through majority-rule institutions. The identification of patterns of preferences that induce cooperation, on the one hand, and conflict, on the other, will show how energy differs from many other issues and, at the same time, will indicate the limits of institutional reform.

The Institutionalist Thesis

The institutionalist argument proceeds from the unremarkable observation that structures shape outcomes. This observation is obscured by the differing conclusions its followers espouse with respect to how well political systems function. The institutionalists of the new political economy by and large believe that institutional design induces stability in a world of egoistic actors; left to their own wits in a formless world, these players would certainly engage in self-destructive behavior (at least with respect to coalition formation).

In contrast, the "older" institutionalists studying U.S. politics perceive a world of more well-meaning actors, but less benign structures. They see strong legislative committees not so much as inducing desirable outcomes as blocking majority preferences within the full chamber. There is a need for some mechanism of central control, particularly party leadership (Bolling, 1965). The Congressional reforms of the 1970's that weakened the committee system led more to anarchy than to centralized decision-making. Many institutionalists blame these reforms for the failure of Congress to make policy (see esp. Oppenheimer, 1980). Some from this school go further. As debilitating to policy-making as legislative structures are, the real problem lies in the constitutional division of powers between the legislative and executive branch. The deadlock in policy formation cannot be changed without a fundamental alteration of the division of powers and a movement toward a majoritarian (Parliamentary) system of government (see Committee on the Constitutional System, 1987).

The differing evaluations of how well the political system functions, and whether political actors would behave in a self- or other-regarding fashion if left to their own devices, should not obscure some fundamental points of agreement between the older and newer institutionalists. Both sides agree that structures drive outcomes. More critically, both sides believe that when the system does go awry, structural reforms will relieve the problem of deadlock or lack of cooperation (cf. Shepsle, 1984, with Committee on the Constitutional System, 1987).

Such a view is quite compatible with the argument that structure is largely exogenous. Reasonable people only need to be shown how reforms will improve policy formation and they will rally to the cause of changes in institutional design. Those who fail to do so are virtually by stipulation unreasonable since they prefer deadlock. In contrast to constitutional reformers, institutionalists who focus on the committee system see the constitutional system as not malleable. What unites them is the belief that structural change is possible and will have desirable results.

The "new political economy" thesis maintains that agreement among legislators leading to the enactment of laws is made difficult because autonomous actors have incentives to renege on any deals that are made (Shepsle, 1986; this idea is elaborated in Chapter 2). Thus legislators construct institutions to enforce the agreements: committee systems are given the power to act as monopoly agenda-setters that present legislators with take-it-or-leave-it proposals so that cooperation among autonomous actors is induced.

I do not propose to consider the mechanics of the models of "structure-induced equilibria" here. But consider the following argument from Shepsle (1986, p. 54):

> If there is a monopoly agenda-setter—someone who is uniquely and completely empowered to pick and order elements of an agenda—then . . . there is always sufficient opportunity for him to manipulate the sequence of votes to produce any final outcome he desires; the preferences of other agents are no constraint on the final outcome. On the other hand, if the agenda is built randomly or by an "open" process in which any agent may propose an alternative, then the results imply that no matter where the process begins, there is no telling where it will end.

Legislative bodies, then, operate in anarchic worlds. Only committees that impose a take-it-or-leave-it alternative against the status quo can be sure of obtaining their most desired outcome.

Can this institutionalist perspective account for cooperative behavior in Congress? I think not. The conditions for committees to act as monopoly agenda-setters are quite restrictive and are empirically very suspect, especially in the light of the radical decentralization of decision-making in the House of Representatives that has occurred since 1974. Those changes devolved power from full committees to subcommittees, and the number of support staff dramatically increased. Jurisdictions were changed and (sub)committees jousted for control over policy areas with each other.

The structure-induced-equilibrium thesis is based on three critical assumptions: (1) committees can control the agenda through closed rules prohibiting amendments; (2) committees can protect their bills from hostile amendments that are not germane to the legislation; and (3) committees maintain control over legislation within their jurisdiction. (Shepsle and Weingast, 1987, also consider the role of conference committees as inducing equilibrium outcomes, but this is not critical for my purposes; for a critique of this position, see Krehbiel, 1987.) All three assumptions are questionable. Closed rules have become very rare in House decision-making since the 1970's (Smith, 1986a). Committee control over the amending process has sharply declined since the mid-1970's. More amendments are being offered to legislation than in the past, especially by legislators who are not on the sponsoring committees. Moreover, this has occurred in both the House and the Senate (Sinclair, 1986; Smith, 1986a). Dilatory tactics, especially those that deal with non-germane items, are becoming more frequent.

Most important among the reforms of the 1970's was one permitting multiple referrals of legislation. While most legislation is sent to only one committee, more and more bills are sent to two or more committees. Such bills are more controversial, are considerably less likely to be reported from committee, take up more time in hearings, are more likely to be amended on the floor, and are much more likely to be defeated on the floor of the House (Schneider, 1980; Select Committee on Committees, 1980b; Davidson, Oleszek, and Kephart, 1986). A committee considering a multiply referred bill acts more like a guardian of constituency interests than as a monopoly agenda-setter. It is a far cry from being a "little legislature" dominated by the baronies of which Woodrow Wilson (1967, ch. 2) spoke.

The three assumptions of agenda control are critical to the model of structure-induced equilibrium. Without them, the bases for cooperation break down and anarchy reigns (Shepsle, 1986). Yet they are empirically very dubious. In particular, they do not hold at all for energy legislation in periods when the issue was very salient. In the 95th House (1977–78), 13.6 percent of all multiply referred bills concerned energy. Only the Budget Committee, which indirectly handles energy legislation anyway, and four minor bodies (District of Columbia, House Administration, Standards of Official Conduct, and Veterans' Affairs) did not receive energy bills.

A total of 83 committees and subcommittees, including every member who served on a committee, held hearings on some aspect of energy policy. The Education and Labor Committee held hearings on a synthetic fuels bill because some of the new jobs the legislation would create fell under the Comprehensive Employment and Training Act. The Department of Energy authorization bill was split among four committees: Commerce, Science and Technology, Interior, and Foreign Affairs. Rep. Toby Moffett (D–Conn.) remarked in November 1979: "We exist in a kind of jungle warfare with regard to [energy] jurisdiction. Many decisions are being made almost exclusively on the basis of who can attain the jurisdiction and who can retain the jurisdiction and guard their turf" (Select Committee on Committees, 1980a, p. 163). Only the health issue ranked with energy in terms of multireferrals, but the former policy area was far less salient in the 95th Congress.

The institutionalist perspective was designed to account for pork barrel politics in which members of Congress secure projects for their districts. As enunciated, it is silent on whether any committees are *not* monopoly agenda-setters. I shall argue below that pork barrel committees do act in this way. Clearly others do not, and this reflects the pattern of preferences on issues that each panel considers. My overall thesis is straightforward: where the conditions for structure-induced equilibria to hold are met, as on the pork barrel, legislators' preferences are sufficient to yield cooperative outcomes (regardless of institutional design). On the other hand, some issues are marked by sharp cleavages that virtually ensure that the institutional setting will *not* correspond to the assumptions of the model of structure-induced equilibrium. Where you need a particular institutional design to promote cooperation, you usually cannot get it; where you can get it, you do not need it, because preference patterns will suffice to produce cooperation. The institutionalist thesis simply does not account either for these differences or for the endogeneity of preferences that gives rise to them.

Not only does this new institutionalism fail to explain differing outcomes across policy areas, but an older institutionalist framework similarly fails to do so. This perspective argues that Congress is too decentralized to enact any type of policy and that, in this regard, energy is no different from any other issue (Oppenheimer, 1980, 1981). Oppenheimer (1980, p. 26) dismisses the idea that the energy issue is distinctive:

One explanation [for the Congressional failure to enact a comprehensive energy policy] is that the House had not previously been called upon to deal with issues as substantively and politically complex as energy policy-making presented in the mid-1970's. If one accepts this explanation, then one might argue that the jurisdictional disputes merely reflect the complexities of energy issues, that the divisions cut across party lines, and that solutions were not readily apparent. But to do so would ignore an important point. The same types of difficulties have confronted the House on a significant number of other issues of varying complexity.

This account derives from a theoretical tradition very different from the new institutionalism. It is pessimistic about the capacity of a decentralized Congress to enact public policy, and its roots are similar to those of constitutional reformers. Both perspectives focus on structural factors as the key to understanding policy success or failure in the Congress, and both propose explanations that cut across policy domains.

The older institutionalist thesis seems oblivious to the simple fact that some major, indeed comprehensive, legislation does survive the "obstacle course on Capitol Hill" (Bendiner, 1964). Notable policy areas include civil rights, the environment, legislation, deregulation, immigration, Social Security, and tax reform (see Chapter 8). Even the radical decentralizing reforms of the 1970's have not stopped all legislative initiatives in their tracks. Indeed, the post-reform 95th and 96th Congresses (1977–80), for all of their fits and starts, performed better in dealing with energy issues than did the pre-reform 93d Congress (1973–74).

The weakness of the new institutionalist thesis is that it fails to recognize how committee systems reflect the policy preferences of legislators. The difficulty with the constitutionalist argument is similar, but more profound. Constitutional structures are even less malleable than committee systems. Yet even if we were able to change the more fundamental basis of our political system, there is no guarantee that policy outcomes would differ. Would a parliamentary system lead to a greater capacity for action on controversial issues such as energy? A quasi-experimental design would examine two polities that are otherwise quite similar except for constitutional systems.

The United States and Canada are two such polities. In the 1970's and 1980's the former had little success in enacting a comprehensive energy policy; in 1980 Canada did adopt such a policy. On the surface, it would appear that the differences are attributable to constitutional systems. Indeed, both the strengths and the weaknesses of Canada's political system have been attributed to its parliamentary form of government (see esp. Cairns, 1968). In Chapter 7 I argue that institutional structure is not the key to understanding why Canada succeeded where the United States had failed. The lessons are not only that structural reforms are exceedingly difficult to achieve but also that tinkering with institutions will not lead to fundamental changes in the policy process. What remains to be demonstrated is that a theory of preferences across issue areas can account for outcomes in both the United States and Canada on controversial issues such as energy.

The All-Pervasive Issue

Prior to 1973 the energy issue was neither distinctive nor terribly salient in the United States. Energy policy was neatly segmented into subsystems of each fuel. Coal, oil, natural gas, electricity, and nuclear power were handled separately. Coal issues included leasing of public lands and miner safety; later, environmental concerns were added to the list. Oil and natural gas were both subject to governmental regulation, but primarily this federal action was sought by producers to stabilize domestic prices against cheap imports. The electricity policy community was another convenient marriage between consumers and producers, as the federal government and state regulators both sought to hold down costs to the former by providing assistance to the latter in achieving economies of scale. Nuclear power policy centered on the development of the new technology and the protection of the security aspects of atomic weapons and nuclear-powered submarines (Kash and Rycroft, 1984, ch. 3; cf. Davis, 1982).

These self-contained policy communities were not free of any conflicts, to be sure. Many of the fiercest labor disputes in the twentieth-century United States were between coal miners and mine operators. Large oil companies were seen by many as robber barons, an image that gained credence in the Teapot Dome scandal over oil leasing during the Presidency of Warren G. Harding. The great issue in electric power generation was private versus public ownership of the production and distribution companies.

The ideological confrontations that marked pre-1973 energy policies were seen by some as having become even more entrenched in the post-embargo period. Wildavsky and Tenenbaum (1981, p. 298) argue that the new ideological issue is between preservationists (environmentalists) and industrialists, which Kalt (1981, p. 293) attributes to "a quarrel over income distribution." Energy, on this view, is an issue like other classical left-right confrontations. Eventually it will be resolved when one side gains sufficient numbers to overpower the other in the political arena. This is very likely to occur at some point if for no other reason than that there are only two sides to the issue.

If the energy issue is simply a classic example of ideological conflict, then there is little reason to adopt a comprehensive energy policy. Critics on the left view energy simply as another aspect of the economy in need of fundamental reform. The markets for energy do not work well because no market performs as economic theory would have us believe. Both price *and* quantity are manipulated by the industry. On the other hand, conservatives argue that supply is responsive to price. At an appropriate price, "new energy in massive quantities can be generated virtually anywhere on the planet" (Stockman, 1978, p. 21). Energy is just another commodity and the price shocks of 1973–74 and 1979–80 were "almost entirely *economic events*" (Stockman, 1978, p. 16; emphasis in original), stimulated largely by the sharp increases in consumption in the years preceding the first embargo. In time, energy markets will behave just like any others. Indeed, there is considerable evidence that this has happened already: world energy prices declined from 1981 through most of 1986, rebounding in the latter part of that year to just half of the peak levels of $36 per barrel. OPEC for much of that period lost control of its role as the price-setter, being barely able to control its own internal discord. Despite claims that a new energy crisis is likely to occur within the next decade, the issue has not risen on the nation's agenda.

The traditional pattern of energy politics hardly differs at all from that found on other issues. The "policy subsystems" (Freeman, 1965), or less charitably, "iron triangles," are based on mutually beneficial relations among reelection-seeking legislators, budget-maximizing bureaucrats, and policy-oriented interest groups. All the demands can be satisfied simultaneously and the system thrives when the legislators can satisfy these narrow interests by enacting legislation that provides constituency benefits and few, if any, perceivable costs.

This entire system of mutually reinforcing relationships depends on keeping the boundaries of political disputes closed. The more salient an issue becomes, the larger the number of groups that want to participate in the decision-making process and the more difficult it will be to reach an agreement. The energy crises of 1973–74 and 1979 transformed the agenda on this issue. Jones (1979b, p. 105) noted that "the *cozy little triangles* . . . had become *sloppy large hexagons*" (emphasis in original). The twin energy crises of the 1970's brought the issue to the top of the nation's agenda. In 1974 and 1979 energy ranked as one of the two or three most salient issues facing the nation according to several surveys. While the issue's salience tended to rise and fall with the rate of increase in energy prices, energy also became one of the most cited issues during Carter's 1977 push for the adoption of a national energy program (Farhar et al., 1979, p. 80; Byers and Fitzpatrick, 1986, p. 43).

The increased salience of energy led to a new style of politics on the issue. Elizabeth Drew (1975, p. 35) said that these resource constraint issues have the following in common:

gue over who must make sacrifices, the political problem may lack an obvious solution. In the United States, however, neither food nor other raw materials are quite so evidently perceived as being in short supply. On the other hand, energy seems to typify all the central features of resource constraint (or what I call shale barrel) politics. Shortages were acute, or at least perceived to be so, the scope of conflict was extremely wide, costs were readily perceived, and cleavages cut across each other.

Other issues share these traits, albeit not always so dramatically. The cleavage pattern on environmental issues is similarly bifurcated (Keeter, 1984), although the costs are less clearly perceived by most citizens and the scope of conflict is smaller because there is greater consensus on the need for environmental protection. Water supply more closely resembles energy. It is in short supply throughout the Western United States; there are centrally important questions about how to allocate it among residential, agricultural, manufacturing, and energy-producing uses, among others.

However, water is not as controversial an issue as energy. First, the scope of the conflict is restricted because shortages are generally limited to west of the Mississippi River, where farming generally cannot be carried out without irrigation (*The Economist*, 1983, p. 42). Second, water, unlike conventional energy resources, is renewable. Third and most critically, the water crunch is reported to be coming. It is not yet here.

Energy is the classic instance of a type of political issue on which cooperation is virtually impossible. It is, to reiterate, not unique, but rather may simply be a forerunner of other resource constraint political issues such as agriculture, trade, water, and the like that have already disrupted U.S. politics in the 1980's and will continue to do so in the 1990's. We have heard calls for comprehensive policies on these other resource constraint issues in the 1980's just as we did for energy in the 1970's. Why did we not hear such clarion calls in earlier years? Very simply, because there was no *perceived* imminent threat of a national crisis in a policy area.

Now, one can make a good case that the United States ought not to have a national energy policy (see Stockman, 1978). One might prefer the market as a teacher, or one may be pessimistic enough about the prospect of resolving all the complex issues of energy to fear that a comprehensive policy might actually make some things worse. Yet such a position does not explain why the United States failed to enact wide-ranging legislation aimed at preventing a future energy crisis. In 1977 Congress was presented with a comprehensive plan, which it proceeded to emasculate by the next year. Two years later the Congress did enact the Energy Security Act of 1980, but few in the legislature would claim, even at the time of adoption, that they were doing much more than taking a riverboat gamble on a quick technological fix. Congress did take a few more limited steps to encourage conservation, raise oil and natural gas prices, and develop new sources of energy, but most of the adjustments were the results of exogenous price shocks rather than legislatively determined policies.

The explanation for the legislative failure to enact a comprehensive energy policy cannot be traced to the members' beliefs that their constituents did not want speedy action. The polls indicated otherwise. Nor did legislators themselves believe in the free market, as the long history of price controls on oil and gas attests. The several attempts at enacting major legislation indicate that members of Congress rejected the entire idea of comprehensive energy bills. North of the forty-ninth parallel, in Canada, comprehensive energy legislation was enacted (see Chapter 7).

The salience of the energy issue, the demands for comprehensive policy formation, and the several attempts at such policy initiatives suggest that it is important to explain why this foray into large-scale policy-making produced paralysis. To argue, with institutionalists such as Oppenheimer, that Congress generally performs poorly in policy-making is to ignore the context of decision-making. Most of the comprehensive policies considered in committee never get much farther because they are not salient enough to force their way onto the agenda (Kingdon, 1984).

To explain why some attempts at Congressional policy-making succeed and others fail, we need to go beyond the traditional variables such as legislative decentralization or the capacity of the President to lead Congress. Presidential influence may account for changes in the way a few key people vote. But most legislators compile very similar roll-call records from year to year (see Clausen, 1973). Leadership activities may make the difference between why a particular piece of legislation is passed or defeated, but it is unlikely to explain a decade of inaction on energy legislation. Thus, however well argued, the thesis that Carter's failure to win approval for a national energy plan can be traced to his inept leadership (see Malbin, 1983) must be rejected. For an approach to be useful in comparative policy analysis, it must be capable of greater generality.

The Scope of the Study

In the pages that follow, I present a theory of cooperation and conflict in legislative institutions employing energy as the classic example of the latter. This preference-based framework acknowledges that institutional design is important in understanding legislative decision-making. But it differs from the new (and the old) institutionalism in arguing that structure is endogenous to preferences and norms. Preferences can overwhelm structural barriers to policy formation. In this sense, institutions such as committees are always "creatures of the House." Yet, perhaps even more critically, the conflicts among legislative institutions reflect those of the larger chamber and of the society. In this sense, structures represent more than what Riker (1980) called "congealed tastes."

Institutional design does not change as quickly as tastes do. Thus there must be something like a meta-preference, or norm, that shapes institutions. It is not within the scope of this study to consider how norms develop from preferences. In Chapter 3 I return to this concern and show that the committees with significant energy jurisdictions and the largest number of multiple referrals have more variegate clientele groups than other committees. This provides support for my claim that structures reflect preferences.

The theoretical framework, derivative from public choice theory, will be developed in Chapters 2 and 3. I argue that both the pork barrel and energy politics are marked by unstable coalitions (in technical terms, cyclical majorities). The framework uses ideas derived from the arguments of the new institutionalism to describe the politics of the pork barrel. However, it makes virtually no reference to institutional structure (see Fiorina, 1981b; Weingast, 1979). To account for differences in the way these issues are resolved, we need additional variables. The scope of conflict and whether voters are likely to perceive the costs of a policy decision are offered as the most promising ones.

This perspective on political structure does not deny that institutions have impacts on decision-making. It does matter that the U.S. Congress is divided into committees, and no one would deny that committees are powerful actors that generally get their way on legislation. My perspective differs from the "new institutionalism" on two fundamental grounds. First, viewing structures as endogenous to preferences implies that institutions are not to be taken as given. The power of Congressional committees, for example, derives from members' preferences. In this sense, rules of procedure and for committee governance can, to varying degrees, be viewed as strategies of legislators. Like any other strategies, these may be challenged by other players. Some, however, reflect more deeply held values and thus become more entrenched and difficult to alter. They may thus appear exogenous, but in actuality are just as endogenous but more difficult to change (since the underlying preferences are more strongly held). When people's preferences—or values—change, institutional structures will likely follow suit.

Second, and more critical, is the notion that tinkering with institutional design is not likely to lead to long-term redirection of policy. A Constitutional amendment requiring a balanced budget is not likely to lead to an outburst of fiscal restraint among reelection-oriented legislators. Nor would a single energy committee in the House of Representatives be a panacea for a lack of consensus on this issue area. Indeed, many legislators who fear the policy effects of structural realignments work to prevent such changes in institutional design for the very same reasons they try to block policy initiatives. In this sense, institutional design is a question of strategic politics. The Socialist government of François Mitterand changed the French electoral system in 1986 to try to prevent a right-wing victory in Parliamentary elections. This strategy did not work, but the new conservative government nevertheless replaced the Socialists' proportional representation system with the old single-member district plurality balloting (which, ironically, worked to the advantage of the Socialists in 1988). The lesson of the French experience is not that institutional tinkering backfired strategically, but rather that even such a critical Constitutional reform must be viewed both as endogenous to actors' goals and as anything but fixed. As such, the answer to the problems of energy policy formation in the United States does not lie in rearranging Congressional jurisdictions or in moving all the way to a parliamentary system of government. We do not get ourselves into policy fixes merely because we have poorly designed institutions.

To demonstrate the utility of the framework, I offer four case studies. Each highlights a different aspect of the framework, although all elucidate the idea of cross-cutting versus reinforcing (ideological) cleavages. The synthetic fuels and natural gas case studies (Chapters 4 and 5, respectively) show how the pattern of preferences is important. In contrast to arguments that energy politics has been marked by sharp left-right ideological shifts, I show that nothing like this degree of coherence is found on those issues. Neither the passage nor the termination of the Energy Security Act of 1980, the largest peacetime authorization in U.S. history, showed evidence of sharp ideological conflict. The six-year life span of the synthetic fuels program ended as the pork barrel was quite literally stood on its head: the all-for-one, one-for-all politics of universalism was replaced by the all-for-none conflicts of destructive coalitions of minorities (see Chapter 2).

The finding of a similar pattern of destructive coalition formation on natural gas is of particular importance since it is price regulation more than anything else that has been held to lead to sharply polariz- -ing politics (Kalt, 1981). If the two parties had been clearly demar- cated in terms of consumer-producer conflicts, and if the issue could have been framed solely on this dimension, then we would have ex- pected a very different result in the regulatory politics of 1978 than the Natural Gas Policy Act (NGPA). The crazy-quilt pattern of regu- lation and deregulation established in the legislation set the stage for the formation of destructive coalitions of minorities just four years later at a time when gas supplies seemed to defy the law of sup- ply and demand.

These case studies focus on preference configurations. The two re- maining examples consider both preferences and institutional design. The attempt to establish an energy committee in the House of Repre- sentatives was based on the fallacious assumption that tampering with institutional design would lead to the establishment of a structure- induced equilibrium on energy politics where no preference-induced equilibrium existed (Chapter 6). Instead, the key actors on energy policy in the Congress "rolled" the committee proposing the struc- tural reform. Institutional design was clearly endogenous to prefer- ences over outcomes.

Canada's adoption of a National Energy Policy in 1980 is instructive because Canada is in many ways (mostly economic, but also cultural) similar to the United States (Chapter 7). Surely, few other nations have as much in common as these two. Why Canada succeeded— although its National Energy Program was effectively repealed in 1985—is the subject of my inquiry. (One does not have to agree with any aspect of the program to argue that Canada was successful in *enacting* a comprehensive program.) The structure of preferences on energy in the two countries is the key to understanding the dif- ferences in policy outcomes, not the more commonly supposed vari- ations in the structures of legislative-executive conflict and over federal-provincial/state relations. Arguments that these regime-level variables are important generally fail to recognize that institutions mirror the underlying values (norms) of the two societies. Thus the Canadian case study shows both how preferences can overwhelm in- stitutions and how institutional structures are rooted in the norms that underlie the pattern of preferences on energy issues.

Finally, in Chapter 8 I consider the implications of the study for models of legislative decision-making, the prospects for reform of institutions, the strategies available to legislative leaders, and the possible spread of the politics of noncooperation to other issue areas.

The criteria for selecting the case studies was that each should represent a major energy initiative either confronting the Congress or relevant to the way the issue is handled in the United States. The rationale for developing the framework was to account for policy failure in legislative institutions by focusing on how preferences are structured and making comparisons with the most prominent models of policy success. Deriving predictions and testable propositions was of much less consequence. Hence, the major criterion for evaluating the framework should be whether the case studies show patterns of conflict that I shall posit.

I make no claim that the framework covers all energy areas. Indeed, I am quite certain that it does not; energy research and development policy is much more like traditional pork barrel politics than the shale barrel (see Chapter 2, n. 7). I do not view this as a serious flaw in the framework. The framework is only in part designed to explain energy politics. Rather, its focus is on a type of political pathology, a breakdown in cooperation. If not all energy issues fit this characterization, this is little cause for alarm. Some other issues might fit better. Thus my agenda is not to test the framework to see whether a whole range of energy issues fit a set of predictions, but to explicate how some of the major energy concerns of the 1970's and 1980's do exhibit the pathology of the framework.

Shale Barrel Politics

> . . . let him spend, and spend, and domineer till his
> heart ache . . . (*Everyman in His Humour*, I.i, p. 27)
>
> Who is so patient of this impious world
> That he can check his spirit or rein his tongue?
> (*Everyman Out of His Humour*, Prologue, p. 285)

I N   T H I S   chapter I develop a theoretical framework that contrasts situations in which cooperative behavior by legislators will
and will not occur. An issue or a set of issues is proposed in a legislative body, but the range of possible outcomes (including the status
quo) is very large indeed. How do legislators form majority coalitions?
Under what conditions will a single alternative secure sufficient support? Do legislators seek outcomes that obtain the support of only a
simple majority of their colleagues?

Consider two polar examples: one in which cooperation among virtually all actors is the norm (universalism), the other in which cooperation generally is not achieved (disaggregation). Technically, a universalistic solution is one in which the coalition that forms on a piece of
legislation includes every member of the voting body. It suggests a
coalition across issue areas in which all members obtain something of
value for their constituencies. All members cooperate for mutual advantage. On the other hand, a disaggregative outcome is one in which
only the core supporters of a proposal, those with a direct constituency stake in it, vote for the bill. At the extreme, a series of bills would
each fail in the House of Representatives by votes of 1–434. This is in
sharp contrast to the simple inability to form any sort of majority
coalition. While neither of these scenarios are very likely to be observed empirically in their extreme forms, they do typify the differences between pork barrel and energy politics.

First I outline some central assumptions of the model to be presented and then move to discussions of the key differences between
these policy areas, the widely known family of models for explaining
universalism, and a derivative framework for the politics of disaggregation. Specifically, both the universalistic and the disaggregative
domains will be modeled as involving cyclical group preferences that
yield strategic Prisoners' Dilemmas. In the former instances, the ob-

stacles to cooperative behavior are overcome, while in the latter they are not. In Chapter 3 I examine several theses about how such cooperative behavior comes about and relate them to the models proposed in this chapter. The scope of conflict in the policy area and the extent to which costs imposed on constituents are readily perceived by the voters are the key variables in the analysis of whether agreement can be achieved.

The guiding assumption behind the entire enterprise is not only that preferences of both legislators and constituents matter, but also that they account for differences in observed behavior (cooperative or noncooperative) in the legislature itself. Members of Congress are posited to be primarily reactive agents. The conflicts in the institution largely, though not exclusively, mirror those in society. One cannot deny that certain powerful members with key institutional positions (chairs of important committees) can and often do set the legislative agenda to their own satisfaction rather than to that of their fellow legislators or the country at large.

Obstructionism is the exception, not the norm. Indeed, it must be for a large chamber with relatively complex rules of procedure, especially one in which each member believes that he or she has been given an independent mandate (Matthews, 1960, ch. 5). Thus it should come as no surprise that the strong public support for civil rights ultimately led to the adoption of such laws even in the face of obstructionist leaders and similar tactics such as Senate filibusters. Indeed, when the tide of public opinion is strong, as it was on the Clean Air Act of 1970, a piece of legislation can be adopted quite readily even when confronted with substantial interest group opposition (Jones, 1975, esp. ch. 7).

The theoretical framework to be developed to explain why universalism occurs in the Congress some of the time and disaggregation at other times employs micro-level assumptions about legislators' behavior. Yet in order to understand the circumstances that give rise to universalism and disaggregation *within the Congress*, we must comprehend the nature of conflicts *outside the halls of Congress*. A strictly institutional account of whether cooperation can be achieved is incomplete.

The Assumptions

Although the framework to be derived relies heavily on concepts of the field of public choice, the study of political problems based on the methods and assumptions of economic theory, it will not be expressed very formally. This is a tale of words, not of symbols, and even the highly technical arguments of others will be presented in as straight-forward a manner as possible. First, of course, we assume that people are rational agents. They have some goals and pursue strategies of ac-tion that will maximize the probability of attaining the goal.[1]

While I agree that legislators also seek power and to make good public policy (Fenno, 1973; Dodd, 1977; Uslaner, 1978a,b), it is at least analytically convenient to assume with Mayhew (1974) and others that the primary goal of legislators is to secure reelection.[2] Con-stituents may have more diverse priorities, but one assumption in such models is that they ultimately add up all the pluses and minuses of the incumbent's perceived behavior across their concerns, make similar calculations based on the challenger's promises, and then de-cide whether and how to vote.

However, legislators typically don't behave as if voters merely weigh up their good and bad points against those of their opponents. In-stead, they avoid taking risks and seek to avoid alienating their con-stituents whenever possible in order to maximize the probability of being reelected. They adopt what we might call a *mitzvah* theory of the electorate. According to Jewish religious law, there are 613 *mitzvot*, or good deeds, that each person must perform in order to achieve salva-tion. However, the scorecard does not weigh each such deed equally (Rosten, 1970, pp. 252–53). In the legislator's calculus, then, certain acts are more critical than others, and foremost is the negative *mitzvah*: thou shalt not alienate thy constituents on a highly salient issue (cf. Kingdon, 1973, pp. 41–42; Fenno, 1978, pp. 141–46). To secure re-election, legislators either shun controversial issues altogether or simply toe the dominant line among their electorates. As Fiorina (1981b) has shown, incumbents have substantial asymmetric advan-tages over their challengers in bringing benefits to the district (the

---

[1] Axelrod (1984, ch. 1) argues that one does not even need the assumption of ratio-nality to analyze coordination problems. His argument is novel, but I am not sure that I agree with it. The assumption, which he also makes, seems harmless enough.

[2] Even more interesting than the claim that the assumption of rationality is not needed (see n. 1) is the argument that the reelection goal is not required to yield univer-salism on the pork barrel. Imagine a legislature selected by lot from a population. It would still be reasonable to assume that farmers would press for agricultural price sup-ports for other farmers (including, at the next selection of the legislature, themselves), and so on. As long as there are social groups and no clear-cut antagonisms between those who govern and the opposition, there will be universalistic politics. Perhaps the only situations in which we would not find such logrolling are behind Rawls's (1971, pp. 136–42) "veil of ignorance" or in a society torn apart between two factions that have little hope of reconciliation. None of this denies that legislators do see electoral benefits in pork barrel activity. What is critical is that legislators would pork-barrel even without an electoral connection.

politics of distribution) and in helping people with personal problems, but not in questions of policy.

However, most members of Congress recognize that even this risk-averse strategy does not curtail their activities drastically. Most Congressional elections do not revolve around issue stands, and legislators generally benefit from providing tangible benefits to constituents even if taxes have to be raised to finance these projects. Olson (1969, pp. 482–94, n. 9) explains this nicely: "In the United States Congress, logrolling probably leads to a greater expenditure when projects of a 'pork barrel' type are at issue. In most of these cases the projects are of a tangible type, and a Congressman is more likely to be identified in his district with such a project than with a general increase, which could not in any case usually be traced to any one package of local projects." This is the argument of the "fiscal illusion": people see only benefits from a policy because the gains are positive while the costs are hidden in a more general tax bill.[3] The citizen-taxpayer-voter does not readily make the connection between the size of a tax bill and the expenditures for which the assessments may be increased.

These assumptions then paint a portrait of a legislature in which the members are myopic. Legislators who are primarily concerned with reelection will be willing to increase the marginal costs to voters of politically popular programs, especially since they believe that the costs will likely not be perceived. As for controversial issues, either they will be avoided or the members will adopt the most popular solution—that of the median voter in each district (Downs, 1957). However, there is no guarantee that any proposed alternative will be the choice of the median voters in a majority of districts. Controversial issues, in particular, are often complex and will thus have more than two possible outcomes. Thus, over a series of votes, there may well be no alternative that has the support of a majority of legislators—or their constituents (Riker, 1958).

Everyman in His Humor: The Politics of the Pork Barrel

Highly salient and controversial issues such as energy stand in stark contrast to the more routine decisions made by the Congress on how to distribute benefits to constituents. In the next two sections I com-

[3] The argument on the fiscal illusion has also been made by Barry (1965, p. 318) and Mayhew (1974, p. 88). There is a limit, of course, and recent years have been marked by tax revolts in various states (California, Michigan) and localities with at least short-term electoral consequences. The task of the strategic politician is to recognize when that limit is being approached.

pare these two polar issue domains. Of course, they do not exhaust the set of policies considered by the Congress, but that is not important for my purpose. Distributive or pork barrel issues are the classic example of "everyman in his humor," of how legislators cooperate with each other. On the other hand, energy and related issues (such as water in the West) are the archetypes of the breakdown of cooperation. Thus, to understand "everyman out of his humor," we must first comprehend the forces that lead to happy endings.

Perhaps no single result is as well established in the literature on Congress as that pork-barreling is believed by members of Congress to help their reelection efforts. By pork barrel I mean *any* project that is basically distributive. The hallmark of pork barrel politics is universalism. Every member shares in benefits and the votes to enact such distributive bills pass overwhelmingly, often unanimously. The benefits to a legislator are projects for the district. Shepsle and Weingast (1981, 1984; Weingast, 1979) have developed a family of models that explain why legislators choose to adopt pork barrel projects even when they are not economically justified and also why virtually all legislators support such legislation. Distributive projects are marked by benefits that are assumed to accrue entirely within single Congressional districts. Costs, on the other hand, are spread diffusely through taxation across all districts. If all proposals are adopted, however, net benefits cannot exceed net costs. This is hardly a recipe for universalism. Instead, a more rational model might appear to be one in which only a minimal winning coalition forms; that is, only a bare majority of members have their projects adopted, while the costs are spread across all districts. If the United States had a strong party system, we would expect coalitions large enough to include *all* members of the majority party rather than a simple majority. But we do not find evidence of such coalitional activity on pork barrel legislation (Mayhew, 1974, pp. 111–15).

Simply noting that the U.S. Congress is not marked by strong parties doesn't fully explain the phenomenon of universalism. Any minimal winning coalition (or variant thereof) that might form is unstable. Nobody but legislator A would support funding for a pork barrel project for A's district. If each proposal were considered separately, all would fail. Instead of considering each proposal on its own, members package projects together in an omnibus bill. Such legislation usually collects all the individual projects for a given issue area, but it may well involve deals cut across policy domains. Each omnibus supported by a bare majority could be upset by a slightly different majority. If the minority Republicans received no projects, for example, they could "lure" some Democrats out of that party's coalition by funding their projects even more generously. But this permutation could be upset by yet another permutation of the 51 percent of members needed to pass a majority omnibus, and the cycle could go on indefinitely.

The problem of cycling or cyclical majorities was brought to the fore in the literature on decision-making in democratic societies by Arrow (1951). Suppose that we have a legislature of at least three members or blocs. For convenience, we shall label them according to the "three-party" system of the United States. The Northern Democrats would prefer a majority omnibus of projects to include themselves and the Southern Democrats, but would be willing to accept a coalition with Republicans if necessary. Southern Democrats would most prefer to coalesce with their ideological soulmates, the Republicans, but the GOP legislators believe that the Northern Democrats are more reliable partners since they have the greater wherewithal to make a deal stick. These preferences are, of course, entirely hypothetical. What we see from the orderings in Table 2.1 is that (1) a majority of the parties prefers an all-Democratic coalition to one involving Northern Democrats and Republicans, and (2) a majority also prefers a coalition of Northern Democrats and Republicans to one of Southern Democrats and Republicans, but (3) a majority would vote for the conservative coalition over an all-Democratic bloc!

Given these preferences, which are inevitable when the parties are composed of members whose strong first choice would be the adoption of their own projects and the defeat of everybody else's, there is no majority bloc that could form once and for all. Someone could always propose a more attractive coalition. What is worse, this is not just an obscure example. Under a wide variety of reasonable conditions, these cyclical preferences will ensure that any attempt to form majority coalitions through logrolling will be unstable (Bernholz, 1977; Miller, 1975; Oppenheimer, 1973; Schwartz, 1977). Even more frustrat-

TABLE 2.1

Majority Omnibus Coalition Preferences of Party Blocs

Preference	Northern Democrats	Southern Democrats	Republicans
First choice	ND + SD	SD + R	ND + R
Second choice	ND + R	SD + ND	SD + R
Third choice	SD + R	ND + R	ND + SD

NOTE: Preferences are hypothetical preferences. ND + SD indicates a possible coalition between Northern Democrats and Southern Democrats.

ing is the result that strategic legislators trying to extricate themselves from these cyclical preferences by trading votes across issues would likely make themselves all worse off (Riker and Brams, 1973; Uslaner and Davis, 1975), at least as long as there is no guarantee that legislators will be prohibited from continually seeking better deals.

Preference cycles lead to unstable logrolling cycles. Minorities are always able to upset existing coalitions. Each legislator or bloc is confronted with a strategic choice: to continue seeking the "cheapest" winning coalition in which the member is included or agree to be part of a coalition of the whole, which would guarantee support for every project but be much more expensive. Every member would prefer the former (Ferejohn, Fiorina, and McKelvey, 1984). The cheapest winning coalition is composed of a simple majority of legislators (for a unicameral body)—and, globally, this means the majority whose projects cumulatively cost the least. Of course, not every member would prefer this outcome, especially the legislators with more expensive demands. This winning coalition thus excludes a large number of members. However, the losers can offer to bribe legislators in the winning coalition with other policy payoffs (Butterworth, 1971). Particularly if the absolute cost of the projects is not a vital concern to members because of fiscal illusion to their constituents, there is plenty of room for maneuvering. If one excluded member can attempt to bribe his or her way into a victorious coalition with a simple majority of legislators, then so can any other.

Each legislator thus faces a strategic dilemma: either continue to seek a better bargain or agree to support a universalistic outcome. But the first choice of every legislator is a cheap minimum winning coalition of which he or she is a member. The second choice is the outcome in which all projects are funded. In both situations the legislator can present the project to constituents as his or her work, but in the first scenario the member can also claim to be a guardian of the nation's pursestrings. The third choice would be the no-agreement point, in which legislators continue to seek out better deals for themselves at the expense of others. Technically, this is a continuation of cycling ad infinitum. Practically, it means that no projects are funded, since sooner or later the legislative clock will stop, even if this means affirming deadlock. Finally, members would least prefer some minimum winning coalition being formed without their pet projects being funded. In this case, the member's constituents would share in the costs of the funded projects but receive no benefits of their own. The strategic problem the legislators face as a result of cyclical group preferences on the projects for each district is analogous to that of the logic of collective action, in which rational actors refuse to contribute to the provision of a collective good because each hopes to be a "free rider" on the other citizens (Olson, 1965).

When no alternative is preferred to the others by a majority of voters, some degree of cooperation is needed to prevent a stalemate. This is the way a simple preference aggregation game, in which we simply count the votes on each side of an issue, is translated into a coordination problem (Schelling, 1960). The most famous characterization of efforts to induce cooperation rather than straightforward competition is the Prisoners' Dilemma or PD (Rapoport and Chammah, 1965). The problem facing each of two prisoners, in the simplest form of the game, is that they have been captured by the police after committing a crime. The authorities offer each prisoner a deal: if either agrees to testify against the other, that prisoner will receive a reduced sentence, while the other will receive a longer jail term. If both refuse to assist the prosecutor, then each will receive a moderately long term, longer than what the tattletale would receive but less than what the prosecutor could obtain with the tattletale's testimony against the other prisoner. If, on the other hand, both testify against each other, both serve longer terms—but since the testimony of each is somewhat tainted, their sentences are less severe than they would have been had only one of them testified. Thus each prisoner must decide whether to cooperate with the other or to defect to the prosecution. A possible configuration of payoffs in the PD game is represented in Table 2.2. Table 2.3 represents the strategies in the game, where C_1 represents cooperation by prisoner 1 and D_1 defection by 1.

TABLE 2.2

Payoffs in the Prisoners' Dilemma

PRISONER 1		PRISONER 2	
		C_2	D_2
	C_1	(1, 1)	(−2, 2)
	D_1	(2, −2)	(−1, −1)

TABLE 2.3

Strategies in the Prisoners' Dilemma

PRISONER 1		PRISONER 2	
		C_2	D_2
	C_1	(R, R)	(S, T)
	D_1	(T, S)	(P, P)

A PD game is defined by the following inequality:
$$T > R > P > S,$$
where

> T is the payoff for "temptation" to defect, i.e.,
> what a player receives when the other(s)
> cooperate(s) but he/she defects.
> R is the "reward" payoff for a player who coop-
> erates when other(s) also cooperate(s).
> P is the "punishment" payoff for failure to co-
> operate when other player(s) also fail to
> cooperate.
> S is the "sucker's" payoff for cooperating when
> other player(s) do(es) not cooperate.

The inequality merely defines the preference order among outcomes that defines the dilemma.

Hardin (1971) first explicated collective action problems as Prisoners' Dilemmas. While most discussions of logrolling have focused on the problems arising from cyclical majorities, many analysts have also noted that the PD characterizes the legislative pork barrel as well (Axelrod, 1984, ch. 1; Barry, 1965, ch. 14; Hardin, 1982, ch. 5; Riker and Brams, 1973; Schwartz, 1981; Uslaner and Davis, 1975; Weingast, 1979). The usual formulation of the pork barrel PD represents the universalistic coalition of the whole as the cooperative outcome and the formation of a cheaper minimum winning coalition (composed of just enough members to pass a bill, or 218 Representatives in the House) as defection. This perspective is marred by two problems. First, because members are uncertain whether they will become members of a minimum winning coalition, they must estimate expected probabilities of inclusion; this does not necessarily correspond to a PD game (Sen, 1967). Second, even though we *can* represent the four payoffs in the PD game (as appropriately discounted by probabilities of inclusion in a winning coalition), the traditional accounts have not specified which strategies such payoffs represent. This is not a trivial omission; no straightforward linkage of strategies, outcomes, and payoffs seems feasible in the n-person game.[4]

This does *not* mean that the pork barrel cannot be fruitfully represented as a PD. Representing it as a PD requires, however, refocusing

[4]The strategic situation faced by each legislator is not simply whether to join some minimal winning coalition, but which coalition to join as well. Without any structuring of conflict, each member must choose among the (435/218) possible such coalitions that might potentially form. This yields (435!)/(218!) (217!), clearly an unmanageably large number of potential coalitions. The number would be only marginally reduced by the exclusion by each legislator of coalitions that did not include that legislator.

our attention to a game between the two Congressional parties, where the defect stragegy of forming a minimum winning coalition will necessarily refer to a bloc of legislators from the (majority) party. The account I offer places the pork barrel PD within the context of explanations of universalism in Congress. It does not imply, however, that the all-cooperate strategy is dominant in a game-theoretic context. All I seek to do is show how the pork barrel can be modeled within the PD framework; explanations of why universalism occurs derive from assumptions about risk and from the framework developed in this and the next chapter.

The major pork barrel committee in the House of Representatives, the Public Works Committee, operates on the basis of a strong norm of unity within each of the legislative parties. At the same time, the major goal of committee members is to bring specific benefits back to their districts (Murphy, 1974, pp. 174, 170). Thus it is not surprising that the most desired outcome of the pork barrel game is the adoption of a purely partisan distributive bill. But according to Murphy (1974, p. 179; cf. Fenno, 1973, pp. 92–94, on the Interior Committee), "the two parties *distrust* each other. . . . Since each party values majority status, each expects the other to porkbarrel—to authorize and appropriate projects on the basis of political clout or favor—when the other is in the majority. Because they foresee the possibility of partisan allocations and because they take the allocation of public works benefits so seriously, congressmen insist on a fair allocation of the goodies" (emphasis in original).

If we think of legislators' calculations in terms of the longer-term threats to their electoral security rather than in terms of the immediate legislative agenda, we can see a strategic Prisoners' Dilemma embedded in the members' preferences. The strategic choice each legislator, as a party member, must make is whether to press for a bill that funds only projects for the member's party or for both parties. All Democrats (or Republicans) prefer a cheap minimum winning coalition that would yield a bill providing funding only for projects in districts of Democratic (or Republican) members. If legislators were to make their calculations solely on the basis of the partisan balance at the present moment, the majority party would always impose its cheap minimum winning coalition on the minority party. But as noted above, the fear of defeat in an election at some future time cautions against such a strategy.

The most preferred outcome for members of the Democratic party would be a Democratic minimum winning coalition, in which only projects for legislators from Democratic districts would be funded. This is clearly the least desirable outcome for Republican members.

Similarly, Republican members would most prefer to fund only their own projects and would least prefer only Democrats to receive pork barrel projects. The fear that one will be excluded from the spoils of elective office leads, as I shall show, to the outcome in which legislators from both parties cooperate by supporting each others' projects.

Strategically, the situation is somewhat more complex. I assume first that legislators vote in blocs with their parties. Each member must decide whether to cooperate (to support projects for the other party as well as for one's own) or to defect (to support only those projects for one's own party). The strategies and outcomes are outlined in Table 2.4. When both parties' legislators cooperate, the universalistic outcome obtains in all cases. Consider next what happens when Democrats decide to cooperate and Republicans opt to defect. In this case, when the Democrats are in the majority, there will be a universalistic outcome. Democratic legislators will vote for their own projects and for those of the minority party, while Republicans will only support funds for GOP-particularized benefits. Because the Republicans are in the minority, however, their votes will not determine the outcome. Thus programs for members from both parties will be approved. Consider now, however, what will happen when the members employ the same strategies but the Republicans are the majority party. In this case, only projects for GOP members will be approved. Thus the Democrats-cooperate/Republicans-defect strategy will yield either a universalistic outcome or a situation in which only Republican projects will be funded. If we reverse the parties' strategies, it is easy to see that the outcomes will be universalism when the Republicans are in the majority and a funding of just Democratic projects when the Demo-

TABLE 2.4

The Pork Barrel Prisoners' Dilemma

| | | DEMOCRATIC STRATEGIES | |
		Cooperate (support projects for all members)	Defect (support only projects for Democratic districts)
REPUBLICAN STRATEGIES	Cooperate (support projects for all members)	Universalism always	Democratic majority: Democratic mwc Republican majority: Universalism
	Defect (support only projects for Republican districts)	Democratic majority: Universalism Republican majority: Republican mwc	Democratic majority: Democratic mwc Republican majority: Republican mwc

NOTE: mwc = minimum winning coalition.

TABLE 2.5

Payoffs, Outcomes, and Strategies in the Pork Barrel Prisoners' Dilemma

Payoff	Outcome	Strategy
Temptation	Defecting party always receives projects, cooperating party receives projects only when in majority.	One party supports only its own mwc.[a] Other party supports projects for both parties.
Reward	Universalistic outcome always prevails.	Both parties forsake their own mwcs to support projects for both parties.
Punishment	Majority party's mwc prevails.	Each party seeks to impose its own mwc. Party with majority wins.
Sucker's	Defecting party always receives projects, cooperating party receives projects only when in majority.	One party supports projects for both parties. Other party supports only its own mwc.

[a] Mwc = minimum winning coalition.

crats are in the majority.[5] Finally, if each party decides to defect, the party that controls the Congress can impose its own cheap minimum winning coalition on the other. Assuming that neither party will command a continuous majority over time, the double-defect strategy will mean that alternating minimum winning coalitions will prevail.

Is this a PD game? In Table 2.5 I outline how the strategies and outcomes correspond to the payoffs in the Prisoners' Dilemma. Let me expand on that presentation. Each party would most prefer to obtain only its own pork barrel projects. However, no outcome produces this simple result. Let us consider how a Democratic member might treat the options in Table 2.4, recognizing that the situation is symmetric with respect to Republicans. The upper right-hand cell in Table 2.4 corresponds to what would normally be the temptation payoff for the Democrats. As such, it should be the most preferred. And indeed it is, under the assumption that neither party knows the frequency with which it will be in the majority in the future. When there is a Democratic majority, this cell indicates the party will obtain its partisan minimum winning coalition. When the party is in the minority, the universalistic outcome will obtain. No matter which bloc

[5] My colleague Karol Soltan provided this formulation, which is far more elegant and plausible than, though logically similar to, one I had developed.

controls the Congress, all Democratic districts will receive projects under this outcome. Furthermore, because at least part of the time Democrats can expect to be the majority party, there will be occasions when the party can reduce the costs of the pork barrel by excluding the costs for Republican projects. Hence, the payoff for this cell is higher than for the upper left-hand cell, in which the universalistic solution is always reached.

It is just as clear that the lower left-hand cell represents the worst situation for a Democrat. Party members will receive either their own projects while Republican members also get theirs or nothing while a GOP minimum-winning-coalition bill is imposed on them. When the Republicans are in the majority, assuming legislators from that party choose to defect, Democrats can never hope to obtain any pork, regardless of the strategy they employ. On the other hand, when the Democrats are the dominant party, still assuming GOP noncooperation, majority members have the choice of either supporting universalism (lower left-hand cell) or imposing their own minimum winning coalition on the GOP (lower left-hand cell). The latter option clearly has a higher payoff.

The only somewhat difficult comparison is that between the universalistic outcome (upper left) and alternating minimum winning coalitions (lower right). If members do not have good reason to assume that their party will be dominant in the future, then the expected values of these outcomes might well be estimated to be the same. On the other hand, risk-averse members would always prefer the security of knowing with certainty that their projects would be funded to the imponderable question of when the other party might attempt to ride roughshod over minority interests. Furthermore, legislators believe that pork-barreling activities aid the reelection attempts of incumbents and that this advantage is not something, like issues, that challengers can match. Thus the more successful a member is at pork-barreling, the more likely the member is to be reelected—and conversely, the smaller is the probability that the other party's candidate will be able to capture the seat. In the aggregate, this means that the minority party will be less likely to (re)capture control of the Congress. For this reason, perhaps above all others, risk-averse legislators prefer the strategy of universalism to imposing partisan minimum winning coalitions.

These preferences correspond to those of the Prisoners' Dilemma. While there is no preference cycle among these alternatives, we can trace the PD characterization to a problem of unstable majorities. Each district (and, hence, the legislator from that district) would most prefer to obtain a program for itself but not to have to pay for any other projects. While the alternating minimum winning coalitions that result from the both-parties-defect strategies are hardly the same thing, in a technical sense, as preferences that cycle, the insecurity that both breed among legislators is likely to be indistinguishable from case to case.

In the two-person PD the outcome depends on the strategy chosen by the other player. Resolution of the n-person PD, on the other hand, does not depend on everyone's cooperation (Schelling, 1978, ch. 7; Hardin, 1971). In a legislature, all one generally needs is a simple majority. However, the bad news in either game is that the dominant outcome is for every player to defect, regardless of the behavior of other players.[6] Once defection occurs, as it surely will, it will become endemic. While the omnibus package appears to be the only stable solution, we need some way to obtain cooperation in the first place. In particular, how can cooperation be secured without some formal institution that can invoke sanctions against defectors?

A simple answer to the cooperation problem is that legislators enforce the reward payment by ensuring that no one is in a position to secure the temptation outcome. They sacrifice the preferred policy solution—to fund only projects where the benefits exceed the costs (Shepsle and Weingast, 1981, 1984)—to the dominant reelection goal. Strategically, legislative leaders get around the problem of diverse, and indeed cyclical, preferences by putting all pork barrel proposals in a single omnibus. Out of chaotic preference orders, the leadership produces order. All members care only about their own projects. Thus vote-trading across independent issues permits majority rule institutions to resolve issues of intensity of preference (Buchanan and Tullock, 1962, ch. 10).

By linking the projects together, leaders create a constructive coalition of minorities. Instead of a situation where minorities tear apart a coalition supporting a candidate or a legislative proposal, we have a situation where everyone appears to gain from joining issues. Such a strategy also provides an escape route from the cyclical preferences that are endemic in coalitions of minorities. This proposal will provide benefits to all even though the costs will be higher. But because of the fiscal illusion, it is highly unlikely that constituents will notice the increased costs—and they certainly will not be able to trace them to

[6] In the PD there is a solution in the core. That is, there is a strategy that is not dominated by any other, as determined by the pay-off matrix: it is all-defect. However, the payoff structure also guarantees that the core is not stable. I owe this interpretation to my colleague Joe Oppenheimer.

the omnibus proposal. Thus the difference in payoffs between the temptation and reward outcomes is reduced and cooperation becomes possible (cf. Cohen, 1982). To be sure, the simple explanation offered does not fully account for the cooperative behavior found in pork barrel politics. In addition to strategic factors, explanations for cooperation in the PD game include the following: (1) trust develops as the game is played many times; (2) most societies have norms inducing cooperative behavior; and (3) the cooperative outcome simply should seem obvious to rational players. I shall consider these accounts in Chapter 3. They become important primarily when they are contrasted with a very different style of politics, that found in much energy legislation. The rationale for discussing the politics of the pork barrel at such length is to prepare the way for a consideration of energy politics. I turn to it now.

Everyman Out of His Humor: The Politics of the Shale Barrel

In contrast to the pork barrel, energy politics is disaggregative. Cooperation is not achieved. In this section I compare these polar cases to demonstrate how energy differs from distributive issues. Both sets of policies are marked by cyclical majorities with their associated unstable logrolling coalitions. Once again this leads to a strategic Prisoners' Dilemma for legislators, but this time everyman out of his humor will not agree to a universalistic outcome. In the pork barrel case we start with a diverse set of policy proposals that ultimately are resolved through the formation of a constructive coalition of minorities. In the politics of disaggregation, on the other hand, we begin with a policy proposal designed to resolve a specific problem (insufficient energy supplies, skyrocketing prices, etc.), which uncooperative legislators begin to attack from an equally diverse set of perspectives. The proposal thus succumbs to a destructive coalition of minorities, each with a different objection to the program to resolve the policy problem. The immediate task ahead is to describe the politics of noncooperation. Then we must ask why legislators are willing to form coalitions of the whole on some issues but cannot even achieve simple majorities on others. The rest of this chapter and all of the next are devoted to the latter question.

Typically, the pork barrel is not marked by loud voices and great ideological battles. Indeed, the reelection imperative is so strong and the belief that pork-barreling helps that goal is so pervasive that some of the key budget-cutters in the Republican leadership have succumbed to the temptations to demand for their districts what John L.

Lewis demanded for his union: more. (On House Minority Leader Robert Michel, see Klose, 1983; on Senate Budget Committee chair Pete Domenici, see Dewar, 1983.) On the other hand, the politics of energy is typified by intense conflicts, much more sharply focused public attention, and an inability on the part of Congress to face up to the problems. In contrast to pork barrel politics, we have shale barrel politics, named after the massive program Congress adopted in 1979–80 to develop synthetic fuels. In contrast to the pork barrel, shale barrel issues involve readily perceived costs. When there are energy shortages, people see the increased price at the pump and in their monthly utility bills. The pork barrel is the politics of abundance, the shale barrel of scarcity or at least shortages. There are few direct costs to the constituents of a Chicago member for a dam on the Colorado River. The farmer is all too happy to have his or her legislator trade votes with a New York member to obtain agriculture price supports in return for school lunch programs.

On the other hand, energy politics is hardly a situation in which everyone can be a winner; it does not even involve clear-cut ideological battles between winners and losers. What is clear, especially during periods of shortage, is that someone is going to have to bear the burden of higher energy costs. On the pork barrel, on the other hand, what costs there are rarely become the focal point of debate. Only benefits seem to count. The shale barrel is the politics of noncooperation. While the pork barrel is typified by constructive coalitions of minorities, the shale barrel is marked by destructive coalitions of minorities. On the pork barrel we start with a series of projects that are of interest only to legislators from each district. On the shale barrel, since everything affects energy, the scope of the issue is very large indeed. Any energy proposal encompasses interests in every Congressional district. Furthermore, since the impact of energy on everything else is so great, any decision about how to allocate either supplies or prices inevitably involves issues affecting agriculture, industry, labor, trade, and virtually everything else.

While the pork barrel was chosen to contrast with the shale barrel because it differs dramatically on key issues such as the dispersion of and perception of costs and the scope of related concerns, the two are similar in that neither is marked by the clear-cut ideological politics of great issues of income redistribution or civil rights. Both involve the politics of coalitions of *minority interests*. Thurow (1979, ch. 2) might well be correct in arguing that energy, unlike the pork barrel, does involve winners and losers and what one side wins must be lost by the other side. But the cash register of politics does not work so finely as that of economics. People don't always see stakes in the same way, so all winners do not feel a common bond with each other. Nor do all losers. Indeed, there is no guarantee that people who are believed by economists to be winners (consumers on price deregulation) perceive themselves in that same light. In short, zero-sum economics does not imply zero-sum politics.

Shale barrel politics is marked by cyclical group preferences and unstable logrolling coalitions. One of the most fundamental questions on the entire energy issue is what direction future supply development should take. Should we pursue a hard path (coal, oil, gas, synfuels, nuclear) or a soft path (solar, windpower, hydropower, etc.)? Virtually every roll-call analysis of energy voting in Congress suggests a clear ideological conflict between either left and right or materialists and postmaterialists (Inglehart, 1977), with awe of big concrete buildings at one pole and support for little furry animals at the other (see Chapter 5). However, nothing like such a straightforward ordering is found in people's preferences. In the midst of the 1979 energy crisis, the Council on Environmental Quality (1980, pp. 22ff) asked citizens which two or three alternative energy sources should receive the greatest concentration over the next two decades. Solar energy, which is not clearly in any feasible set of total solutions given present technology, was mentioned by 61 percent of the respondents; no other alternative came close. Coal (36 percent) was second, followed by conservation (35), water power (31), oil and natural gas (28), synfuels (26), and nuclear power (23). Given these rankings, one or more preference cycles (excluding solar energy) are not only possible but likely since no alternative has majority support and the range of support for the various proposals is not large.

Minority interests place strains on leaders because they make it impossible to procure the sort of automatic majorities that simple ideological issues yield. Only coalitions of minorities make logrolling possible. However, while leaders get around the cyclical majority problem and the associated instability of logrolling coalitions by forming constructive coalitions of minorities on pork barrel issues, this strategy is not feasible on the shale barrel. What makes vote-trading potentially profitable for a universalistic coalition under the pork barrel is that the issues are largely, though not completely, separable. Issues are separable (Schwartz, 1977, p. 1000) if the legislator's preferences on one proposal are independent of those on another.

We thus ignore any spillover, or external, costs imposed on neighboring districts and any external benefits, as a hospital constructed in one district may serve clients and even provide jobs for people in others. These assumptions are typically made in models of the pork barrel (see Shepsle and Weingast, 1981, p. 101, n. 2). On the other hand, shale barrel issues generally are not even relatively separable. The price of natural gas affects the price of other energy supplies, whether it is even worthwhile to develop alternative energy supplies under current market conditions, and a whole host of other economic issues: whether farmers can make sufficient profits not to require large governmental subsidies, whether trucking deregulation will work, inflation rates in general, and so on. Thus, as we shall see in Chapter 5, each affected interest will weigh carefully any proposed change from the status quo on an issue such as gas pricing.

These groups have little in common with each other for the most part. They are not, therefore, natural allies either on ideological grounds or because they have fought together in the past on issues of mutual concern. Rather, they all gang up against a policy proposal they believe will adversely affect each one. The effects of any such proposal are thus not readily separable as are the components of an omnibus pork barrel bill. Futhermore, the spillover consequences of a piece of shale barrel legislation cannot be ignored; they are the lightning rods for attracting opposition. Thus shale barrel legislation cannot readily be logrolled along the same lines as public works programs.[7] Each proposal by itself might be enacted by majority vote, but the minority on each is very intense. When coalitions of minorities form, they will destabilize potential majorities. Hence, I refer to them as destructive coalitions of minorities.

What brings constructive coalitions of minorities together is concentrated benefits. On the other hand, the perception of costs leads to destructive coalitions of minorities. In linking the proposals together in a single package, the omnibus bill becomes a ready target for defeat. Indeed, this is what Downs (1957, pp. 55–60) and Oppenheimer (1973) originally envisioned when they formulated the problem of the coalition of minorities.[8]

[7] This statement only holds for attempts to make national energy policy. It does not hold for research and development policy on energy, on which the various energy constituencies such as nuclear, coal, oil, natural gas, electricity, and the softer paths of renewable fuels may work together to support a universalistic energy pork barrel. I am indebted to John Chubb for pointing this out to me. See the very useful discussions of this in Chubb, 1983, ch. 3, and Cohen and Noll, 1983.

[8] Cohodas (1983, p. 2154) commented on such coalitions in the context of social legislation: "It is difficult, if not impossible, to pass omnibus social legislation. While Congress has been willing to lump all sorts of spending and budget matters into one piece of legislation—witness the massive budget reconciliation and stopgap appropriations bills of recent years—it has been unwilling to use a similar process for anything that directly changes social policy."

Destructive Coalitions of Minorities: A Lesson in Legislative Strategy

Consider a situation in which a single proposal for comprehensive legislation is offered, but falls prey to minority vetoes by groups that do not like provisions of the legislation. This is what happened in the Senate in 1977–78 to Jimmy Carter's national energy proposal. In this section I show how the Senate was marked by a destructive coalition of minorities and how shrewd legislative strategy by Senate leaders rescued the parts of the bill that had barely escaped emasculation. This example sets the stage for comparing PD situations on the pork and shale barrels in our quest to determine why one is marked by cooperation and the other by disaggregation.

The situation described in Schema 2.1 demonstrates how a destructive coalition of minorities operates. Let (a) be the outcome in which all bills in an omnibus pass, (b) represent a situation in which k of the n bills pass, but $n-k$ fail, and (c) be the outcome in which all bills fail. Let abc be the preference order of a 4-member bloc, bca that of a 5-member bloc, and cab that of three legislators. Then, collectively, aPb by a vote of $7-5$, bPc by $9-3$, and cPa by $8-4$. Alternatively, we could construct a more complex case in which each of the bills individually had the support of some majority coalition. The largest majority occurs when some of the bills pass and others fail. Because of the small majority preferring a to b, any attempt to manipulate the agenda to yield a contest between only these alternatives is likely to be resisted. If the choice is between a and c, all bills will fail.

On the other hand, if the leadership can arrange for the agenda to be a contest between b and c, it can ensure that at least k of the n bills will pass. But agenda control may be more difficult when there is a destructive coalition of minorities. It is quite possible that there will be cyclical preferences within the chamber on the k proposals that have majority support so that coalitions of minorities might form to defeat

SCHEMA 2.1

Destructive Coalitions of Minorities and Voters' Paradox

Let: a = (all bills in package pass)
      b = (bills /1, . . . , k/ pass; bills /K+1, . . . , n/ fail)
      c = (all bills fail)

Preference over outcomes:
4-member bloc a b c
5-member bloc b c a
3-member bloc c a b

specific items in b. Thus Kadane (1972) has proved that the optimal leadership strategy is "division of the question," that is, separating the omnibus bill into its component parts when a coalition of minorities threatens to defeat the bill. This is what leaders did in the 97th Congress (1981–82) on tax reform legislation and in the 98th Congress (1983–84) on criminal code revision.

Perhaps the most prominent of recent attempts to circumvent a destructive coalition of minorities defeating an omnibus bill was the decision by Senate leaders in 1977 to split up the comprehensive energy legislation proposed by President Jimmy Carter and enacted almost intact by the House in that year. The President was worried about the potential for a destructive coalition. In an address to the nation in April 1977, he stated (Congressional Quarterly, 1977, p. 710): "I am sure each of you will find something you don't like about the specifics of our proposal. . . . We can be sure that all the special interest groups in the country will attack the part of the plan that affects them directly." In the House Speaker Thomas P. O'Neill (D-Mass.) had built up support for the bill by establishing an Ad Hoc Select Committee on Energy to shepherd the legislation through that chamber. However, the Senate party leadership was less committed to energy legislation, and rather than press for the sort of comprehensive legislation the administration wanted, it sought only to avoid the possibility of the formation of a destructive coalition of minorities (Jones, 1979a, pp. 171–73).

The bill was split into multiple components and many of them died in committee in the Senate (see Cochrane, 1981). Six bills finally did make it to the floor, all attached to minor House legislation to expedite the process, that led to five key votes; two Senate bills, providing for greater use of coal and for conservation in public schools, were joined to the same House legislation. To examine the strategic situation in the Senate, key roll calls on these five bills are considered in Table 2.6. Three final passage votes are included (on deregulation of "new" natural gas, public utilities regulation, and tax incentives for conservation), together with two votes on which a majority of Senators took positions different from the House's (a ban on gas-guzzling cars and a ban on forced conversion to oil in the coal conservation bill).

Majorities in the Senate ranged from a comfortable 86–7 on the utilities regulation bill to a slender 50–46 on gas deregulation. The pattern of opposition to the various bills was far from clear-cut. Indeed, a coalition of minorities was pervasive: fully 85 of the 100 Senators were on the minority position in the Senate on at least one of the five votes considered! (Pairs or announced intentions to vote yea or

TABLE 2.6

Senate Votes on Five Key Energy Bills, 1977

Date of vote	House bill	Page No., 1977 CQA[a]	Subject	Vote
9/8/77	HR 5146	53-S	Coal conservation, vote to ban forced conversion gas to oil	55–31
9/13/77	HR 5037	55-S	Conservation incentives, vote to ban gas-guzzling automobiles	52–28
10/4/77	HR 5289	75-S	Natural gas deregulation	50–46
10/6/77	HR 4018	76-S	Public utility regulation	86–7
10/31/77	HR 5263	87-S	Energy tax; tax incentives for conservation	52–35

NOTE: Number of Senators taking minority position on at least one vote = 85; number of Senators taking minority position on at least two votes = 51.

[a] *Congressional Quarterly Almanac.*

nay are included in these computations, although not in the vote totals in Table 2.6.) The fragility of the support for the omnibus package is highlighted by the result that 51 Senators took the minority position on at least two of the roll calls. Lest the actions of the Senate leadership appear to have saved a doomed bill, it must be noted that only two administration proposals were adopted unchanged by the Senate: a distributive package of tax benefits for home insulation and the setting of mandatory energy efficiency standards for home appliances, whose costs to the individual consumer were largely hidden. The Senate leaders produced a package quite different from the House legislation; it facilitated producer interests (Jones, 1979a, p. 174). By giving many groups much of what they demanded, the leadership effectively separated many of the most controversial issues from each other, but simultaneously it greatly weakened the legislation's claims to reduce energy consumption. A destructive coalition of minorities was averted largely by conceding to each interest before the voting began.

The Prisoners' Dilemma in the shale barrel case is similar to that for the pork barrel and, indeed, more like the traditional logic of collective action problem as discussed by Olson than is the distributive politics case. In the most general case the cooperative strategy involves conserving energy. Defection, as the above examples indicate, lets people use as much energy as they wish. The temptation payoff would have others conserve even as you yourself use all the energy you need. For reward, everyone agrees to accept the costs of conservation. The punishment payoff would have everyone use whatever amount of energy they choose (or can afford). Finally, the sucker's payoff would see a player saving energy while others do not. Clearly, for each player, T > R > P > S. This is the classic PD of collective action problems.

There are two complications, however. First, conservation is in part a "lumpy good" (see Chapter 3). It works best when most people cooperate. When a few people begin to defect, the benefits to all are considerably reduced. Moreover, the incentives for others to defect rise as they see their compatriots refusing to conserve. Yet this is no different from other collective action problems involving public goods. Second, the environment of energy policy is less predictable than that of many policy areas. Does the uncertainty in payoffs lead to a departure from the PD characterization? Since only a few defectors can be tolerated before this strategy becomes rampant, any probabilistic decrease in R will also lead to a reduction at least as great in S, who conserves while others consume. Similarly, free-riding (payoff T) will continue to be attractive if a sufficient number of others do in fact cooperate. Thus the uncertainty of the energy environment does not destroy the PD game, but rather adds an element of risk regarding exactly which strategy one is employing in the n-person game when both external costs and benefits and the expected behavior of the other players are not known.

In contrast to the pork barrel, then, the lack of collective action on energy typifies the electoral situation: voters are less concerned with what a government does *for* them than with what it might do *to* them, as emphasized by the *mitzvah* theory. The reelection imperative induces cooperation in the legislative game even when players face cyclical preferences and a PD in strategy over how to resolve such cycling. But energy supplies are not so abundant that coalition builders can form cooperative coalitions. In the energy PD game, even if the payoff for R is no greater than current standards of living, the threat regarding what the P payoff will be should energy supplies run out might be sufficient to induce cooperative behavior. But the capacity of most economies to absorb at least a few free riders makes the T payoff even more tempting, and the fear that the future even with a reward payoff may be worse than the present clearly can lead to a consume-now strategy. As the gospel song goes, "Everybody wants to go to heaven, but nobody wants to die."

At the heart of the PD, of course, is mistrust of the other player(s). National surveys conducted for the Federal Energy Administration in 1975 by the Opinion Research Corporation (1976a, b), show this mistrust to be widespread on even the most basic issues in energy conser-

TABLE 2.7
Self-Willingness and Perceptions of Others' Willingness to Conserve Energy, 1975

Conservation activity	Self [a]	Others [b]
Drive small economy car	70/12/15	35/43/15
Set thermostats at 68 degrees or lower during day	59/37 [c]	28/40/29
Do laundry/wash dishes after 9 p.m.	57/22/18	18/35/39
Turn down control on water heater from hot to warm	61/25/14	30/42/25
Employ a variety of measures to conserve natural gas	76/18/2	31/51/11 [d]

SOURCES: Opinion Research Corporation, 1976a,b.

[a] Person's own willingness to engage in activity, from very willing to somewhat willing to not too willing. Percentages do not add to 100; remainder are don't knows.

[b] Others' perceived likelihood (very/somewhat/not too likely) of engaging in these activities.

[c] For self-willingness, the question concerned the setting people would choose. The dichotomy here corresponds to that for perceptions of others.

[d] The question concerned others' perceptions of the seriousness of the need to conserve natural gas.

vation. Over three-quarters of respondents indicated a willingness to engage in conservation activities, while between 57 and 70 percent gave positive responses to particular options. However, only about a third expected *others* to do the same. Some of the key results are presented in Table 2.7. The optimistic forecast of the survey team (Opinion Research Corporation, 1976a, p. v) focused on people's willingness to conserve even as they perceived others as less public-regarding. Economic considerations, rather than social norms, are the major determinant of changes in people's energy consumption behavior (Sears et al., 1978; Olsen, 1981).

On the other hand, the reported behavior of consumers gives us less cause for optimism. Just 5 percent of the population engage in such conservation activities as servicing their furnaces, lowering their water heater thermostats, or using cold water detergents in the laundry. Only half of the homes lower thermostats (from a mean of 70 degrees during the day) at all during the night (Milstein, n.d.). Note that these measures involve relatively little cost. They rarely impose severe hardships on people. Yet even on such easy options, people don't trust others to coordinate behavior to save energy. If anything, responses to the 1975 surveys reflected what people thought they ought to do (or ought to tell pollsters that they do) rather than any real willingness to change behavior. When the issues become more clearly redistributive and complex, we would expect even less trust. Milstein (1978) reports majority support for governmental programs such as automobile taxes *and rebates*, forcing utilities to lower off-peak rates, and tax rebates for insulation. On the other hand, in the late 1970's strong majorities opposed increasing taxes on gasoline and home heating fuels, decontrolling fuel prices, taxing public parking to encourage the use of public transportation, and gasoline rationing. All these proposals involve readily perceived costs. People don't trust each other to comply with conservation norms voluntarily, but by 70 to 20 percent they favor exhortation to conserve more over the Olsonian solution to the logic of collective action, passing and enforcing laws (Milstein, 1978, p. 87).

To extend this logic to the strategic situation confronting legislators, members are faced with the problem of allocating costs or the responsibility for such costs across Congressional districts. If a proposal for comprehensive energy legislation is under consideration, each legislator realizes that such a bill will impose readily perceived costs on his or her district. The temptation payoff would be for the member either to seek a solution that will minimize the negative effects on the district or at least will relieve the member of any direct responsibility for the ensuing problems. Thus, strategically, the legislator should stand up for district interests and vote no, thereby joining a potential destructive coalition of minorities. The reward payoff would involve attempting to break a preference cycle by agreeing to have each member's district share equitably in the costs of such a policy. Each legislator could then claim responsibility for helping to achieve a national policy while also arguing that no other district fared better. The punishment payoff would entail voting no and again joining a coalition of minorities that would defeat the bill, while the sucker's payoff would find the cooperator having to explain to constituents why he or she voted to impose costs on them even as the proposal failed. Indeed, because the scope of energy issues is so broad, the legislation under consideration need not even be a comprehensive bill, but only one with multiple lines of cleavage and clearly perceived costs along each dimension. The outcomes and strategies in the shale barrel PD are presented in Table 2.8.

The strategic Prisoners' Dilemma on the shale barrel is more straightforward than that on the pork barrel precisely because there is no need to invoke long-term perspectives on mistrust. Mistrust is immediate, as the very idea of a destructive coalition of minorities indicates. On the pork barrel, legislators are worried about some future partisan coalition disrupting a dominant majority that will no longer be able to impose its own winning coalition. On the shale barrel, legislators do not aggregate specific demands into a comprehensive bill. Rather, they start with a policy problem and a proposed solution.

TABLE 2.8

Outcomes and Strategies on the Shale Barrel Prisoners' Dilemma

Outcome	Result	Strategy
Temptation	Comprehensive energy bill is enacted without Legislator A's support.	Legislator A votes against comprehensive energy bill; at least a majority of others vote yea.
Reward	Comprehensive energy bill is enacted with everyone's support.	Legislator A and all others (or at least a majority) vote for comprehensive bill.
Punishment	No comprehensive energy bill is enacted.	Legislator A and all others (or at least a majority) vote against comprehensive bill.
Sucker	No comprehensive energy bill is enacted, despite A's support.	Legislator A votes for comprehensive energy bill; at least a majority of others vote nay.

There is no bidding war except to see who can yell the loudest among groups that would be adversely affected by the proposal most prominent on the agenda. Instead, people with diverse—and generally cyclical—preferences put aside these differences to gang up against a resolution of the policy problem. There are few partisan or ideological anchors for a coherent attack, so no coalition is initially favored. No one is willing to make sacrifices, so each attacks the comprehensive bill on different grounds. Legislators then set out on a search-and-destroy mission for the legislation in question, as whatever support the bill might have quickly dissolves amidst pressures from constituency groups. These forces cannot agree to do anything, but they can agree to stop something.

Because legislators perceive any imposition of costs as hurting their reelection prospects, the reward payoff is unlikely to be achieved. Furthermore, while roll-call voting in the Congress requires only majority support for a bill, the logic behind this PD formulation is that no member would be willing to join only a majority coalition that imposes on constituents costs that are clearly attributable to the voting behavior of legislators. If an unpopular bill is going to be adopted, a legislator would argue, I would be better off letting others take all the responsibility for it, so that I can at least argue to my own constituents that I did whatever I could to prevent costs from being imposed on them. Everyone thus seeks the temptation payoff, but the outcome is all-defect, so that each receives the punishment payoff. No player is willing to let others free-ride on the accountability issue, much less on actual costs imposed on constituents. Thus, if we assume that the re-election goal is based on an asymmetric perception of benefits and costs, the expected outcome would be for all members to refuse to compromise. As soon as the cooperation norm breaks down, it breaks down completely as one legislator after another seeks to avoid responsibility and negative effects on the district. And there will always be members whose electoral situation is far from secure and who will therefore be ready to defect.

Summing Up

The politics of the pork and shale barrel are polar opposites in outcomes, but there is much similarity in the underlying structure of the issues. Both involve cyclical group preferences that can be represented as strategic Prisoners' Dilemmas. Lest one think that every possible political and social problem can be so characterized, I remind readers that there are some truly redistributive issues in the politics of advanced industrial nations that must be formalized differently. The civil rights struggle is one such domain, as is the issue of government control and ownership of major industries that dominates debate in some nations with strong Socialist parties. There are also great issues of public morality such as freedom of speech, abortion, and capital punishment that must be discussed outside the Prisoners' Dilemma framework. Thus, finding two polar cases with similar bases is not unimportant. Indeed, it leads directly to the question of why some types of issues lead to cooperation while others lead to disaggregation. This is the subject of the next chapter.

The Bases of Legislative Cooperation

> O, sir, it holds for good policy ever, to have that out-
> wardly in vilest estimation, that inwardly is most
> dear to us . . .   (*Everyman in His Humour*, II.ii, p. 32)
>
> I fear no mood stamped in a private bow,
> When I am pleased to unmask a public vice.
> (*Everyman Out of His Humour*, Prologue, p. 286)

H AVING set out the model for analyzing energy politics and showing the linkages between it and the more traditional pork barrel framework, I now turn to the important differences between the two areas. If both the pork and the shale barrels involve cyclical group preferences leading to strategic Prisoners' Dilemmas, why do we observe cooperative behavior on the one hand and noncooperative outcomes on the other? To be sure, the answer must lie in the payoffs for the two types of games. But in the world of politics it is next to impossible—and certainly implausible—to attach numbers to payoffs for a complex policy area such as energy.

In the absence of direct measurement, we must proceed conceptually. In this chapter I offer first two key variables that help to account for the differences between the pork and shale barrels: the scope of conflict on an issue and whether there is a fiscal illusion. I relate these concepts to proposed resolutions of the collective action problem in the Prisoners' Dilemma, including Axelrod's conflict-of-interest theory, fairness norms, the idea of a prominent solution, and sequential games. These are not competing explanations. They are consistent with the thesis to be offered about the scope of conflict and the presence of a fiscal illusion. Then I consider once more the implications of the preference-based framework for the analysis of institutional design, showing that the scope of conflict of committee jurisdiction reflects the demand pattern of interested constituencies.

Accounting for the Differences

Unlike distributive politics, shale barrel politics involves intense minorities with preferences that cannot be readily separated across issues. The result is a situation in which bargaining is much more difficult. The focus shifts from benefits to constituencies to costs. Wilson (1973, pp. 333–34) and Ferejohn (1974, p. 53) have suggested that the critical distinction is between concentrated benefits/dispersed costs, on the one hand, and diffuse benefits/concentrated costs on the other. When we consider issues as disparate as omnibus public works bills and natural gas deregulation, we immediately notice that on both there are concentrated benefits. In each policy area, it is not terribly difficult to determine who at least some of the beneficiaries are. If the benefits from price deregulation were so diffuse, then the major oil and gas producers would hardly be expected, on Olson's logic, to have striven so hard for such a collective good. The economists who argue that price deregulation will ultimately benefit consumers—hence yielding diffuse benefits as well—might be correct. But this does not get us out of the bind that the benefits are perceived as basically concentrated.

However, it does make sense to argue that when costs are concentrated, universalistic solutions cannot be obtained. Constructive coalitions of minorities can only be based on diffuse costs. Destructive coalitions, on the other hand, will form when *at least some of the costs* are concentrated. In the case of natural gas deregulation again, interstate pipelines and many utilities attacked the idea of lifting of price restrictions. On the other hand, so did other groups, including many representatives of consumer organizations. One could hardly call consumers a readily identifiable interest group with particular claims upon a set of legislators. If there is any diverse group in politics, it is the consumers' movement. This suggests that while the concentration of costs tells us something about the way destructive coalitions form, it does not explain why the PD game on the pork barrel will yield cooperation while that on the shale barrel is expected to produce defections.

Several other possibilities might account for the differences. These are distinguishing features of the conflicts on energy. First is the general question of supply. Pork barrel legislation is not about dire shortages of parks, dams, hospitals, agricultural commodities, and the like. It is about distributing goods. Indeed, the underlying logic behind the entire system is the idea that resources are unlimited (Dodd, 1980) so that the diffuse costs really don't matter. Even when there is a current budgetary problem, we are willing to keep up current projects at a cost (the public debt) to future generations. In typically Keynesian fashion, politicians work under the assumption that the new projects will stimulate enough growth that they will eventually pay for themselves. They must believe this because they realize that the costs of an omnibus pork barrel bill will exceed the district benefits (Shepsle and Weingast, 1981). In contrast, the debate on energy in 1973–74 and 1979–80 focused on the less politically tractable question of how to allocate shortages. The pork barrel politician doesn't know how to play this game, much less play it well. Are shortages the key to the difference?

Closely connected to the issue of shortages is that of stakes. The impact of most pork barrel items on the budget (or the gross national product) is rather small. We study them because they have interesting political benefits, not because our macroeconomic system depends on the goods and services brought home to the district by our representative in Washington. Even agriculture price supports, then, are small potatoes compared to energy. If energy were not so important in terms of stakes, then economists would not conduct so many arguments among themselves about whether rising energy prices during the two embargos were the major cause of the inflationary spirals that shook the nation and helped undo at least two Presidents. Are stakes the answer?

One reason people clamored so loudly about rising energy prices in the 1970's is that they had relatively few market options. I heat my house with natural gas, but if the price skyrockets when the fuel is finally decontrolled, I can't simply shift to oil or electricity or solar power. Every other alternative requires huge start-up costs that might be available to big industrial users but not to myself and my neighbors. Is substitutability the answer?[1]

The pork barrel provides tangible benefits to constituencies. An energy policy, even if passed, only promises somewhat diffuse benefits to most people—and those in the long run. The benefit most people would receive is *no reduction* in the standard of living. Any program such as synthetic fuel development—or even research into solar energy—will not have payoffs for many years, perhaps long after the incumbent legislators are even around to claim credit for their foresightedness. Is the imminence of benefits the answer?

Some pork barrel projects are rather large, such as a dam. Others are of more moderate size—a hospital, a post office, a park. But energy development inevitably requires large, lumpy programs. "Lumpiness"

---

[1] Taking OPEC's lead, seven Latin American nations decided in March 1974 that they were no longer content to be poor banana republics and formed the Union of Banana Exporting Nations (UBEN). They raised their prices between one and two-and-a-half cents a pound to consumers in the same nations of North America and Europe that were so badly hit by the OPEC price hikes. Prices had held steady at $.25 a pound for 30 years and the UBEN seven saw the opportunity to get rich quick by following the same cartel strategy as OPEC (New York *Times*, 1974). What they failed to appreciate is that bananas, like most other food products, are not an absolute necessity for people, while energy is. Consumers could—and did—readily adjust their eating habits to face the market. One need only remember the beef boycotts to realize just how flexible people can be.

means that the project, such as a bridge, is of no use unless it is completed. Canadians have a term for such enterprises: megaprojects. With such enterprises politicians have a more difficult time providing whatever more specific and concentrated benefits there are to a large number of districts. One cannot locate synfuels plants throughout the country. Does lumpiness make the difference?

In pork barrel politics some districts can receive parks, others dams or post offices, and so on. The demand for public housing is far smaller in rural Kansas than it is in New York City, where constituents have little interest in wheat price supports. Vote trading is easy because cleavages are cross-cutting (Dahl, 1961; Miller, 1983). What one legislator wants, another is willing to give—for a price. This market works very well for most pork barrel issues. To be sure, in recent years there have been very sharp conflicts over some traditionally distributive issues, including price supports, particularly for dairy products. But the general thesis still seems valid, particularly in contrast to shale barrel issues. The problem with energy (or water) is that cleavages are not cross-cutting. Everybody needs energy (water), and if the commodity is in short supply there are likely to be very messy fights indeed in the Congress. Are cross-cutting versus reinforcing cleavages the answer?

All these factors contribute to the distinction between the pork barrel and the shale barrel, but they are reducible to two broader concepts: (1) the fiscal illusion problem and (2) the scope of the conflict on the different issues. The fiscal illusion on the pork barrel hides the costs of the projects, but when energy is in short supply, the costs become quite apparent. People see their energy bills rising directly, in their monthly bills for gas, oil, or electricity, and at the pump. Politicians recognize this; Key (1964, p. 568) noted that the electoral "god of vengeance" is more severe than the "god of reward" (Fiorina, 1981a).[2] Legislators thus face a conundrum: if the energy situation becomes very serious, constituents will demand some action to alleviate the crises. There may be electoral costs if the members do nothing. However, any action will impose costs on voters as well, so the legislators must determine whether they are better off acting in some way or not acting at all. They may seek, as we shall see in the next chapter, a policy that is largely symbolic and imposes relatively few costs on constituents at least in the short run. But such a policy is unlikely to resolve the energy crisis; it is more likely to defer difficult decisions to

---

[2] Shakespeare also made the point in Mark Antony's soliloquy in *Julius Caesar*: "The evil that men do lives after them. The good is oft interred with their bones."

another day, which might be a reasonable strategy for a myopic politician facing an electoral cycle of very short duration.

Similarly, the issue of stakes is tied to people's perceptions of those costs. What matters is not simply how large the stakes are. The defense budget is much larger than that for the pork barrel, and its impact on the economy is arguably even greater than that of energy. However, there is precious little evidence that most people make any direct connection between the size of their taxes and defense expenditures. Indeed, as people became very irate over energy prices in 1979–80, they were demanding larger expenditures for defense (Miller and Shanks, 1981, pp. 325–26). Energy prices were simply not hidden by any fiscal illusion.

Substitutability is similarly related to clearly perceived costs. When prices rise dramatically for a good that cannot be readily replaced, consumers readily recognize that they have no alternative and very well may hold legislators accountable, even if there is nothing the politicians can do (at least in the short run). The less imminent the benefits of a program are, the lower the probability that any immediate negative effects of perceived costs can be mitigated. Similarly, mega-projects often have much more visible costs than smaller programs do. A synthetic fuels boom town creates all sorts of environmental, health, social, and other economic effects that force people to stand up and pay attention. A new post office or park has far fewer costs. Finally, cross-cutting cleavages lead to the sort of vote-trading that thrives on the fiscal illusion, while reinforcing conflicts only make the stakes seem higher.

The scope of conflict has long been recognized as a critical factor in determining whether cooperation can be achieved in a policy area. Banfield (1961, p. 318) argued: "As the number of autonomous actors increases, control tends to become less structured." But the number of autonomous actors is itself a function of the scope of interests affected. Pork barrel issues are narrow in scope. By assumption, each project only affects—at least in the sense of the fiscal illusion—the district of the Representative sponsoring the program. Energy, on the other hand, affects everyone and virtually every other issue. Its scope is about as broad as one can imagine. Schattschneider (1960, p. 15) states the case well: "The best point at which to manage conflict is before it starts. Once a conflict starts it is not easy to control because it is difficult to be exclusive about a fight. If one side is too hard-pressed, the impulse to redress the balance by inviting in outsiders is almost irresistible." Furthermore (p. 65), "the development of one conflict may inhibit the development of another because a radical shift of alignment becomes possible only at the cost of a change in the relations and priorities of all the contestants."

Schattschneider's first statement points to a key distinction between the pork and shale barrels. Discourse on the pork barrel is kept within the bounds of comity. Everyone makes a deal and nobody makes a fuss. On shale barrel issues, on the other hand, it is well near impossible to control the conflicts between producers and consumers, among regions, and among all who conceivably might have an interest in the issue—which is basically just about everybody. Because shale barrel issues are not readily separable, people readily join in the fight. Issue positions are not necessarily marked by a clear-cut ideology because the scope of the issue is so broad. Thus preference cycles are likely, and the level of intensity of the conflict will increase further as enemies become friends and vice versa as minor components of proposals change. Shortages, high stakes, the lack of substitutability, the absence of immediate benefits from a policy proposal, and lumpiness only serve further to expand the scope of conflict by drawing into the process additional groups who might have a tangential interest in the specific proposal under consideration. This too is the message of Schattschneider's statement.

When allocating abundance, politicians can respect the narrow demands of various clientele groups, which are not perceived as conflicting with each other. In times of shortages, however, there simply is not enough to go around, so claims must clash and the number of actors involved in each decision correspondingly increases. Similarly, when the stakes are high, the situation is ripe for a fight because there are few disinterested constituents. If one good can be readily substituted for another, there is more maneuvering room for mutually beneficial exchanges; such leeway in bargaining becomes progressively more narrow as the range of possible alternatives decreases. If there are few immediate benefits from a policy, legislators are robbed of their chief source of political capital for exchanging votes and the debate shifts to the allocations of costs. Once again, the scope of conflict expands. Finally, lumpy goods, or megaprojects, will certainly have higher external costs, negative effects that are by-products of the provision of such goods, than projects that have more readily disaggregated benefits. Increased negative externalities, such as environmental effects of energy development, of course lead to an increased scope of conflict. To be sure, a lumpy good such as a dam also has large external costs, but the politics of the pork barrel on rivers and harbors legislation is based on keeping such concerns out of the realm of public debate.

What distinguishes the pork barrel from the shale barrel is, first, the scope of conflict. Pork barrel issues are of narrow scope, with few legislators taking an active role in the policy area. This permits members to make deals behind closed doors because nobody else is looking, or even cares to look. Not coincidentally, it also permits elites to lead, indeed even manipulate, the citizenry because the range of participation is limited. Once the scope of conflict expands and more people get into the fray, as Schattschneider noted, it becomes virtually impossible to contain the fight. An expanding conflict attracts even more participants, and preferences that have not been previously expressed must now be taken into account. New actors are not easily disenfranchised or ignored. The genie cannot be put back into the bottle, although many political leaders have devoted considerable energy in trying to do so—either by trying to redesign an institutional structure in the hope that politics will become more orderly (see Chapter 6) or by simply refusing to recognize that the scope of conflict has greatly expanded (Shefter, 1985, p. 70). In each case, the attempt has failed.

It matters less whether costs are concentrated or dispersed than whether they are clearly perceived. The perception of costs, together with the scope of conflict, largely determines whether cooperative or noncooperative outcomes will result. The more directly costs are perceived and the broader the scope of conflict, the lower is the probability that the issue will be resolved by cooperative behavior. On the other hand, when costs are largely hidden and the scope of the issue is narrow, the prospects for coordinated behavior are much greater. The relative presence or absence of fiscal illusion determines the willingness of participants to bargain cooperatively, while the scope of the issue determines the range of bargaining alternatives. As the scope widens, more interests must be accommodated. Other things being equal—including, of course, the willingness to seek a cooperative solution—negotiations become more complex and difficult when the number of issues to consider is great. I turn now to a consideration of these issues.

Fiscal Illusion and the Scope of Conflict

Axelrod (1970, p. 5) argues that the key to strategic behavior in bargaining games is "the state of incompatibility of the goals of two or more actors." He develops a measure of the amount of conflict of interest in games in which bargaining can take place, including Prisoners' Dilemmas. The amount of conflict of interest is a function of the four payoffs in the PD game. Axelrod argues that the amount of conflict will increase, and hence the probability of mutual cooperation will decrease, if the temptation or punishment payoffs are increased *or* if the reward or sucker's payoffs are decreased (Axelrod, 1970, p. 69).

The level of conflict of interest is an appealing account of the conditions for cooperation (cf. Dodd, 1976, p. 60, on the idea of a priori willingness to bargain). Under what conditions will the level of conflict of interest be large or small? Precise measurement is out of the question, but a conceptual approach may offer us some help. I suggest that two variables, (1) whether citizens clearly perceive the costs of alternative outcomes and (2) the scope of conflict, determine the level of conflict of interest.

Consider first the idea of fiscal illusion. Models of universalism on the pork barrel focus on the benefits that voters perceive, rather than costs. Some completely downplay the role of costs (Fiorina and Noll, 1978; Olson, 1969), while others regard external costs (spillover effects from neighboring districts) as extraneous (Shepsle and Weingast, 1981). In the pork barrel example presented in Table 2.4 (see Chapter 2), the difference between the temptation and reward payoffs for majority party legislators is small. In each case these members obtain their projects; the only difference is the cost to the taxpayers of the extra projects (for minority party legislators) when both parties cooperate.

If voters do not readily perceive the costs of the additional projects, which are hidden deep in the recesses of the overall budgetary and tax systems, then legislators have little incentive to refuse to cooperate with each other. Fenno (1978, pp. 137–41) argues that failure to secure benefits is likely to be more costly to a member's reputation than securing cost savings in other constituencies. Pork barrel expenditures are protected by a fiscal illusion, which helps induce cooperation among legislators.

On the shale barrel, in contrast, citizens (and legislators) readily perceive costs—at the pump, in monthly utility bills, and so forth. Voters in particular concentrate on costs rather than benefits. Risk-averse politicians worry about minimizing the costs to their constituents, and there is no politically advantageous way of allocating shortages.[3] The incentives to shift costs to other districts thus become

---

[3] Consider the statements of two House members regarding potential sucker's payoffs as the House of Representatives defeated by a vote of 159–246 President Carter's first proposal on emergency gasoline rationing in 1979 (*Congressional Record*, daily ed., 96th Cong., 1st sess., May 10, 1979, pp. H2997, H2992). Rep. Tom Hagedorn (R-Minn.) argued: "I care less about supplies in the Washington area and more about the citizens of the Second District of Minnesota who would be forced to wait for their ration checks in the mail. . . . I care about the citizens of the Second District who would be forced to pay the white market value for extra coupons that could be sold in downtown Manhattan and brought out to the Midwest and sold for 3 to 4 times as much." Even

paramount. Relative to the pork barrel, then, the value of the temptation payoff is higher and the risk of being seen as a "sucker" for
providing benefits to other districts is greater. Thus the incentives to
cooperate are fewer.

On the pork barrel the scope of conflict is narrow. Legislators all
seek the same goal—reelection. While members often run for the
Congress by running against the institution, they rarely attack other
incumbents (Fenno, 1975; Mayhew, 1974). Again, legislators gain
little on the pork barrel by arguing to their constituents how much
they saved at the expense of other districts. It is precisely the narrow
scope of conflict that facilitates cooperation across partisan and ideological divisions on the pork barrel (Axelrod, 1970, p. 56). The value
of the temptation payoff relative to that of reward is small for majority
party legislators, so that cooperation becomes attainable.

On the shale barrel the scope of conflict, the domain of the set of
issues under consideration, is considerably larger. Since resource constraint issues, including energy, affect so many other issues and because preferences over the range of alternatives are likely to be nonseparable, the scope of conflict will be very wide. The larger the
domain of issues is, the greater the likelihood that we shall find one or
multiple preference cycles and a high level of conflict of interest. A
wide scope of conflict, with more actors and a more diverse set of
preferences, will increase the probability of a satisfactory compromise. The more complex policy space makes negotiating more difficult and raises the stakes to all participants, especially in comparison
to pork barrel issues.

When costs are readily perceived, actors are less likely to be willing
to compromise. Legislators seeking reelection do not wish to vote
for legislation that will be costly to their constituents. If other districts
are perceived as beneficiaries while their own is seen as a loser or a
"sucker," members fear electoral reprisals from the electorate. Thus,
when costs are high—and therefore clearly perceived—the perceived
benefits from cooperation are small. This is equivalent, in Axelrod's
(1970) terms, to a large difference between the reward and sucker's
payoffs, precisely the condition leading to a high level of conflict of
interest. The energy issue is often defined in terms of winners and

---

more dramatic were the remarks of Rep. Edward Beard (D-R.I.): "This is not in the
interest of my people or the State of Rhode Island. I do not represent California, nor
do I represent New York or any other State but Rhode Island, and so for that reason
and for the fact that it is very unfair to my State I will vote against this particular bill."
What is surprising, then, is not so much that the proposal was defeated as that it received as many as 159 yea votes.

losers, and legislators are not willing to impose sacrifices on their constituents for some greater good. On the other hand, if constituents do not readily perceive that a policy imposes direct costs on them, the benefits of defecting while others cooperate—so that one receives the temptation payoff—relative to full cooperation (the reward payoff) are small. This is clearly the case on the pork barrel. Legislators point to projects they have brought to their districts. Benefits to other districts are generally out of sight and therefore out of mind to constituents. Legislators are hardly better off if they bring projects home *only* for their own district than if they support benefits for all districts. Thus there is little conflict of interest. Similarly, because the goods provided in pork barrel legislation are district-specific, the scope of conflict is narrow—and hence the costs of cooperation with other members are very small. When an issue is a national one and includes many actors with different perspectives on the problem, as in the energy crises of the 1970's (and the associated gas lines), the incentive not to be among the losers is powerful.

The relative presence or absence of fiscal illusion and the scope of conflict generally work in the same direction, but they are not identical. A Federal Trade Commission ruling in 1984 required funeral homes to provide comparative prices over the telephone to anyone who inquired. The scope of such an issue is relatively narrow, at least in comparison to energy or water. While most people have infrequent dealings with funeral homes, the costs are not hidden. Airline deregulation, particularly when the cost involves either loss of service to a city or greatly reduced service, is another example of absence of fiscal illusion but a relatively narrow scope. When there is a wide scope of conflict and costs are clearly perceived by constituents, the prospects for cooperative behavior are minimized; these variables, albeit imprecisely measured, correspond quite well to the situation in which a high level of conflict of interest will occur.

The extent to which actors' preference structures conflict with one another clearly affects the potential for negotiations. Is the game one of pure bargaining or total conflict? PD games fall somewhere in between; players have mixed motives to the extent that cooperation is in everybody's interests, yet each player believes that he or she will be better off by defecting. Even within PD games, however, the cardinal utilities of the payoffs will affect the probability of cooperation. The closer to pure coordination a game is, the more likely its players will be to arrive at an acceptable compromise. Furthermore, the agreement achieved will be an "obvious" stable point, or a "prominent solution" (Schelling, 1960, pp. 56–57).

Mixed-motive games with low degrees of conflict of interest, such as the pork barrel, may also have prominent solutions (e.g., universalism). Such games with higher levels of conflict of interest are less likely to have such stable points. As the number of dimensions of conflict increases, the likelihood of finding a point of agreement decreases—especially if the stakes are perceived as quite high and costs are readily apparent. Indeed, games in which destructive coalitions of minorities form often have solutions that are prominent in the sense that they are *rejected* by all parties (see Chapters 5 and 6). Such solutions may be widely favored by outside observers and by some participants (see especially Chapters 6 and 8), but they are highly charged politically in an atmosphere of strong conflict of interest and thus serve as lightning rods for attracting opposition.

When we do observe cooperative behavior, how do we account for its stability? The structural account, which I argued was deficient in Chapter 1 (see also below), stresses the need for an enforcement mechanism, particularly the committee system. An alternative account does not depend on such structural considerations. Legislators have incentives to police their own agreements. Members who propose to disrupt universalism, as Senators Paul Douglas (D–Ill.), William Proxmire (D–Wis.), and James Buckley (Conservative–N.Y.) have done, may be threatened with retaliation (Ferejohn, 1974, p. 114; Weingast, 1979, p. 253). To be sure, any successful monitoring must be aimed not only at defectors but also at legislators who fail to punish norm violators (Axelrod, 1986). Players will learn that being provocative can be costly, as in Axelrod's (1984) computer simulations of PD games and in the dictate of the late Speaker Sam Rayburn (D–Tex.): To get along, go along.[4]

Policing can work in legislative bodies because mutual trust devel-

---

[4] Axelrod's (1984) examples include the pork barrel in Congress. However, even with quite long memories in a system based on reciprocity and the shared reelection goal, it is possible that some will choose to defect. There are always some "meanies" (in Axelrod's language) who are willing to defect for their own electoral advantage even when others are adhering to the norms of the institution. In 1984 several conservative Republican House members upset the general understanding that legislators' extended remarks at the end of each day's debate were to be of limited duration. Furthermore, no individual or group was to monopolize the debate. The daily "soap opera" with a continuing cast of characters became a strong irritant to the Speaker and other Democrats, who retaliated in May by violating House rules to show on television Rep. Robert Walker (R-Pa.) addressing an empty assembly. Generally such departures from the rules are ultimately resolved universalistically, but with a new equilibrium. In 1988 a proposal was under discussion to permit all members of Congress to use tapes of House debate in their campaigns in the hope that this change in rules would end the GOP members' "filibuster." In the words of House Minority Leader Robert Michel (1984), unless some solution is reached, "the process of civility and the nature of comity that have been the foundation of our legislative process will be eroded beyond repair."

ops over a time into a set of norms (Matthews, 1960, ch. 5; Hardin, 1982, chs. 10–11). These norms sustain a pattern of universalism (Fenno, 1966, p. 318, 1973, chs. 3–4; Murphy, 1974). Cooperation requires institutional memory (Axelrod, 1984, ch. 3), as well as the absence of a clear-cut end to the game. When players know that a game has a fixed number of plays, they will rationally defect on the last round (Rapoport and Chammah, 1965). A stable set of expectations develops as legislators play the pork barrel game year after year. The incentives to police the universalistic solution are found in the narrow scope of conflict and the fiscal illusion. There is relatively little for members to gain from forming narrow, partisan minimal winning coalitions, and much to lose should one's party lose its majority in the legislature. The norm of cooperation is sustained by strategic calculations. Compromise is possible, in Axelrod's terms, because there is little conflict of interest.

On the shale barrel, on the other hand, we begin with mistrust. As Wildavsky and Tenenbaum (1981, p. 11) have argued, "within a polarized issue context . . . search is simple and subjective. Whatever will discomfort the enemy is wanted." Norms do not develop on shale barrel issues. Fortunately, they do not appear quite so regularly on the political agenda. Each crisis appears to be a single play of the game. Legislators do not seem to learn very much from the history of previous crises (see Chapter 4 and Goodwin, 1981a, passim). Hence there is no sense of institutional memory, and equally important, there are few incentives for cooperative behavior. Legislators believe that any cooperative effort leading to legislation that will impose costs on their constituents will have adverse electoral consequences. The high stakes and the panic mentality that are part of resource constraint crises effectively work to prohibit the development of trust that can be socialized into coordinated behavior. The wide scope of conflict narrows the range of potentially acceptable solutions—quite often to zero. Conflict of interest is maximal. There is no obvious point around which a coalition can be built.

The explanation of cooperation as induced by institutional structure is deficient because it *only* accounts for stability; similarly, an account based on norms will be circular (Krehbiel, 1986). The concepts of the fiscal illusion and the scope of conflict are useful precisely because one can provide an explanation for rationally based norms that can lead to cooperation (the pork barrel), as well as the absence of such a system of norms (the shale barrel). The institutional structures within the legislature reflect such patterns of preferences. I now examine how this reflection is manifested in energy.

The Scope of Conflict and Institutional Structure

The models of structure-induced equilibria leading to universalism are based on pork barrel politics (Shepsle and Weingast, 1981, 1984). However, it is precisely when the scope of conflict is narrow and voters do not clearly perceive the costs of policies, that committees can act as monopoly agenda-setters. In policy areas of interest to only a few actors, legislators have little to gain by attempting to impose on others' turf. Jurisdictional disputes are highly unlikely to arise and there will be no demands for multiple referrals. Nor will there be any resistance to proposed restrictive rules for the consideration of legislation, or any incentive to gain by attempting to attach non-germane amendments to pork barrel bills. The conditions for structure-induced equilibria are clearly met for this type of legislation.

In contrast, on energy legislation the scope of conflict is wide and citizens readily perceive the costs of alternative policies. The issue virtually invites multiple referrals (see Chapter 1) because so many actors have interests in energy legislation. Legislators who do not want to levy costs on their constituents will seek to block attempts to impose restrictive rules (cf. the example of the attempt to reform energy jurisdictions in the House in Chapter 6 below). They will also be quite willing, even anxious, to retain control over the agenda by offering non-germane amendments either on the floor or in committee. The problem, of course, is determining precisely what is non-germane to an issue that has such a wide scope. Almost any issue sticks like glue to energy legislation and becomes entangled with other items in bills. The lack of separability further confounds the agenda. In contrast to the pork barrel, shale barrel issues have very large conflicts of interest and thus are unlikely candidates for attaining structure-induced equilibria.

Energy issues are perhaps the most conflictual of those put before legislative committees. Their preeminent position can be demonstrated in comparison with the environment as a policy arena. Since the two clearly overlap, one might expect that the environment would be as highly charged politically as energy. Yet *only* 44 committees and subcommittees currently have jurisdiction over the Environmental Protection Agency (Kurtz, 1983).[5] These figures overestimate the

---

[5] Jones and Strahan (1985) demonstrate that in more recent Congresses the number of Representatives and Senators serving on committees with energy jurisdictions has continued to increase, but the turnover on those bodies has been significantly higher than for either chamber. This is consistent with what one would expect of a policy arena marked by issue networks—and it suggests that rational risk-averse legislators may simply prefer to opt for a less controversial area of responsibility. After all, they can always carp at policy recommendations from the floor.

cross-cutting nature of environmental cleavages, however, because the conflicts over clean air (based primarily in the Energy and Commerce and Interior Committees) do not bear heavily on decisions on water projects and pollution (Public Works) or ocean dumping (Merchant Marine). The latter programs have passed easily while debate over clean air has been marked by more clear-cut development/environment struggles in committee and on the floor of both the House and the Senate (Congressional Quarterly, 1977, pp. 605ff).

Committees with major energy jurisdiction in the House do not represent clearly defined constituencies that make for ready compromise and possible universalistic solutions to policy problems. In fact, they are more diverse than other House committees. To be sure, committees and subcommittees are primarily instruments of interest representation: since most farms are in the Midwest and the South, it is not surprising to find the Agriculture Committee dominated by members from those regions. To the extent that committees represent purely regional interests, the scope of conflict on those bodies will be reduced. With a narrow range of issues coming before the chamber, it will be well positioned to put forth its proposals as a monopoly agenda-setter. In Table 3.1 I present data on the regional fractionalization or heterogeneity among House committees in the 98th Congress (1983–84). The index of fractionalization (from Rae, 1967, pp. 56–57) measures the probability that randomly selected members will come from different regions, assuming sampling with replacement. Four regions (East, Midwest, South, and West) are employed. The higher the value of the fractionalization index, the more diverse the regional representation on a committee.

In Table 3.1 the 22 House committees are listed in order of their fractionalization scores, together with the dominant region(s) and the percentage of members from that region, as well as the fractionalization score and rank. Five committees have significant energy jurisdiction, but two are generally considered to be the lead energy chambers in the House: Energy and Commerce and Science and Technology. Of all House committees, the former has the most diverse membership while the latter ranks third, just behind Budget. Only Interior, which has jurisdiction over public lands and is thus considered primarily a Western committee, falls below the median. To be sure, the jurisdiction of Energy and Commerce is also quite broad, encompassing just about everything that can be bought, sold, bartered, or traded (see Plattner, 1983). Issues that are generally considered to be handled in more distributive ways—farm supports (Agriculture), defense plants (Armed Services), parks (Interior), post office construction

TABLE 3.1

Regional Fractionalization in House Committees, 98th Congress, 1983–84

Committee	Dominant region (percent)[b]	Fractionalization (rank)
Energy and Commerce[a]	Midwest (31.0)	.7474 (1)
Budget	South (29.0)	.7471 (2)
Science and Technology[a]	East/South (29.3)	.7412 (3)
Education and Labor	East/Midwest (30.0)	.7378 (4)
Standards of Official Conduct	West (33.3)	.7361 (5)
Public Works and Transportation	South (32.0)	.7321 (6)
Banking and Housing	East (36.2)	.7271 (7)
Judiciary	Midwest (38.7)	.7222 (8)
Government Operations[a]	South (36.8)	.7218 (9)
Foreign Affairs[a]	East/Midwest (32.4)	.7178 (10)
Small Business	Midwest/South (32.5)	.7163 (11)
Merchant Marine	East (38.2)	.7138 (12)
Post Office/Civil Service	Midwest (41.7)	.7118 (13)
House Administration	West (42.1)	.7092 (14)
Ways and Means	South (40.0)	.7053 (15)
Appropriations	South (33.3)	.6979 (16)
Veterans' Affairs	South (42.4)	.6906 (17)
Armed Services	South (33.3)	.6864 (18)
Agriculture	Midwest/South (36.6)	.6723 (19)
District of Columbia	East (46.7)	.6528 (20)
Interior[a]	West (52.4)	.6485 (21)
Rules	South (46.2)	.6271 (22)
Total membership	South (30.0)	.7453

NOTE: The index of fractionalization is from Rae, 1967, pp. 56–57. The data are arrayed in Cohen, 1983. The 11 Eastern states run from New England to Maryland; the 12 Midwestern states extend from Ohio to Kansas and states further north. The 14 Southern states include those in the Confederacy, together with West Virginia, Kentucky, and Oklahoma. There are 13 Western states.
[a]Committee has significant energy jurisdiction.
[b]Region(s) with greatest percentage of membership on committee and that percentage.

(Post Office), and veterans' benefits (Veterans' Affairs)—are marked by committees with substantially lower fractionalization scores.

Three of the four committees that handled the largest number of multiply referred bills in the 94th and 95th Congresses (1975–78) have major energy jurisdictions: Interstate and Foreign Commerce (now Energy and Commerce), Interior, and Science and Technology. The committees with no multiple referrals have much more narrow interests as clientele groups: District of Columbia, Small Business, and Veterans' Affairs (see Schneider, 1980, p. 445, for the data). Other committees dealing largely with distributive benefits, such as Agriculture and Post Office and Civil Service, fall below the median on multiple referrals.

Not only do the Energy Committees have high rates of multiple referrals; their bills, in both the House and the Senate, are more likely to be subject to amendments. The institutionalist theory of structure-induced equilibria insists that committees be able to control their own agendas by limiting both germane and especially non-germane amendments (Shepsle, 1986; see Chapter 1). Not only do committees now have to share jurisdictional claims, but in recent Congresses there has been a dramatic increase in amendments to committee bills offered on the floor. Smith (1986b, p. 35) found that Interstate and Foreign Commerce and Interior experienced the largest increases in the number of amendments offered to *any* House committee bills between the 92d (1971–72) and the 93d (1973–74) Congress. The number of amendments offered to Commerce bills jumped from 51 to 168, while those for Interior increased from 55 to 163. Smith attributed these spikes to the controversial nature of the energy issue (and, to a lesser extent, to environmental legislation). In the second Congress, of course, the first energy crisis of the 1970's occurred.

In addition, energy related committees seemed to lose control of amending activity. Five committees met two criteria from the 92d to the 93d Congress: (1) more than twenty amendments were offered to their bills in each year, and (2) each chamber experienced an increase of 30 percent or more in the *success rates* of amendments to their bills (computed from Smith, 1986a, tables 12a and 12b). The committees (and the percentage increase in success rates) were Commerce (30), Science and Technology (76), Government Operations (37), Armed Services (95), and Appropriations (35). The first two committees have primary energy jurisdiction, and the fourth and fifth also have at least considerable interest in energy legislation. Appropriations, of course, handles all types of bills. Sinclair (1987) finds that the Interior and Energy Committees in the Senate had the greatest percentage increase (364 percent) of all committees in the mean number of roll calls per Congress from the 1960's to the 1970's and 1980's.

Energy, then, became much more controversial in the 1970's. By some measures it was the most disputed issue on the Congressional agenda. By others it was at least among the most explosive—insofar as the rate of increase in challenges to committee power was among the highest in any issue area. By any standard, committee control over energy policy was dramatically reduced in the 1970's. These "little legislatures" not only had to share jurisdiction with one another, but they also could not count on the floor to bow to their wishes. Members were more likely to propose amendments to all bills, but especially to energy legislation, and these amendments were more likely to pass.

If structure-induced equilibria do exist, they reflect the underlying patterns of conflict and cooperation in the Congress. When the scope

of an issue is quite broad, however, it is unlikely that legislative structure can impose a cooperative outcome on the membership. Indeed,
the structure is likely to mirror the lines of cleavage in the institution.
Even with shared jurisdiction by several (sub)committees, a stable
outcome might be achieved if the interests of members setting the
agenda were similar. They most emphatically are not, however. If, as
Shepsle (1986) suggests, the problem is one of enforcing cooperative
agreements, then there is little reason to presume that legislators will
design their institutions to impose unpopular outcomes. Even when
the rules can be used strategically by the leadership to enact controversial legislation (such as Carter's energy package in 1977), the outcome will still reflect only the lowest common denominator of acceptable proposals. It is thus hardly surprising that the most satisfactory
application of the monopoly agenda-setter model to the Congress involves pork barrel legislation (Shepsle and Weingast, 1981), where
costs are not readily perceived and the scope of the issue is narrow. In
such circumstances, what seems to be an example of committee power
may really be the illusion of committee supremacy. Behind the mirage
is a very low degree of conflict of interest; successful bargaining can
occur under virtually *any* institutional structure.

I do not argue that institutional structures have no impact on policy outcomes. Anyone who has studied the Congress and the extraordinary power that committee chairs wielded prior to the reforms of
the 1970's cannot deny institutional effects. Both legislative committees and the separation of powers in the U.S. constitutional system can
frustrate the will of the majority of citizens. The most malleable of institutional structures, rules for the consideration of legislation on the
floor of the legislative body, are most strongly linked to preferences
over policy outcomes. Other institutional variables have greater staying power, largely because they generally *do not* frustrate the will of
the majority. When structure and policy preferences consistently
clash, calls for reform might actually lead to changes in institutional
design—depending on whether actors can achieve agreement on
what policies ought to be enacted.

It is critical to understand that we cannot base an explanation for
cooperation or noncooperation solely on institutional structure, for
the very division of powers that makes bargaining essential in U.S.
politics—the separate legislative and executive branches and the two
houses of Congress themselves—was not given by a *deus ex machina*. It
is part of an American tradition of individualism that distrusts majoritarian government and seeks to restrain governmental excess by institutional design.

As Hartz (1955, ch. 5 and p. 60) argues, this problem of how to construct the U.S. polity has its roots in the Lockean ideology of individual rights and the need to establish some basis of cooperation. Individualism without binding mechanisms to enforce agreements is a poor recipe for cooperation. American society has always faced this problem of collective action. Yet the rugged individualism in American life (most notably associated with the "yeoman myth" of the farmer) and the distrust of authority have led to a politics of cooperation that could not be induced by an institutional structure: a voluntarism apart from authority (Hofstadter, 1955, ch. 1; Tocqueville, 1945, ch. 8). The collective action problem has roots deep in U.S. ideology and its Lockean basis and, in particular, a rejection of the strong state of majoritarian democracies (see Chapter 7). To the extent that institutions can effect cooperation, they must reflect this distrust of authority, and thus they serve primarily to splinter power rather than to aggregate it. When institutions appear to reflect a tendency to cooperate, they must therefore mirror a narrow set of cleavages with few perceived costs—the conditions identified for voluntary cooperation.

Pluralism, Universalism, and Disaggregation

The appropriate question to ask when we observe a legislature typified by cooperative behavior is *not*, Why is there so much cooperation? I shall argue in this section that no enforcement mechanism is needed to resolve Prisoners' Dilemmas arising from preference cycles. Instead, we should be more interested in failures of collective action. I have referred to the politics of energy policy-making as a pathology; Lindberg (1977a) has called it a syndrome. A body politic could not survive if it had many such pathologies. The dilemma of collective action and the need for an enforcement mechanism are salient issues at the stage of constitution-making. However, we are not born into a state of nature. We inherit both institutions and norms that give them their forms. We expect them to function well, to reach cooperative solutions to the major problems we face. When they do not, we demand to know why.

Norms enforce the cooperative solution. A threat of sanctions that both is realistic and potential offenders know will be enforced polices the norms of a society (Schelling, 1960, pp. 35–43). Some of these norms, such as tax collection, must be affirmed by statute. (Of course, under systems such as the French in which tax evasion is reportedly rampant because enforcement is lax, one wonders why so many people are honest! Again, norms must account for such behavior.) Others, however, become internalized more readily because there is so little advantage in attempting to defy them. I have continually been impressed that most people I ask will say they will not go through a red light on an isolated road late at night, even when they can clearly see that no traffic is blocking their passage at the intersection and they know that the local police are on a work slowdown (and refusing to issue moving violations). Even after removing almost all of the costs of noncompliance, the gains from defying the norm are relatively small. We are not led into temptation, but neither do we fear being a sucker. Similarly, the benefits from noncooperation in a legislative pork barrel game are slight indeed, particularly compared to the cost of the punishment payoff.

Take another example of a PD game: market exchange (see Hardin, 1982, pp. 206–7). It is always possible that the seller will give me the goods for free or at a ridiculously low price, but few of us are typically willing to risk mutual defection. We realize that the other player is also rational, so we have a pretty good idea how the exchange will ultimately be worked out. After playing the game often enough, a rational player would not even think of beginning to bargain each time a seller is confronted. In real-life exchanges, such behavior would violate our norms of comity in interpersonal transactions. The norms serve as our conventions of daily life (Lewis, 1969). We could not operate without them. They hold together our language of civil and political discourse.[6]

The U.S. political system is held together by a set of beliefs in the democratic creed regarding the allocation of power, influence, and

[6] The differences between the temptation and sucker's payoffs in the Prisoners' Dilemma is associated with the willingness of legislators to cooperate on the pork barrel and to defect on the shale barrel. There is no mechanism to enforce cooperation (Shepsle, 1986), but the prospect of small relative gains from defecting on the pork barrel increases the probability of players' cooperating. I speculate that it should also increase the likelihood that legislators will be willing to police violations of legislative norms. When (T − S) is small and the probability of cooperation is relatively high, potential cooperators have a stake in ensuring that few legislators defect, for once defection begins, it becomes endemic. On the other hand, if (T − S) is relatively large, a legislator intending to defect will have little interest in policing the cooperative behavior of others even though that legislator would be better off if all others did cooperate. The costs of policing action when defection is already endemic would be prohibitively large. (Note that it is not simply a matter of one's ability to detect "cheating," which is the same in both cases.) Thus, punishing recalcitrant legislators such as Proxmire and Buckley on the pork barrel (see Chapter 2) is much easier than doing so on the shale barrel—because the incentives for policing are higher and, similarly, because the costs of defection are clearly specified. On shale barrel issues there is generally no equilibrium policy that can be imposed on defectors (other than the status quo, which may be preferable to many alternatives under consideration) compared to the possible majoritarian solutions on the pork barrel associated with the T and S payoffs. Because the likelihood of punishment is high and the benefits from defection are relatively low, cooperation on the pork barrel becomes the norm.

more tangible resources (Dahl, 1961, ch. 28). This is the theory of pluralism, with its emphasis on dispersed inequalities. Miller (1983, p. 740) argues that the conditions underlying pluralist politics are the same ones that typically result in cyclical majorities. Furthermore, pluralist theorists at least implicitly welcome cycles. Such belief patterns indicate dispersed preferences and a potential for conflict resolution through logrolling: "Precisely because social choice is *not* stable . . . there is some range for autonomous politics to hold sway, and pluralist politics offers almost everybody hope of victory" (Miller, 1983, p. 743; emphasis in original).

Furthermore, pluralism welcomes Prisoners' Dilemmas. More appropriately, it encourages PDs in the same way that it does preference cycles: so that they can be resolved. Few things express the American democratic creed better than the national motto: *E pluribus unum* (One out of many). The question becomes how one makes the many cooperate to yield one, a universalistic solution. Again, the answer is logrolling and the enforcement of democratic norms, backed up by the guarantee that no one will be totally lacking in political influence (Dahl, 1961, p. 228). In contemporary terms, this means that everyone will obtain some of the rewards of the system. Indeed, the expectation of receiving benefits has become a virtual entitlement for any group with even a modest degree of political clout (Wilson, 1980). Even the social welfare legislation of the 1960's has been converted into a "social pork barrel" (Stockman, 1975). But that very broad sweeping package of Great Society reforms was in conception a massive social public works program. There were no great claims for redistribution to the poor even in the anti-poverty program. Pluralism is characterized by continuing attempts to enlarge the pie so as to make the "universalistic" coalition ever more inclusive. What has made the Democratic party so dominant electorally over the past five decades has been its attempt to be all things to all people (Mayhew, 1966, pp. 146–60), to make one out of many. If anyone has to be charged with the costs of our prosperity and distributive politics, it is future generations who will bear the costs of our national debt. We hide the costs from ourselves by placing them on unborn citizens in the ultimate form of fiscal illusion. We restrict the scope of conflict since there is no one to represent them in our contemporary legislature.

On the other hand, shale barrel issues lead to noncooperative outcomes because at least some costs are directly perceived and the scope of conflict is expanded. Shale barrel issues, even if not zero-sum, are redistributive in the sense that both benefits and costs are perceived. Unlike the great ideological issues of civil rights and class antagonisms, shale barrel issues involve many subsidiary concerns in which preferences are likely to cycle. Thus it is difficult to build an electoral coalition in the manner of the economic alliances of the realignments of the 1890's and 1930's (Burnham, 1970). Such realignments change the nature of political discourse from the whisper of logrolling to the street language of two-party conflict (cf. Schattschneider, 1960, p. 3). In periods of electoral realignment, or more generally in political systems with polarized parties taking opposite positions on key public issues, political language is clearly understood by the citizenry. The issues are well defined and the stakes are generally known to one and all. We are speaking a common language.

In pluralism, under normal bargaining, participants may well be speaking different languages, but each is content to let the others communicate with their own groups.[7] The task of the legislators is to maintain as much consensus as possible within their communication networks. The proliferation of new interest groups, many of them with larger and more ideological bases of support, has in recent years produced a situation where few interests are unchallenged in the legislative process (Walker, 1983; Gais, Peterson, and Walker, 1984). Issues are no longer as separable as they once were. Our affluent society spawns interest groups that then seek out issues and people to organize. The expanding scope of conflict replaces closed systems with policy-making as "an intramural activity among expert issue-watchers, their networks, and their networks of networks" (Heclo, 1978, pp. 105–6). The issue networks place a lower value on achieving consensus than on "informed skepticism" and are marked "by continuously weighing alternative courses of action on particular policies, not by suspending disbelief and accepting that something must be done" (Heclo, 1978, pp. 120–21). The networks, in sharp contrast to iron triangles, are fluid. Their members have fewer long-term ties to their organizations (which may be quite new themselves) and are likely to circulate from position to position in Washington.

The growth of issue networks threatens subsystem politics. To be sure, some iron triangles continue to thrive, mostly for obscure groups whose benefits are hidden deep in the recesses of the federal budget such as kiwi and peppermint farmers (Sinclair, 1983). Yet, increasingly, the scope of conflict is becoming wider across most issues.

---

[7] This is equivalent to the idea of a monopoly agenda-setter, of course. But the very notion of such an agenda-setter leads to another impossibility result in public choice. If we permit actors to impose their individual preferences on a single issue of greatest salience to them, the net result will be suboptimal social welfare, given the same allowable preference patterns as in the more general issue of cycling. This is the problem of the "Paretian liberal" (see Sen, 1971).

This makes structure-induced equilibria more difficult to obtain even on issues that heretofore have been marked by narrow scopes of conflict. Yet Heclo's issue networks do retain a common language, that of the technocrats. This at least makes communication possible, and policy-making can proceed, even in a more highly charged environment.

Shale barrel politics, however, is characterized by a linguistic tower of Babel and a high pitch. What is worse, such disagreement cannot be traced entirely to technical difficulties of estimation. The figures are highly charged politically and there is no common language among the experts. Thus one of Heclo's key conditions for an issue network, a common frame of reference, may not be met, making energy a virtually formless policy area in which each actor competes as if in a state of nature. There are difficulties in enforcing the norm-based social contract because each actor has a different idea of what the stakes are.

Pluralism, Miller argues persuasively (1983, pp. 740–44), resolves conflicts by ensuring that no group is consistently a loser on issue after issue; party government, on the other hand, highlights conflict by clearly identifying winners and losers. But shale barrel issues mostly raise questions about how costs will be borne by people. When people are preoccupied with direct costs and negative externalities, they are likely to perceive themselves as losers, particularly during shortages. Such concerns go to the heart of the problem of hyperpluralism, the system of entitlements that has replaced pluralism as the dominant public philosophy in the United States. Hyperpluralism is the belief that any organized group has some almost divine right to dictate that its policy preferences be reflected in governmental decision-making. Without an ever-increasing budget to reward all actors, there will be fewer opportunities for each group to achieve its goals. Furthermore, there is no assurance that as the number of groups multiplies, the traditional pluralist assumption that the multiplicity of demands yields nonconflicting claims will hold.

When cleavages become overlapping, or reinforcing, interests pay more attention to preserving their turf than to expanding it. This leads to attempts to block new initiatives that might be harmful to a group's interests and provides the seeds for the formation of destructive coalitions of minorities. As Dodd (1982, p. 65) argues, "the orderliness of the past may vanish and a potentially quite durable era could dissolve under a series of rapid 'flashpoint' shocks because institutions fail to process the most basic policy decisions, or because policy problems exceed the capacity of this (or possibly any) institutional/constitutional setting to manage. . . . We cannot simply assume that the descriptive patterns of past periods are perfect guides to the present." This is what electoral disaggregation is all about. Issues that could be resolved in terms of party politics would destabilize existing logrolling agreements, to be replaced first by a more clearly defined method of political discourse and ultimately by a return to the more traditional method of conflict resolution. However, the newer issues, again with the shale barrel being the archetype, are not so readily aggregated into winning and losing coalitions.

Instead, a turf battle in the legislature mirrors the conflicts in the society at large. The scope of conflict is expanded, on the one hand, but each (sub)committee insists on sharing control over the agenda. Dahl (1971, p. 120) warned that, "to contrive a political system that works by unanimity and minority veto, or by shifting coalitions, and guarantees that no majority coalition will act adversely toward any of its subcultural minorities, may be a perfect recipe for governmental immobility, for a system, that is to say, in which major problems, as these are defined by the political stratum, go unresolved because every possible solution is vetoed by some minority whose leaders feel that its interests are threatened." Shale barrel issues are thus a warning about what might happen if norms break down, if such issues come to dominate discourse on how we distribute our national resources. We cannot conceive of destructive coalitions of minorities becoming the norm, for it violates our very understanding of what the concept "norm" means. But norms depend on a common language, so we must consider how our communications can break down.

The framework developed in this and the preceding chapter contrasts the traditional pluralist politics of the pork barrel with the hyperpluralist politics of the shale barrel. In the former, everyman is in his humor. Despite cyclical preferences for legislators over a series of distributive issues that threaten to disrupt decision-making, members of Congress resolve the strategic Prisoners' Dilemma by cooperating in an all-for-one, one-for-all scenario in which everyone lives happily ever after (by being reelected). Pork barrel issues are marked by cleavages that are not reinforcing. More critically, the scope of each issue is narrow and the costs of projects are neatly hidden from constituents. There is little conflict of interest among the actors. The distributive game is played over and over and a set of norms enforcing agreement on the cooperative outcome develops. This narrow cleavage pattern permits interest groups, legislators, and the bureaucracy to form iron triangles of likeminded actors who can serve as monopoly agenda-setters in the legislature. What appears to be a vice from the perspective of public choice—theory-cyclical group preferences—is converted into a virtue. Instead of cycles leading to the disequilibrium that Riker (1980) and others so worry about, a shared reelection goal leads to one of the more stable equilibria in legislative politics.

In contrast, shale barrel politics is also marked by preference cycles and strategic Prisoners' Dilemmas. But the issues here raise questions of costs more than benefits to constituents. These costs are readily perceived. Mostly they are beyond the reach of legislators, as citizens see increased prices at the pump and in their monthly utility bills. Furthermore, the scope of shale barrel issues is very wide so that no group can serve as a monopoly agenda-setter. The electoral incentives for legislators center on the prevention of high costs to constituents, and this is a recipe for failure to cooperate on legislation. It is easier to mobilize people against the imposition of burdens than for the common good. Furthermore, people distrust each other's motivations for cooperation. High costs and the pervasiveness of shale barrel issues mean that there is a great deal of conflict of interest, and few benefits are to be reaped at least in the short run from cooperating. Thus there is the potential for a destructive coalition of minorities. Since shortages come and go, there is little memory component in the current struggle to avoid the mistakes of the past. Thus norms do not develop over shale barrel issues. Indeed, for both pluralism and hyperpluralism, shortages are anything but the norm. The disequilibrium that some theorists warn of reaches full force when everyman is out of his humor.

FOUR

Living in Syn

Unless your breath had power
To melt the world and mould it new again,
It is in vain to spend it in these moods.

(*Everyman Out of His Humour*, Prologue, p. 286)

THE PRICE shock for petroleum following the Organization of Petroleum Exporting Countries' oil embargo in 1973–74 led to greater conservation efforts and to government programs to decrease U.S. dependence on foreign energy sources. Between 1978 and 1979, oil consumption dropped by almost half a million barrels a day, the first decline since 1975. Imports were also down—by 200,000 barrels a day. On the rocky road to energy independence, coal usage increased by 17 percent and production reached an all-time high. Even without substantial government intervention, the energy situation was beginning to stabilize. However, the ascension of Ayatollah Khomeini in February 1979 led to a sharp cutback in Iran's oil production and exports. The price of oil nearly doubled, reaching $30 a barrel, and pump prices rose beyond the incomprehensible dollar-a-gallon level. Half of U.S. oil was imported, a record level, and rising energy costs directly induced about 20 percent of the 13.5 percent inflation rate for 1979 (Congressional Quarterly, 1979a, p. 601). We had returned to the days of 1973–74 with a vengeance. Indeed, the price shocks—particularly considering the shorter time frame—were more severe than in the first boycott. As Iran demodernized, Americans waiting on gas lines began to shoot it out as well. Violence was even reported at a few service stations.

A panic mentality swept the Congress. Legislators were twice as likely as the public at large to perceive the 1979 energy situation to be of crisis proportions (Sussman, 1979). The theoretical framework developed in Chapters 2 and 3 suggests that the situation should have been an ideal scenario for inaction. The scope of conflict was wide indeed: everyone was affected by skyrocketing energy prices. The energy shortage dominated the national political agenda. There was certainly no fiscal illusion. The United States stood at the mercy of foreign nations. Attempts to impose conservation met with widespread

Congressional resistance as legislators were unwilling to impose costs on their constitutents. However, in 1979–80 the legislators enacted with relatively little controversy a massive program to develop synthetic fuels. The Energy Security Act of 1980 provided $88 billion in federal funds over five years. It was designed to create a privately run industry that would yield 500,000 barrels of fuel a day by 1987 and 2 million barrels by 1992. The scope of the investment was unparalleled. Never in U.S. history had such a massive dollar commitment been made to any domestic program. The authorization for 1981, the first year of the program's operation, was $20 billion.

How did this legislation get passed? The politics of the situation seemed to preclude any legislation action on energy, much less one of such broad scope. This chapter attempts to answer that question. Briefly, the argument will be that Congress responded to widespread public concern over energy shortages and the perception of demands that something must be done by enacting legislation that would bring only benefits rather than readily perceivable costs. Synthetic fuels were basically unknown to most of the people. Indeed, a massive compilation of public opinion polls on energy from 1973 to 1978, with as many pages as there are members of the House of Representatives, contains no reference whatsoever to synthetic fuels (Farhar et al., 1979). A Harris survey finally posed a question about synfuels just after Carter announced his massive subsidy plan. With gas lines still long, one might have expected strong support for this new energy source, even if that meant making some environmental trade-offs. But when the question was posed in terms of the idea that synthetic fuels development might mean relaxing environmental standards, the public expressed its support by a margin of only 56 percent to 35 percent (Farhar et al., 1980, p. 153). In 1980, at the height of Congressional debate on Carter's energy program, there was little public concern for the potential of the emerging technology. Only 26 percent of a national sample said that synthetic fuels should be one of the two or three energy sources to receive the most attention over the next 20 years. Nuclear energy, for all of the problems associated with its development after the accident at Three Mile Island in March 1979, fared only marginally worse at 23 percent (Council on Environmental Quality, 1980, pp. 22ff).

Given all the ballyhoo about synfuels from the White House and Congress and the relatively restrained criticism from opponents, it can only be concluded that the poor showing resulted not from public hostility, but rather from indifference or sheer lack of knowledge. For the members of Congress, this untapped source of energy was like manna from heaven. It might be expensive, at least at the beginning, but it was abundant beyond a policy-maker's wildest dreams. It was the ultimate quick fix, if the nation could only hold out against international events for two more decades. Even if the cruel world were to intervene with further shocks, politicians could always argue that energy independence was just around the corner.

The politics surrounding the passage of the Energy Security Act of 1980 will be shown to conform much more to the traditional pork barrel model than to that of the shale barrel. Since synthetic fuels were of low salience, a constructive coalition of minorities was needed to enact the legislation. This is precisely what happened, as the bill was loaded down with funds for more popular although less promising energy sources such as gasohol and solar power. House leaders also deftly brushed aside the potential effects of a destructive coalition of minorities by separating a key section of the bill dealing with less restrictive environmental regulations for synthetic fuels and letting that proposal go down to defeat on its own demerits. The natural question, then, is, If the story of synfuels is that of the pork barrel, of what relevance to key energy issues is the shale barrel model? The answer is straightforward: in the rush to enact the Energy Security Act, legislators failed to pay sufficient attention to the negative aspects of the program. An issue on which there would eventually be a wide scope of conflict and clearly perceived costs would be temporarily transformed to a pork barrel program by satisfying most of the key elements in the energy community. Expenditures would be largely hidden by a fiscal illusion, much as those for the Pentagon are routinely handled regardless of their sheer magnitude. With the term "security" neatly placed in the bill's name, the huge expenditures could be justified on the basis of defense against foreign blackmail.

Yet, other costs such as boomtown effects, damage to the environment, public safety, and health are much more visible to constituents. Unlike a new post office or veterans' hospital, megaprojects such as synfuels plants do not bring constituents only benefits. Unlike pork barrel projects, they have spillover costs to other districts that simply cannot be ignored. While many pork barrel projects do have environmental costs, the traditional model of universalistic politics assumes that politicians will not weigh such factors in their voting decisions (see Chapter 3). This does not mean that citizens will be united in their demands that plants *not* be placed in their backyards, for there remain many people who profit greatly from boomtown effects. It does suggest that destructive coalitions of minorities are set loose only once the costs have been perceived—and in this instance, after the legislation has been passed. The story of synthetic fuels, then, high-lights the different aspects of the pork barrel and shale barrel models rather than issues of institutional design. These latter issues will be considered in greater detail in Chapters 6 and 7. After a brief descrip-tion of what synthetic fuels are, I shall analyze how a constructive coalition of minorities was formed on the Energy Security Act of 1980 and then how it split apart just a few years later.

What Are Synthetic Fuels?

Synthetic fuels are fuels derived from other products. A lump of coal cannot be put into a gasoline tank, but it can be liquefied into a fuel to power automobiles. While oil reserves are declining at a pre-cipitous rate, world coal supplies are 350 times the volume of recover-able oil. Much of these reserves are located in the United States, in-deed in sufficient supply to sustain an industry based on synthetic fuels for up to 175 years (Darmstadter et al., 1983, pp. 57–63; Her-shey, 1980). Synthetic fuels include not only liquefied coal, but also oil shale, tar sands, unconventional gas from Devonian shale, gas in geopressurized zones, methane from coal seams, and biomass fuels (which include gasohol, a mixture of gasoline and alcohol, and fuels derived from agricultural and wood products, as well as municipal wastes). We are rich in energy indeed.

If we are so rich, why aren't we smart? Why haven't we exploited this load before? The problem has been one of cost. For most of the twentieth century, oil has been very cheap and its real price has gener-ally been declining. On the other hand, the estimates of price for syn-thetic fuels have always been much higher than for other fuels—up to 3.5 times the cost of oil—and the costs of constructing plants to produce these alternative fuels are also high (Morgenthaler, 1981). Furthermore, such costs are affected by the same inflationary forces as other commodities (largely driven by increases in energy prices), so a vicious circle envelops the drive to make synfuels competitive with oil.

Nevertheless, there have been modest attempts to develop syn-thetic fuels since the end of World War II.[1] The Truman administra-tion proposed a $10 billion program, but the idea foundered when the petroleum industry opposed a government role in energy produc-tion, so only a small demonstration project was enacted. It was termi-nated during the Eisenhower administration. The Johnson admin-

[1] This paragraph is based on Congressional Quarterly, 1979a,b; Cochrane, 1981; Goodwin, 1981b; and Rudolph, 1983. Rudolph's study provides useful background on synfuels development outside the United States.

istration considered restarting the pilot program, but could not obtain permission to lease federal lands for shale development.[2] The oil embargo of 1973–74 led President Gerald R. Ford to renew the call for synfuels development, but conflict over who would benefit from the projects and whether the technology was cost-effective led to defeat of his proposals in the House of Representatives in 1974 and 1976. Two years later a small pilot program finally began under the Energy Research and Development Administration authorization bill.

The Energy Security Act of 1980:
The Political Setting

The gasoline shortages of the spring and summer of 1979 set the stage for the massive synfuels subsidies program enacted the next year.[3] Congress did not choose among alternative energy futures for the United States, nor did it attempt to ensure that supply disruptions would not occur again. No single strategy had sufficient support for a major political commitment, so most major alternatives were included in a pork barrel bill. Such a course of action paid little attention to whether any of the energy sources could provide relief from future shortages or what the environmental (and other societal) consequences might be. Politically, however, this strategy had much to offer. First, it indicated to the public that Congress was doing something. The size of the commitment made it seem that Congress was doing a lot. Second, forming a constructive coalition of minorities among supporters of the many alternative paths postponed the difficult decision about the nation's energy course and made the task of building a legislative coalition considerably easier. The scope of the conflict was reduced because the longer-term implications of the choices that would have to be made were simply ignored. Ultimately, however, this was to set the stage for the unraveling of the universalistic coalition and the formation of a destructive coalition of minorities.

The impetus for synthetic fuels legislation actually predated the 1979 embargo. In 1978 the chair of the House Banking Subcommittee on Economic Stabilization, William Moorhead (D–Pa.), introduced a bill providing $3 billion for synfuels development aimed at

[2] The national government owns 36 percent of the surface of Colorado, 49 percent of Wyoming, and 30 percent of Montana. It holds approximately 40 percent of all coal in the country and 61 percent of all reserves west of the Mississippi River, compared to just 26 percent for private individuals and firms. Seventy percent of the shale land in the West is under federal control. It is also split into crazy-quilt tracts, so that federal consent is a necessity for any development (Masselli and Dean, 1981, p. 8).

[3] This section draws heavily on Congressional Quarterly, 1979a, 1980; Hamlett, 1982; and Rudolph, 1983.

producing 500,000 barrels a day by 1990. As with future legislation, the package was a mix of loan guarantees (which would insure private firms against financial disaster), purchase guarantees (which would obligate the government to buy specified amounts of synfuels from producers), and price supports. Turf battles with Rep. John Dingell's Energy and Power subcommittee on Interstate and Foreign Commerce delayed consideration of the Moorhead measure until after the oil embargo hit the nation.

In June 1979 this modest proposal sailed through the House by a vote of 368–25. A handful of House Democrats, mostly from California, who favored "soft" energy paths such as solar and other renewable fuels, opposed the legislation, as did a few fiscal conservatives, mostly Republicans.[4] The overwhelming vote was explained by Rep. Millicent Fenwick (R–N.J.): "[Constituents] want action. They don't really care how much it costs" (Congressional Quarterly, 1979a, p. 633). Without even a recorded vote, the House accepted a proposal to quadruple the target of 500,000 barrels a day to 2 million by 1990, with the lower figure set as an intermediate goal to be reached by 1985. No additional funds were provided for the new figure.

Less than a month later, on July 15, President Carter delivered a televised address to the nation in which he spoke of "a crisis of confidence" that was "threatening to destroy the social and the political fabric of America." He laid the blame almost everywhere: his own weak leadership, OPEC, a Congress isolated from the people but insulated by the special interests, the unproductive U.S. labor force, and citizens who used too much energy. He offered as a solution: (1) faith ("We simply must have faith in each other, faith in our ability to govern ourselves, and faith in the future of this Nation"); (2) hope ("We know the strength of America. We are strong. We can regain our unity. We can regain our confidence"); and (3) not a little charity ("I propose the creation of an Energy Security Corporation to lead this effort to replace two and a half billion barrels of imported oil per day by 1990. The corporation will issue up to $5 billion in energy bonds").[5]

[4]The votes discussed here and later in this chapter were obtained from Congressional Quarterly, 1979a, pp. 54S, 55S, 64S, 65S, 80–81H, 164–65H, and 1980, 34–S, 100–103H.

[5]The text of the address is reprinted in Congressional Quarterly, 1979a, pp. 45E–47E. The President also proposed oil import quotas (which he imposed by executive order), the creation of the nation's solar bank that would provide 20 percent of the nation's energy in the form of renewable power by the year 2000 (a very popular goal, even if unlikely to be attained), a standby gasoline rationing program (which seemed even less feasible politically than the solar energy program was technically), a $10 billion public transportation program, and an Energy Mobilization Board to speed up development of synfuels.

The goal of energy independence, which was based on an overall savings of 4.5 million barrels of imported oil a day, was within reach.

The administration's bill would create an Energy Security Corporation to be run by a board of seven members that would manage the investment of the funds. In addition to the $5 billion mentioned in the speech, $83 billion in revenues was anticipated from the windfall profits tax that was enacted along with a partial decontrol of domestic oil prices. The Synthetic Fuels Corporation (SFC) would run the program and would be given extraordinary latitude: it would not have to follow Civil Service rules and would be freed from most conflict-of-interest requirements, and it could decide without Congressional interference how to invest the money, possibly in government-owned plants. An Energy Mobilization Board (EMB), a companion to the SFC board, would cut through red tape on environmental regulations to ensure that synfuels production could begin promptly. The President set a target of 2.5 million barrels of fuel a day by 1990, which was 500 percent more than some sources estimate could be produced in reasonable circumstances (Perry and Landsberg, 1981, p. 263). Four Senate committees claimed jurisdiction over the bill: Energy, Banking, Governmental Affairs, and Budget. The Budget Committee only held hearings on the legislation, while Energy and Banking did battle over how the bill would take shape. In a September meeting with members of all three committees, Carter agreed to split the funding for the bill into two phases: the first would provide $20 billion for building some initial plants, after which Congress would evaluate the program and could approve the remaining $68 billion. The President also agreed to a reduced goal of 1.75 million barrels of synthetic fuel a day by 1990.

The Battle of the Committees

Even before the President submitted his proposal for an $88 billion synthetic fuels program, the House Interstate and Foreign Commerce Committee's Energy and Power Subcommittee held hearings on five different synfuels proposals, which were competitors with the bill from the Economic Stabilization subcommittee. The proposals called for between $2 billion and $100 billion in expenditures. The hearings yielded a surprising amount of support for a large government program to develop these technologies (Interstate and Foreign Commerce Committee, 1979a). Of the various witnesses from the government, utilities, private consultants, and academics, only two cited any real reservations against large-scale government programs to develop synthetic fuels. The story was basically the same in the Senate.

There was, however, substantial criticism of a major synfuels effort at the Senate Banking, Housing and Urban Affairs Committee (1979) hearings. Environmentalists concentrated on defeating the EMB. They refrained from a full-stage attack because they did not want to be seen as standing in the way of energy development while the nation was undergoing severe shortages. There was little excitement about the President's legislation. As Sen. J. Bennett Johnston (D–La.) admitted, "Many of our members were just not that interested in synthetic fuels" (Congressional Quarterly, 1980, p. 477). While the opposition was restrained, there simply did not appear to be sufficient support for these technologies to enact a massive program. The strategic response was a growing constructive coalition of minorities. While a core in each house supported synfuels development—including Johnston, Energy Committee Chair Henry Jackson (D–Wash.), Sen. Pete Domenici (R–N.Mex.), and House Majority Leader Wright— the potential for a destructive coalition of minorities clearly existed. Westerners were divided, as Democrats in both chambers and Republicans in the House perceived constituency benefits in the program, but GOP Senators were skeptical of a government role in energy development. Many legislators from non–energy-producing states worried about massive commitments of funds to an untested technology that might have severe environmental consequences.

The first test came on an amendment to prevent the SFC from owning any synfuels plant; it was defeated by the narrow margin of 47–44. Proxmire tried to substitute the Banking bill for that of the Energy Committee and lost by 57–37 in the second test. Yet he drew support from what Congressional Quarterly (1979a, p. 640) called an "odd coalition." Within the Senate, members moved by environmental concerns joined with those suspicious of government involvement in the energy industry. Outside the Senate, the United States Chamber of Commerce, the American Petroleum Institute, the Sierra Club, and Common Cause all pressed for the more limited Proxmire approach to synfuels development.

Yet the Energy Committee proposal passed the Senate by an overwhelming majority of better than three-to-one (65–19). Why did the Energy Committee proposal receive such a lopsided vote, even from critics in both parties? The answer probably does not lie in the President's power of persuasion. Carter was not known as a master of handling Capitol Hill. While there was pressure on legislators to take some action, there is precious little evidence that the citizenry insisted that the solution to our energy problem be synthetic fuels. What moved the Senate—and later the House—was a series of changes that

Jackson and Johnston had made to Carter's original proposal. The scope of the program was greatly increased by adding funds for biomass (alcohol fuels and urban waste), renewable energy (wind, hydroelectric), solar energy, conservation, geothermal energy, and filling the strategic petroleum reserve. This raised the initial authorization in the bill from $88 billion to $95 billion, and potentially more than $7 billion more might be spent on the additional sections. The legislation was no longer just a synthetic fuels bill; it had become an energy pork barrel. There was even a small authorization for a study of acid rain from coal. As Hamlett (1982, p. 8) argued, "a single-goal energy plan had become a massive omnibus energy program, in which nearly every pet project had found a place." Furthermore, as Costain (1981, p. 6) noted, "almost every method of government aid or subsidy ever proposed was included."

The funds for alternative energy sources appealed to a diverse group of legislators. The major portion of the bill was still devoted to synthetic fuels. Western legislators in both parties in the House saw constituency benefits from shale and coal development, although Republican Senators from the affected states were more responsive to industry's concern about government interference in energy development.[6] Legislators from Eastern coal-producing states such as Kentucky and West Virginia saw the bill as a boon to this depressed industry. The provision for alcohol fuels from corn and grain had great appeal to members from the Midwest, whose farming constituents touted gasohol as the ultimate solution to the energy crisis. Energy from urban waste would appeal to members from large cities since it would solve two problems at once, offering both more dependable fuel supplies and trash removal. Advocates of solar energy in the South and Southwest were placated, as were the environmentalists with conservation funds and support for other renewables such as wind, hydroelectric, and geothermal in addition to the acid rain study and filling the strategic petroleum reserve. The latter issues appealed to members from the two coasts.

Many of the provisions had been stalled in House committees for lack of sufficient support, and the size of the bill grew from its initial Senate passage to the final conference report that reached the two houses almost a year after Carter's televised speech. The conference bill was the product of four House and three Senate committees. The

[6]One can only speculate why GOP Western Senators, unlike their House counterparts, were more responsive to industry than to constituent interests. One fruitful line of thought may be that Senate elections are generally more closely contested than House races and that money from large contributors might make more of a difference there. For a congenial argument, see Uslaner, 1981.

conferees, according to Congressional Quarterly (1980, p. 478), "specialized in particular sections and almost no one was able to talk about the bill as a whole." While some House members, particularly Moorhead, argued that the various portions of the bill ought to be considered separately, Johnston argued that the omnibus approach was the only way to "hold the coalition together. There's something there for the left and for the right." When asked if the bill was not like a cookie jar with something for everyone, he responded affirmatively but added, "All of the cookies are good for the country" (Congressional Quarterly, 1980, pp. 477–78).

The supporting coalitions for each energy source were largely non-overlapping. Congressional Quarterly (1980, p. 477) described the situation well: "Supporters of conservation and solar energy . . . realized their proposals might never pass if detached from synfuels. And synfuels needed their votes." Thus, if every legislator had voted for only the proposals that he or she most strongly favored, the outcome would have been a destructive coalition of minorities against the omnibus bill. The lukewarm reactions of most members to the synthetic fuels proposal would have led to defeat for the large commitment of funds to that portion of the legislation in particular.

The support for synfuels was tepid indeed. The legislation was more of a symbolic effort to placate constituents that something was being done about the energy crisis than a comprehensive approach to a complex policy problem. No one knew what the ultimate cost of the bill would be. There was certainly no guarantee that synthetic fuels would cost less than imported oil even in any future energy crisis. Indeed, there was not even a consensus on *which* synthetic fuels should be developed. What mattered most was that the high price tag of the legislation would not be readily perceived by constituents, while members of Congress could claim that they had provided the basis for an energy "insurance policy."

I demonstrate these claims of symbolism and pork barrel politics in this instance of Congressional policy-making by a content analysis of the debate in the House of Representatives on the conference report on June 26, 1980. The results are presented in Table 4.1. I compare the amounts of authorized monies for the various programs with the column inches of debate devoted to each source and with the percentage of total column inches favoring the energy alternatives. What is striking is the relationship between dollars and rhetoric: 93 percent of all authorizations were for synthetic fuels broadly defined, but only 39 percent of the debate centered on them. Synfuels were mentioned only 1.45 times as often as gasohol, but funds for the former were

TABLE 4.1

Energy Security (Synfuels) Act of 1980:
Federal Expenditures and Congressional Rhetoric

Title no.[a] energy source	Program authorization (in billions of dollars)	House debate (mentions in column inches)	Percentage of debate favorable[b]
I Synthetic fuels (genl.)	88.000	165.43	72.3
Coal/coal gasification		11.66	84.3
Oil shale/tar sands		1.00	0.0
Subtotal		178.09	72.7
II Alcohol from biomass urban waste	1.450	122.82	88.4
IV Renewable energy (wind, hydroelectric)	.230	1.75	100.0
V Solar energy	.525	15.50	100.0
Energy conservation	2.625	96.41	90.1
VI Geothermal	.085	12.00	100.0
VIII Strategic petroleum reserve	2.000	34.25	90.0
TOTAL	94.928[c]	460.85	83.8

SOURCES: Compiled by author from Pelham, 1980, and from *Congressional Record*, daily ed., 96th Cong., 2d sess., June 26, 1980, pp. H5691–H5741.
[a]Refers to title in act; Title III sets energy targets and authorizes no money to be spent.
[b]Percentage of favorable references to energy source of all mentions in House debate on conference report.
[c]Includes $.008 billion on Title VII for studies of acid rain.

greater by a factor of more than 60. For conservation, the figures were 1.85 and 33.5, while for the strategic petroleum reserve the ratios were 5.2 and 44.0. The debate indicated more concern for gasohol and other renewable fuels than for coal and oil shale specifically, which *together* accounted for less than 3 percent of the column inches devoted to all alternative energy sources. Furthermore, virtually all the debate on every alternative except synthetic fuels was positive. Only synthetic fuels received less than 88 percent favorable mentions. Indeed, the correlation between the dollar amount of authorizations and the percentage of favorable mentions in debate is slightly negative ($-.17$).

This lack of concern and support for synfuels suggests that the legislative base for Carter's program was quite narrow. There was little opposition to synfuels development in the debate, but the lack of enthusiasm for the program suggests that it must be viewed as something other than a guaranteed entrance ticket into the Promised Land of energy independence. Instead, legislators felt pressured to do *something* about the immediate energy crisis, and the synfuels program was the only option on the table that offered them even the hope of shelter from enraged constituents who were demanding action. Despite the size of the authorization for synfuels, the scope of conflict was restricted. Seven committees handled the omnibus bill in the two houses, but there was little overlap in their areas of concern in each chamber. The nature of the final bill, as well as the overwhelming support for the bill in both chambers, suggests that the pork barrel model accounts for the passage of the Energy Security Act of 1980 rather well. The 317–93 vote for the conference report under suspension of the rules was similiar to the Senate's better than three-to-one vote on that house's Energy Committee bill. The Senate vote on the conference report was even more lopsided: 78–12.

The Strategic Politics of Synfuels

If we accept Congressional Quarterly's argument that the various parts of the bill might not have been passed without the omnibus approach, we have the makings of a preference cycle among legislators on possible resolutions to the energy crisis. These cyclical preferences create a Prisoners' Dilemma over the strategies for legislators. The only prominent solution was to enact a bill that would be politically popular because it would demonstrate to constituents that the Congress was doing something to resolve future energy shortages while perhaps simultaneously ensuring increased fuel supplies in the future. There were substantial incentives for legislators to pursue the cooperative solution, which had potential electoral benefits and few risks. The multifaceted approach of the conferees ensured that the quest for energy independence would not be viewed in either-or terms of hard versus soft paths. Even though the scope of the commitment, perhaps more than $100 billion, would be large, it would not be readily perceived by constitutents. Energy prices at the pump and in the home were beginning to ease and the costs of the new program were as neatly hidden by fiscal illusion as those in the Pentagon's budget.

The strategic Prisoners' Dilemma facing the Congress is outlined in Table 4.2. As in the pork barrel, we first must divide the legislators into two blocs. In this case, the two blocs are generally exclusive although not exhaustive. On the one side, are the synfuels advocates; on the other, the supporters of soft energy paths such as solar and hydroelectric power. Thus, for synfuels advocates, the temptation payoff would be a bill that only funded synfuels projects, while the

TABLE 4.2

The Synfuels Pork Barrel Prisoners' Dilemma

| | | SOFT ENERGY ADVOCATES | |
		Cooperate	Defect
SYNFUELS ADVOCATES	Cooperate	Both vote for omnibus; funds voted for synfuels and soft paths. Outcome: omnibus passes.	Synfuels supporters vote only for all projects; soft energy advocates vote only for soft paths. Outcome depends on voting decisions of rest of members. Most likely outcome: only soft paths approved.
	Defect	Soft energy advocates vote for omnibus; synfuels advocates only vote for their projects. Outcome depends on voting decisions of rest of members. Most likely outcome: only synfuels approved.	Both vote against omnibus and for their own projects. Outcome: no energy bill adopted.

GROUP PREFERENCES:

Synfuels advocates: Only synfuels approved, omnibus bill, no energy bill, only soft paths approved.

Soft energy advocates: Only soft paths approved, omnibus bill, no energy bill, only synfuels approved.

sucker's payoff would be legislation that only funded solar projects, wind power, and so on. The payoffs are reversed for advocates of soft energy paths. On the other hand, the reward payoff for both would be an omnibus providing funds for both energy alternatives. Punishment would be no energy bill whatsoever. While this might seem the least desirable alternative politically, it must be stressed that advocates of each energy path strongly believed that the other one would not lead to energy security. Soft energy supporters worried about the environmental effects of synfuels and doubted claims that the technology would ever live up to its promises. Synthetic fuels advocates, on the other hand, strongly believed that "passive" technologies could not provide sufficient energy to resolve long-term supply problems. They argued that legislation providing only support for soft paths would raise expectations about solving the energy crisis. Since these hopes would prove to be unfounded, such legislation would be less attractive than no bill at all.

There was little conflict of interest. Neither side objected to funding projects of the other as long as both paths were pursued. Nevertheless, in a Prisoners' Dilemma there are strong incentives for each side to defect. As in the pork barrel, however, the small degree of conflict of interest is associated with electoral incentives to avoid stalemate. Neither side was so opposed to funding projects for the other that cooperation could not be achieved. The crisis atmosphere in the Congress made compromise not only possible but likely. Taking some action that could be presented to constituents as an attempt to relieve energy shortages would have electoral rewards. More critically, failing to reach any agreement could have severe consequences for incumbents at the next election. Thus the electoral game provided the incentive for reaching an accomodation in the policy game. The prominent political solution, as in the pork barrel generally, is the omnibus.

This outcome was not assured. Both blocs remained minorities within each house, as noted above. (Their relative sizes were never estimated in any account of the legislative battle.) Which outcome would ultimately be selected depended on the votes of other members of Congress. We have no knowledge of the preferences of these legislators, but it is reasonable to assume that the political climate of the time dictated that they would favor any energy proposal that had a chance of being passed. Thus they would prefer some package to no bill at all. If synfuels advocates and supporters of soft energy paths were to reach an accomodation, the uncommitted members would support that. On the other hand, if only one of the blocs with strong preferences were to cooperate and the other were to defect, the uncommitteds would go along with the defector. The legislators in the middle would then support a soft path bill if that were the only feasible outcome (upper right-hand cell of Table 4.2), or synfuels funding if that seemed to be the only legislation that could command a majority (lower left-hand cell). On the other hand, if neither side appeared to have the strategic advantage, no bill would be passed, since the uncommitted members had no alternative of their own. Thus it is appropriate to model the game as one between the synfuels advocates and soft energy path supporters only. The existence of a third bloc without strong preferences only serves to introduce some uncertainty into the prospect of achieving the temptation (and sucker's) payoff(s). There is no evidence that this uncertainty changed anyone's order of preferences over the alternatives. Rather, given the key role of the electoral game, uncertainty more likely reduced the overall level of conflict of interest by making the difference between the temptation and reward (as well as the punishment and sucker's) payoffs smaller. The incentives for cooperation therefore increased.

The disappearance of the gasoline lines and the abating of the price shocks by the summer of 1980 certainly reduced the scope of conflict, but we should not make too much of this factor in seeking to explain the universalistic outcome. The conference report merely extended the range of benefits already included in the Energy Committee bill that the Senate approved the previous winter. Once the decision had been made by the administration to pursue a massive program, there was little doubt that if a popular bill could be put together, it would pass overwhelmingly (cf. Hamlett, 1982, p. 16). The coalition formation strategy was as prominent as it was expensive and cumbersome. What fell by the wayside was the technical arguments over whether synfuels would yield the energy promised by its most ardent supporters (Hamlett, 1982, pp. 15–16).

Seeds of Destruction

If the leaders of Congress, or at least those on the Senate Energy Committee, are to be credited with cool sophistication in turning a potentially divisive issue into a pork barrel bill, then they must be given even more credit for knowing where to cut their losses. Carter's proposal for synfuels development included an Energy Mobilization Board that would cut through both red tape and environmental regulations to pave the way for the exploitation of shale and coal resources. But the EMB proposal was itself ultimately derailed in the House of Representatives, and it clearly had the potential to drag the Energy Security Act with it. However, the two proposals were considered separately.

The Senate approved an EMB as part of an omnibus energy bill in October. The EMB vote was 68–25, with most of the support coming from Democrats, who supported it by a margin of 47–10. In November the House approved by 299–107 an EMB that could override any federal law, specifically environmental statutes, that blocked a priority synfuels project. However, the President and both houses of Congress would have to support the waiver. The House vote appeared overwhelming, but an amendment offered by Rep. Morris K. Udall (D–Ariz.), chair of the Interior Committee, failed by just a handful of votes. The Udall amendment would have severely restricted the powers of the EMB and was supported by most Northern Democrats and 40 percent of all Republicans. The next spring, environmentalists were joined by the national League of Cities and the National Governors' Association (both of which feared federal intrusion into subnational laws), the Nader-affiliated Public Citizen Litigation Group, and some large oil companies (Exxon and Gulf) and their lobbying group (the American Petroleum Institute) in the battle to defeat the EMB conference report. Many Westerners worried that the board would plunder their water rights (Lyons, 1980b), while Republicans charged that the EMB would actually result in bureaucratic interference with synfuels development. The conference report was recommitted by an overwhelming margin, with only Southern Democrats providing majority support for the board. The defeat of the EMB can be traced to the earlier jurisdictional battle between the Commerce (Dingell) and Interior (Udall) committees. The turf fight represented very different perspectives on future energy paths. Without the waiver of environmental regulations, the Energy Security Act of 1980 became more of a symbolic piece of legislation because the President's ambitious targets could not possibly be met. The destructive coalition of minorities on the EMB was entirely predictable. Had the board been included in the Energy Security Act itself, this legislation probably would not have passed the Congress, let alone by overwhelming majorities.

Immediately after the synfuels legislation was signed, environmental groups mobilized to slow down or even halt the new technologies. Key actors in the new Reagan administration in 1981 also launched broadsides against the program on the ground that it invaded the domain of the private sector. As the energy crisis gave way to the oil glut and prices began dropping, synthetic fuels lost much of their appeal. It became less and less likely that they would ever become cost-effective. The fiscal problems of synfuels only served to highlight the environmental, health, social, and boomtown effects.

Only so long as the scope of conflict is kept manageable and costs are not readily perceived can the problem of failure to cooperate in the Prisoners' Dilemma be resolved. The bargains struck on the Energy Security Act provided just the vehicle for doing so. However, once the salient issue of the environment was brought into the debate, the compromises between supporters of the hard and soft energy paths were bound to be upset. The scope of the environmental issues involved in any energy development, and particularly synfuels, is very broad indeed. There is also little fiscal illusion: dirty air and water will in time be noticed by residents, but the toxic wastes involved in the coal and shale synfuels processes will be perceived immediately.

I shall not detail all the technical arguments here (see Masselli and Dean, 1981, and Lash and King, 1983), but rather I shall highlight some of the most important concerns. Paramount for many were the environmental and health effects. Most dramatically, spent shale is dangerous to breathe. It has all the problems of more conventional toxic waste and is more dangerous than coal-fired power plants. Water resources are also critical, especially in the water-starved West, where virtually all the shale is located. There is considerable controversy over how much water will be required for synfuels development (cf.

Energy and Natural Resources, 1981; Rycroft and Monaghan, 1982), but there are real fears that such projects could lead to legal conflicts over preexisting claims on the water. There are also boomtown effects. While the Eastern coal regions have well-established infrastructures for megaprojects, those in the West do not (Lebus, 1981), Spiraling populations lead to increases in the prices of commercial property, increases in crime, the disruption of agriculture, strains on municipal services, conflicts between newcomers and longer-term residents, and ironically, growth in unemployment (Hershey, 1981e). When a synfuels plant shuts down, the bust effect can bankrupt a municipality (New York *Times*, 1982a).

None of these concerns loomed large during Congressional consideration of the Energy Security Act of 1980. As the budget deficit preoccupied Washington in the second Reagan administration, the fiscal illusion for such a mammoth project as synfuels vanished. Deficit reductions meant that popular programs would have to be cut; synfuels were largely unknown to most Americans, with most of the publicity the program received dealing with mismanagement by the SFC. The stage was set for a broad-scale attack on the most expensive domestic program in U.S. history.

Fall from Grace

By late 1980 hundreds of companies were preparing proposals for subsidies under the Energy Security Act, and five small-scale coal gasification plants were operating (Rudolph, 1983, p. 10). Energy prices began to decline in 1981 in the midst of a worldwide oil glut. Within the Reagan administration, Secretary of Energy James Edwards fought with Budget Director David Stockman over abolishing the SFC; in the meantime, the President did not fill any vacancies on the board, and interest in the program waned. Even though Reagan ultimately sided with Edwards in maintaining the SFC, he appointed as its chair an Oklahoma business executive who appeared openly hostile to the program. By late July the Energy Department (not the SFC) announced plans to fund two projects in Colorado (Union Oil's Parachute plant and the Colony project of Exxon and TOSCO) and one in North Dakota (the Great Plains coal gasification plant). In January 1982 the SFC board put forth a list of small projects that might qualify for funding (Omang, 1982).

However, the decline in oil prices took its toll on investments in synfuels (Hershey, 1981b). In early 1982 Occidental and Tenneco announced a delay in the construction of their Cathedral Bluffs, Colorado, shale project. In May, under pressure from the SFC, which worried about cost overruns, Exxon announced that it was terminating its joint venture with TOSCO. Other projects began falling like dominoes, at a cost of $17.7 billion (*Oil and Gas Journal*, 1982b; *Newsweek*, 1982). None of these projects had been funded by the SFC, however. The first loan the SFC made was to a peat-to-methanol project in North Carolina that it doubted would ever succeed (Anderson, 1983). The jewel in the SFC's crown, the Great Plains gasification plant, later won a grant despite charges by the General Accounting Office that investors would reap tremendous tax benefits even as the project was losing billions of dollars (Benjamin, 1983c,d; Pasztor, 1983). Yet the SFC pulled the plug in 1985, leaving private backers to withdraw, and forcing the Department of Energy to assume temporary management of the plant (Isikoff, 1985). The third project funded by the SFC, the Cool Water gasification plant in California, collapsed in 1984 (Isikoff, 1984).

The SFC continued making grants, but was torn by internal conflicts, as well as by charges of conflict of interest among board members. Ultimately all but one board member was forced to resign, which led to a confrontation between the Senate and the President over the confirmation of new nominees (Hershey, 1984a). Faced with growing pressures from House Democrats (led by Michigan Democrat Harold Wolpe, one of the very few Northern Democratic opponents of the Energy Security Act of 1980) and moderate Republicans in the Senate for cuts in SFC funding, the administration reached a compromise in May 1984. It would restore $2 billion in domestic spending cuts from the SFC authorization. However, Senate Democrats refused to go along with the compromise.

On July 25, however, the House did something very unusual. By a vote of 261–148 it overturned a Rules Committee prohibition on voting upon amendments to the appropriations for the Department of Interior that would have cut back $5–10 billion of the $13.2 billion still available to the SFC. According to the Washington *Post* (1984), the 261 votes came from "the same coalition of fiscal conservatives and environmentalists that [in 1983] succeeded in scuttling the Clinch River Breeder Reactor" nuclear facility in Tennessee. Democrats could only muster a single-vote majority in favor of the Rules Committee (127–126).[7] Republicans voted 21–135 to permit the amendments to be voted upon.

[7] The roll-call vote is reported in *Congressional Quarterly Weekly Report*, July 28, 1984, pp. 1858–59, and the Americans for Constitutional Action (ACA) scores in the *Weekly Report* for July 14, 1984, pp. 1696–97. The ACA ratings were selected over those for the Americans for Democratic Action because the former do not penalize members for absences.

Fiscal conservatives tended to vote against synfuels, but far more so if they were Republicans trying to help the President find a place to slash the budget (Davis, 1984a). Legislators from energy-producing districts displayed a somewhat greater tendency to support synfuels than Representatives in general.[8] We would expect "interested" members (cf. Mayhew, 1966, pp. 146–60), those from districts with specific stakes in synfuels, to be even more supportive, although the range of externalities suggests that even this group is likely to be split. The 35 interested Representatives split 20–15 in favor of upholding the Rules Committee, demonstrating 21 percent more support than did the full House. Even among legislators with a direct constituency stake, however, the split was close to even and it was marked by clear partisan divisions.

If, as argued in Chapter 3, cooperation requires institutional memory, one potential source of disruption of a stable logrolling coalition is membership change. New legislators readily learn the norms of Congress, especially those dealing with vote-trading and other forms of reciprocity (Asher, 1973). However, there is less reason to suppose that such new members will feel committed to a program that no longer has universalistic support. Indeed, since they were not parties to the original compact, they would be more likely to defect than those who were in the House in 1979–80. The following tabulation shows that legislators who did not serve in the House when the Energy Security Act was originally passed were substantially more likely to vote to permit amendments to cut synfuels subsidies than were all House members for every party group or region group (percentages are the percentage voting with the Rules Committee):

Group	Full House	Members not in the House in 1979–80
Northern Democrats	39.5%	31.9%
Southern Democrats	70.9	52.0
Republicans	13.5	7.0

[8] Altogether, I identified 36 districts that were directly affected by synfuels projects and one that was indirectly affected (manufacturing supplies). The districts directly affected were determined by obtaining from the SFC a list of active projects. This list was culled from various SFC new releases. I then matched up locations of the projects with Congressional districts by employing various atlases, including the *Congressional District Atlas* for the 98th Congress, published by the Bureau of Census. In two cases it was not possible to determine exactly which district a project was located in, so the project is assigned to both districts within a county. In two other instances, three or more districts within a state were possible sites for a project. Those two projects were deleted from the analysis. The district indirectly affected was the California 39th. Roger Staiger, Jr., of the House Energy and Commerce Committee's Subcommittee on Synthetic Fuels pointed out the interest in that district. I include it in the analysis, even though I did not have similar data on other districts, because I felt that the data base should err on the side of inclusiveness.

The changes are particularly notable for Southern Democrats, who have become more like their Northern colleagues on many issues (including the environment) in recent years.[9] But the new members constituted only 37.5 percent of the Representatives who voted against the rule. We must seek an explanation that goes beyond membership change to account for the attack on synfuels. The environmental issues and the concern for deficits approaching $200 billion played important roles here. The program was marked by high costs and provided few immediate benefits except to a few constituencies (and even those communities were split on whether the projects were beneficial).

The defeat of the rule set a showdown between supporters of synfuels, led by William Ratchford (D–Conn.) and Joseph McDade (R–Pa.), who hoped to limit the cutback to $5 billion, and opponents who sought a cut twice as large. The latter were also led by one member from each party: Silvio Conte (R–Mass.) and Wolpe. The irony of the coalition formation process was apparent when Rep. James Broyhill (R–N.C.) took to the House floor to attack the synfuels program as environmentally damaging despite his own low rating by the League of Conservation Voters (LCV). Rep. Marilyn Lloyd (D–Tenn.), who had a slightly higher LCV rating than Broyhill (see Barone and Ujifusa, 1984, pp. 892, 1101), took the floor to note the "curious alliance . . . of free-marketers and dispersed-technology advocates who would have us believe that there is no need for a Government role in synthetic fuels development" (*Congressional Record*, daily ed. 98th Cong., 2d sess., Aug. 2, 1984, p. H8300). The Ratchford-McDade amendment passed by the surprisingly large margin of 236–177, with only moderate partisan cleavages noted. Interested members were substantially more likely to support the smaller cutback, as demonstrated in Table 4.3. The House action left the SFC with $8.25 billion, of which only $1.9 billion had been committed.[10] A Congressional Re-

---

[9] Another possibility is that the new members were less supportive of synthetic fuels because (1) the Reagan landslide of 1980 brought to Congress more conservative members who were less sympathetic to a strong government role in the economy, or (2) many new members moved to a more laissez-faire position in response to what they perceived as a national trend to the right. These explanations cannot readily be tested against the norm-based thesis offered in the text, except to note that all categories of freshman members, including Northern Democrats, showed less support for synfuels than their senior colleagues.

[10] The 1984 House action included another amendment, adopted without even a roll-call vote, that prohibited the SFC from granting loan guarantees or price supports to the second phase of the Union Oil shale project or the Tenneco/Occidental Cathedral Bluffs facility. The SFC had signed letters of intent to fund both of these projects, with a total price tag of $4.9 billion. Furthermore, both projects were in the same Congressional district (Colorado's Third). The overwhelming approval of this amendment stands in sharp contrast to the norm of pork barrel projects in the Con-

TABLE 4.3

House Votes in 1984 and 1985 on the Synthetic Fuels Corporation

Group	Ratchford-McDade, 1984	Vote to kill SFC (Conte amendment), 1985
All members	236–177 (57–43)	312–111 (74–26)
Northern Democrats	94–76 (55–45)	119–48 (71–29)
Southern Democrats	75–7 (91–9)	48–31 (61–39)
Republicans	67–94 (42–58)	145–32 (82–18)
Interested members	26–7 (79–21)	21–15 (58–42)
Northern Democrats	6–1 (86–14)	5–3 (63–37)
Southern Democrats	11–1 (92–8)	7–5 (58–42)
Republicans	9–5 (64–36)	9–7 (56–44)
Interested members vs. all members[a]	+24%	−16%
Northern Democrats	+31%	−9%
Southern Democrats	+1%	−3%
Republicans	+22%	−26%

SOURCES: The vote on the Ratchford-McDade amendment can be found in *Congressional Quarterly Weekly Report*, Aug. 4, 1984, pp. 1932–33; the vote on the Conte amendment, ibid., Aug. 3, 1985, pp. 1566–67.

NOTE: Numbers in parentheses are percentage yea and percentage nay, respectively.

[a] Percentage support from interested member minus percentage support from all members.

search Service report estimated that by 1987 synfuels production would reach only 5,000 gallons a day (Shapiro, 1984).

The Senate approved a $5.2 billion cut in synfuels funding, rejecting a $9 billion reduction proposed by Sen. Bill Bradley (D–N.J.). The House-Senate conference, however, slashed more than either house individually ($5.375 billion), but set aside $750 million for demonstration projects fostering the cleaner burning of coal (Gettinger, 1984b). The administration agreed to the reduction in synfuels funding and also promised to nominate at least two members to the SFC (Hershey, 1984b). The two members selected, former Rep. Tom Corcoran (R–Ill.) and Paul MacAvoy, were regarded as at best lukewarm supporters of the new technologies. Amid reports that President Reagan was considering abolition of the SFC, the new board (which finally acquired a quorum) delayed grants of $774 million to projects in Colorado, Utah, and Texas.

The next year saw a replay of events in the House. The Energy and Commerce Committee voted to abolish the SFC, but the Rules Com-

---

gress, in which legislators all support each other's pet programs. The member in question, Ray Kogovsek, had developed a reputation as a moderate with good ties to traditional Democratic constituencies (Barone and Ujifusa, 1984, pp. 191–92). While his district was never politically safe, Kogovsek was not a ripe political target since he had already announced his retirement from Congress.

mittee once again sought to prevent a vote on that proposition. The House rejected the rule on July 24, 1985, by a vote of 251–179. Seven days later the House voted to reduce the SFC's funding to $500 million, which could only be used for administrative functions, by a vote of 312–111—almost an example of universalism in reverse. The vote has been detailed above. Support for the SFC was now concentrated in a few blocs: (1) members from districts where projects were active, (2) legislators from constituencies where coal or major oil companies had an important presence (the independents were not important actors on synthetic fuels), and (3) members with close ties to Majority Leader Jim Wright (D–Tex.), who remained a strong advocate of synfuels. Six states provided virtually one-third of the support (32 votes) for keeping the SFC alive: Colorado, Utah, Pennsylvania, Kentucky, West Virginia, and Texas. The interested members were effectively isolated.

The Senate was somewhat more reluctant to kill the program, while the administration actually seemed to support it in the fall. The SFC began to award funds for synfuels development even as the House directed it not to do so and even threatened legal action to prevent the disbursement of funds. In December the Senate finally capitulated to the House and agreed to dismantle the agency within 60 days after the President signed the fiscal 1986 appropriations for the Interior Department (Davis, 1985). The agency expired in April 1986, still facing conflict as the Energy Department sought to find a purchaser for the now-abandoned Great Plains gasification plant. Two other shale projects closed and the administration was preparing to propose the transfer of 82,000 acres of public land rich in shale to four major energy developers for a nominal fee (Peterson, 1986). The pork barrel had been stood on its head.

The strategic politics of the destructive coalition of minorities indicates how the politics of the shale barrel can be divorced from the policy implications. By 1985 the prominent political strategy was for legislators to vote to kill synthetic fuels. Concern over long-term energy security had subsided among the public. There were heated cries to cut the deficit again—another type of resource constraint politics. Since synfuels promised only long-term benefits, while costs were more clearly perceived (in terms of impact on the budget and the environment), the massive program was a natural target for a destructive coalition of minorities. The core supporters of synthetic fuels had been reduced to a small minority in the Congress. Furthermore, they had no natural allies. Other issues were of greater salience politically.

Perhaps the program's future would have been brighter if a coalition could have been maintained among supporters of other energy alternatives. However, the Reagan administration cut funding for renewable fuels drastically in its 1981 budget. It also took a much more hostile attitude toward environmental regulations and tried by administrative appointments to cripple the Environmental Protection Agency. In the face of such confrontations, environmentalists (who were also advocates of soft energy paths) came to see synfuels as something very different from an energy alternative that might lead to greater funding of their own projects. In a period of fiscal constraints, synfuels and other energy alternatives were competitors for scarce resources. Only by stressing the environmental problems of coal- and shale-based technologies could soft path advocates stress the need for more funds for their own programs. Tax credits for solar energy were due to expire in 1985, and the two major alternative paths were seen as competitors for the same shrinking pie of energy funding. The policy arena was thus once more a fight between alternative energy scenarios, as described in Table 4.2 above. The payoffs remained essentially the same. The motivations for cooperation had changed. Synfuels supporters looked upon environmentalists as opposing any large-scale energy development. Rep. Carl Perkins (D–Ky.) even charged the SFC itself with treating "coal as a four-letter word that should not be mentioned in polite company" (*Congressional Record*, daily ed., 98th Cong., 2d sess., Aug. 2, 1984, p. H8307). Synfuels supporters also charged that concern for budget deficits was a rather recent phenomenon among environmentalists. Soft energy advocates argued that synfuels had had its day.

The level of conflict of interest had clearly increased. Ironically, the easing of the energy shortages led to the breakup of the coalition that supported the Energy Security Act. There was less of a clearly perceived need to adopt, much less maintain, an energy policy with a high price tag. Indeed, as concern over the budget deficit grew, the cost of projects perceived as unneeded became a major issue within the Congress. The value of the cooperative outcome relative to each player's temptation (each player's own fuel) had declined. An omnibus strategy could perhaps have commanded a majority in the Congress, but the various players saw little reason to cooperate.

Environmentalists could claim to be budget-cutters on synfuels, while harder path advocates could make the same argument with respect to solar tax credits. The electoral rewards for doing so were perceived as greater than those for cooperating with each other. When neither group proved willing to compromise, both stood to lose: synfuels and solar energy credits both appeared to fall prey to larger forces. In contrast to the demand to do something, almost anything, at the height of an energy crisis in 1979, softer energy markets led to a noncooperative outcome. In the pork barrel game, the electoral incentives led legislators to put aside mistrust and cooperate. By the mid-1980's, however, there were no longer electoral rewards for achieving something that could be called an energy policy. Thus there was no way out of the traditional Prisoners' Dilemma, and the all-defect outcome resulted.[11]

The decline in oil prices that began in 1981, just one year after the adoption of the Energy Security Act, clearly set the stage for the termination of the synfuels program. Yet the argument that the law of supply and demand was sufficient to kill the program is too simple. Energy prices did not decline monotonically throughout the 1980's, nor were the drops prior to 1985–86 precipitous. Throughout the decade, virtually from the day the program was enacted, opponents of the original legislation lay in wait trying to terminate the program. As projects failed and as scandals grew in the administration of the SFC, opposition slowly mounted within Congress. Each drop in energy prices clearly weakened the support base for the program, but the pattern of growth in the anti-synfuels coalition indicates that other factors were clearly at work as well. One of the most important was the size of the deficit. The debates in the *Congressional Record* indicate substantial concern about funding such a high-priced program while deficits were at such high levels. Furthermore, even though there were few specific references to environmental issues in the debates, it is noteworthy that several of the rescission motions involved not deficit reduction but transfers of funds to environmental programs. The uneasy alliance of soft and hard technology advocates of the 1970's had clearly fallen apart.

Perhaps most telling was the growing disaffection of members from interested districts. Congress virtually never terminates a pork barrel program, regardless of costs. Indeed, one of the hallmarks of such programs is that they are not presumed to be cost-effective (Weingast, 1979). While there were many good arguments for killing the SFC, the action taken by the Congress is highly unusual. Had the members from interested districts been more united, the synfuels program might not have died so readily. By 1985 fewer than 60 percent of interested members supported retaining the program. Other

[11] In Chapter 2 I made the distinction between the incentives of the policy game and the electoral game (also noted earlier in this chapter). My colleague Karol Soltan has noted, with some insight, that this distinction corresponds to the differing motivations of interest groups and legislators, contingent, of course, on there being different pressures placed upon each. For an example in which this does not appear to be the case, see the discussion of natural gas politics in Chapter 5.

members could hardly be blamed for concluding that these legislators' own constituencies saw costs as well as benefits in the synfuels
program—especially since much of the information provided to Congressional offices urging defeat of the synfuels program came from
organizations such as the Environmental Policy Institute. The drop in
energy prices played a major role in killing the SFC, but by sowing the
seeds of a destructive coalition of minorities rather than through energy economics alone.

Every Project Out of Its Humor

The universalistic coalition of 1979–80 that supported synfuels in
return for the funding of gasohol, solar fuel, and other renewables
came apart rather quickly as the Reagan administration sharply cut
back support for all energy programs except nuclear power and synfuels. The distinctly non-universalistic budgetary politics practiced by
the Reagan administration, particularly in its first two years, met with
considerable resistance from well-entrenched clientele groups. But a
newly formed coalition is much easier to disrupt, and this is precisely
what happened on synfuels. The breaking up of this coalition wid-
ened the scope of conflict as Congressional environmentalists who
were "bought off" in 1979–80 by the funding of renewables now felt
free to attack synthetic fuels.

The linking of energy and environmental issues always expands
the scope of conflict. It also makes the costs of synfuels easier for legislators to perceive. The environment is a high-profile issue area with
many committed activists. Legislators believe that these activists may
make a difference in elections—and that difference is all in one direction. The public is strongly pro-environment (Miller and Shanks,
1981, p. 321). A program that threatens to pollute the environment,
cost the government a lot of money that will go into the hands of unpopular large energy companies, and produce little energy will have a
small base of support indeed. Add to that some scandals at the governing board of the SFC and the rather obscure vision of synfuels by
the mass public and one wonders why the SFC did not die even
sooner. Unlike the natural gas–pricing issue (see Chapter 5), synfuels
ultimately confronted a destructive coalition of minorities even without widespread public furor over the program. The low salience of
these new energy technologies made it much easier for the program
to become the hostage of conflicting issues that ranked higher on the
public agenda (cutting the deficit and reducing environmental decay),
at least in the minds of legislators. One does not have to pose the question of what (or who) killed the SFC. As in the mystery *Murder on the*

Orient Express, everybody did it, since all had sufficient reason to do so. Indeed, the shale barrel model suggests that this is inevitable.

The scope of conflict expanded because the amount of conflict of interest had increased. In 1979 the immediate need of legislators was to find some resolution to the current energy crisis. Virtually all members of Congress felt pressured to act. Differences of opinion, when there were any, focused on which fuels were to be developed and at what environmental cost. The first problem was resolved by providing funding for a wide variety of synthetic (and renewable) fuels. That the pork barrel approach was feasible demonstrated that the conflicts were not severe. The environmental issue was never directly addressed. Energy supplies were of greater importance at the moment, and advocates of the environmentalist position had to be content with the defeat of the Energy Mobilization Board. The EMB battle was really a sideshow in the synfuels war; environmentalists could not garner sufficient support from the Congress even to reduce the size of the massive authorizations. By 1984, on the other hand, the traditional coalition had broken down. No longer could backers of energy security through synfuels be sure of support from advocates of renewable fuels or tolerance from most members of Congress who were strong environmentalists. The problems that had arisen in synfuels development destroyed the 1979–80 coalition as the various actors saw their interests in conflict four to five years later. As the scope of conflict became larger, former allies became adversaries. To put it simply, energy security no longer provided electoral security.

Could the program have been handled in such a way that it could have succeeded? Consider the following evaluation of synthetic fuels development:

It is far from clear whether different actions should have been taken. But it is crystal clear that the process of reaching decisions was far from satisfactory. The dispute was left mainly in the hands of those interests most directly involved . . . the synfuels staff, whose future depended on the continuation of the program, and the petroleum industry, which felt seriously threatened by public encouragement of a potential competitor. The real costs and benefits were never set forth clearly and fairly by either party. Not only were senior staff members . . . confused and uncertain, but Congress and the public seldom heard more than occasional extravagant, self-interested pronouncements. Even the best calculations that were made seldom contained persuasive analyses of demand and supply elasticities for outputs and inputs, estimates of the effects of technical change, and the external costs of environmental changes in different processes.

Few neutral observers would disagree with the characterization of the program. However, it was not made in response to recent synfuels developments but about the program in the Truman administration (Goodwin, 1981a, p. 166).

One can argue that we don't learn from our own history. More critically, the structure of preferences on the issue area seems to dictate that conflicts will repeat themselves. A more successful synfuels program is not impossible. The Canadian experience is evidence of this. But to make U.S. energy policy like the Canadian would require making Americans think about politics the way Canadians do. As we shall see later, Canadian energy politics is marked by partisan and ideological cleavages that reinforce constituency interests. There was never any evidence that such clear-cut lines of conflict existed in the U.S. synfuels experiment. In 1979–80 the omnibus Energy Security Act was fashioned to gain political support precisely because there was no majority support for any single energy strategy. By the time the universalistic coalition began to fall apart, synfuels supporters were divided not along partisan or ideological lines, but rather along constituency lines that cut across parties and political philosophies. Indeed, the two stalwarts in the Congress who *really believed* in synthetic fuels were House Majority leader Jim Wright, a Democrat, and Senate Energy Committee chair James McClure, a Republican. Not only was there no consensus on the role of synfuels, but coalitions shifted on the more straightforward issues of the environment and the role of government in providing for energy security. A destructive coalition of minorities was inevitable because there was no underlying philosophical basis of support for the most expensive domestic program in U.S. history. There was no majority position in the Congress on an appropriate energy strategy because there was no such consensus in the country, and neither the legislative leadership nor any committee of the Congress could induce a stable outcome.

Gas Pains

Oh, but you must pretend alliance with courtiers
and great persons.

(Everyman Out of His Humour, I.i, p. 299)

C LEAN-BURNING natural gas is regarded by many students of energy as the king of fuels. Unlike synfuels and coal, it
affords no serious environmental problems. In contrast to nuclear
power, it only rarely poses safety problems. For most of U.S. history it
has also been very cheap indeed. For decades, when oil dominated the
domestic energy market, producers had so much excess gas that, like
the old lady who lived in the shoe, they didn't know what to do with
this stepchild of petroleum production. They simply flared it away. In
1938 producers beseeched the government to bring some order to the
oversupply problem, and the history of natural gas regulation began.
Forty years later the gas markets were in disarray because of these
regulations as consumers in the industrial heartland saw prices sky-
rocket and even then were often unable to obtain enough gas to heat
homes and factories. Gas production was declining and consumption
was growing.

Congress passed a law that partially deregulated gas prices so as to
relieve the shortages in 1978, but five years later the battle was re-
enacted as prices soared once again. In 1983 the situation was different, even perverse: natural gas prices were rising as production was
increasing. Instead of shortages there was excess capacity. Oil prices
were declining. Some members of Congress called for renewed price
controls on gas, while others demanded that all regulations be lifted.
The 98th Congress responded in precisely the manner that the shale
barrel would predict: it rejected all attempts to impose any sort of
order on gas markets. Out of chaos it produced chaos.

As gas prices increased dramatically in the mid−1970's, a consensus developed in the industry that only a free market could alleviate
shortages. Thus producers, both majors and independents, as well as
pipelines and distributors worked together to secure the decontrol of
prices. Most consumer groups thought the price was already too high

and fought the Natural Gas Policy Act (NGPA) of 1978, at least in the initial stages of the decontrol battle. The compromises that were ultimately reached established a multi-tier gas market, and this set the stage for the battle of 1983.

The disorder in the natural gas markets brought forth a wide range of proposed solutions. The crucial question, on which all other subsidiary issues hinged, was whether to decontrol natural gas prices immediately or to reinstitute strict price regulations. Ultimately the debate in the Congress in 1983 centered on these alternatives. Yet both were soundly defeated in the Senate (neither came to a vote in the House). Why were both proposals killed? In this chapter I argue that the battle was not simply an ideological fight between decontrol advocates on the right and recontrol supporters on the left. The NGPA of 1978 had brought forth a whole host of subsidiary issues that had to be confronted five years later. These concerns simply could not be separated from those of pricing. For many actors in 1983, especially gas pipelines, these subsidiary issues were even more important than pricing. What occurred was the creation of a destructive coalition of minorities against both the decontrol and the recontrol bill. Unusual alliances were the rule rather than the exception, and—in conformity with the shale barrel argument that posits a virtual war of each against all—the patterns of alliance formation almost seemed to defy the notion of a clear-cut structure.

Before the story of the clash can be told, I must briefly explain the structure of the gas industry and the history of regulation up to the Natural Gas Policy Act of 1978. The NGPA set the stage for the gas surpluses and price increases that led to the 1983 debates. How could oversupply and overcharges occur simultaneously? I argue that the 1978 legislation produced a new alignment of actors, which inevitably resulted in the formation of a destructive coalition of minorities in 1983 rather than ideological coalitions. I test this thesis by examining the roll-call behavior of Senators. Finding little support for the framework of the shale barrel, I seek to explain why this is so. Interviews with key actors, supplemented by an examination of Congressional hearings and press accounts of the coalitions that formed, suggest that legislative votes can hide more than they explain. Like Chapter 4, this chapter delineates the preference patterns of the shale barrel model rather than questions of institutional design. In particular, I shall demonstrate that the destructive coalition of minorities found on synthetic fuels is not just symptomatic of a pork barrel program gone awry. Gas pricing, generally presumed to be one of the most strongly ideological issues in the energy constellation (see esp. Kalt, 1981), fell prey to the same set of forces in 1982—and there is reason to believe that the left-right confrontations of earlier years may not have been quite as coherent as previously thought. Before examining the range of issues involved in the legislative battle, I briefly consider the gas industry in historical perspective and examine how a topsy-turvy market, appearing to violate the simple laws of supply and demand, set the stage for a political battle that was anything but purely ideological.

Gas in Perspective

Natural gas is the largest domestic source of energy, accounting for more than 25 percent of all primary energy consumed in the United States.[1] Fifty-five percent of all residences and commercial establishments utilize natural gas, which also makes up 40 percent of the energy consumed by U.S. industry and agriculture (Interstate and Foreign Commerce Committee, 1979b, p. 71). Furthermore, gas consumption increased dramatically from 1960 to 1973, rising from 13 trillion to 22 trillion cubic feet a year (Kash and Rycroft, 1984, p. 62) and leveling off to somewhat less than 20 trillion in the 1980's as prices increased relative to oil.

Rate regulation of gas started at the local level in the nineteenth century and at the state level in the early twentieth. The first federal regulation occurred in the Natural Gas Act of 1938, which both producers and pipelines welcomed. In 1954 the Supreme Court ruled in Phillips Petroleum v. Wisconsin that intrastate markets were subject to federal regulation, but future rate-making would exempt this gas from price controls. A dual market for interstate and intrastate gas developed, leading to severe inequities during the 1973 energy crisis.[2] Producers of interstate gas clamored for decontrol, amid charges by consumer activists that they were "shutting in" existing supplies in the hope that the future would bring higher prices. The confluence of the OPEC embargo, colder-than-average winters, and pressure by the Environmental Protection Agency on utilities to switch from dirty coal to clean gas led to curtailments of as much as 3 trillion cubic feet by 1976. A Ford administration decontrol plan passed the Senate in 1976 but was stymied in the House. Congress and the Federal Power Commissions took some steps in 1977–78 to relieve the shortages through Presidential initiative and financial breaks for pipelines, but the dual

[1] Most of what follows in the discussion of pre-1978 activities is a synopsis of the excellent discussions in Sanders, 1981, and Tussing and Barlow, 1984.

[2] The unregulated intrastate price increased apace with the cost of imported oil, jumping fivefold from 1966 to 1974, while regulated interstate gas increased in price by barely more than 1.5-fold (Stobaugh and Yergin, 1983, p. 76).

market remained: as the crisis worsened for regulated pipelines, customers in intrastate markets "were literally awash in gas" (Tussing and Barlow, 1984, p. 110).

Not all the pressures were for decontrol. Although public opinion surveys show varying responses owing to differences in question wording (Farhar et al., 1980, p. 149),[3] some polls that specifically mention price increases (Inter-University Consortium for Political and Social Research, 1982) and others that do not (Miller and Shanks, 1981, p. 321) show almost 80 percent opposition to price deregulation. Rising prices had removed any fiscal illusion from the impact of decontrol. However, the shortages led to pressure for some action. The Natural Gas Policy Act (NGPA) of 1978 was an elaborate compromise, replacing the dual system with a 27-tier market whose rationale was more political than economic. The key distinction was between new gas (from the Outer Continental Shelf or from complicated production/discovery formulae focusing on 1976–77) and old gas. The former was to be controlled for a short time and then deregulated, while the latter was to be forever controlled but subject to annual increases (a system of "indefinite price escalators") pegged slightly above the rate of inflation. Equally important to understanding what the NGPA wrought were provisions other than pricing. These factors, even more than pricing itself, were the bases of the destructive coalition of minorities that formed five years later.

The NGPA established another dual-tier system called incremental pricing. Industrial users would be charged higher prices by interstate pipelines (intrastates were exempted) while residential customers would pay lower rates. Residential users were thus sheltered from large price spikes, but the Federal Energy Regulatory Commission (FERC) could implement the program to reduce the incentives of industrial users to switch to other fuels and thereby further increase residential price rises (Kumins, 1983, p. 5). Agricultural users were exempt. A companion measure, the Power Plant and Fuel Use Act, prohibited new power plants and boilers from using natural gas and required electric plants to switch to alternative fuels by 1990.

The decontrol forces, including major and independent producers and industrial and agricultural users, opposed the NGPA and its

[3] Nivola (1980, p. 509) discusses a Harris survey in which 56 percent of respondents favored deregulation of oil and gas to "encourage companies to explore for and develop new oil and natural gas supplies," although a majority was opposed to decontrol just two months earlier. A poll by CBS News and the New York *Times* found only 34 percent support for "allowing natural gas companies to increase the prices they charge you, so they can pay for the cost of finding more gas," including only 37 percent who had also expressed more concern for producing energy than for protecting the environment.

gradual approach to decontrol (Sanders, 1981, p. 170). What made the bill palatable to many was provisions that prices would not immediately escalate. Most of the gas sold in the United States would remain subject to price controls: the percentage of regulated declined only from 66 percent to 56–59 percent between the pre-NGPA period and 1982 (Stobaugh and Yergin, 1983, p. 70; Hershey, 1983). Estimates of the amount that would remain under control by the end of the decade ranged from one-third to two-fifths (Schuller, 1982, p. 9; Interstate Natural Gas Association of America, 1984a, p. 5). Even new gas would remain partially regulated for more than eight years.[4] One of the fiercest opponents of a market-based system, Sen. James Abourezk (D–S. Dak.), recognized this use of fiscal illusion to make the bill politically acceptable: "It is the frog-boiling method, fostered by the notion that a 10 percent increase each year until 1985 will go by virtually unnoticed, until the great day comes when total deregulation will be achieved without complaint" (quoted in Nivola, 1980, pp. 500–510). The legislation did not, however, solve the price problem. That it caused chaos is indisputable, and this is the story to which I now turn.

The Post-NGPA Shock

The logic behind the NGPA was simple even if the legislation was complex: the removal of price restraints on natural gas would increase supply and thus ease the supply problem. This was straightforward supply-and-demand economics. It was not what happened. The jury-rigged set of categories under the NGPA once more created an imbalance in a dual market, this time between regulated and unregulated gas rather than simply between interstate and intrastate supplies.

In 1979 the American Gas Association, a trade association of pipelines and distributors that had supported the NGPA, reported that gas well completions set a record in 1978 and were increasing apace in

[4] Residential customers did not have much opportunity to switch from oil to the less expensive gas, since they are tied to a single supplier, the local utility (DeParle, 1983), and the costs of converting one's heating unit is prohibitive for most people. However, processed gas users (paper, food, primary metals, etc.) and petrochemical firms can replace up to 45 percent of the gas with other fuels (Department of Energy, 1984, pp. 2-1, 2-2). The impact on gas prices was substantial since industrial users used 43 percent of total deliveries, compared to 25 percent for residential customers (computed from Stobaugh and Yergin, 1983, p. 73). For evidence of fuel shifting, note that Energy Secretary Donald Paul Hodel told the Senate Energy and Natural Resources Committee in 1983 that 38 percent of gas was now consumed by industry and 26 percent by residential users. This represents a 5 percent decline by industrial users and a 1 percent *increase* for residential users during a period in which prices were rising rapidly (1978–83). Hodel's comments are found in Energy and Natural Resources Committee, 1983a, p. 97.

1979 (Interstate and Foreign Commerce Committee, 1979b, p. 67). Yet prices continued to rise sharply. The wellhead price of gas, the cost to pipelines, more than quadrupled from 1973 to 1978, and virtually doubled again to $1.79 per thousand cubic feet by June 1981.

This rise cannot be attributed to the immediate price decontrol of "deep gas," as expensive as this fuel was, because it constituted only 3 percent of the market (Corrigan, 1981, p. 2063).[5] Between 1979 and 1982 the annual increase in wellhead prices ranged from 14.1 to 24.2 percent in real dollars (Department of Energy, 1984, p. 2). The price effects produced no national outcry because they were far from uniform throughout the country. While residential rates increased by an *annual* average rate of 20 percent from 1978 to 1983, some rates increased by as much as 50 percent annually and even 20 percent in one month alone (Hershey, 1982a, 1983; Murray, 1983a, pp. 443). The shocks were pronounced in the Midwest, but barely felt in the Northeast (Hershey, 1982b; Energy and Natural Resources Committee, 1983a, pp. 616, 626). Higher prices meant drops in consumption (Benjamin, 1983b), but again the effects were asymmetric. Industrial users could and did shift to other fuels. Residential demand barely declined at all (Department of Energy, 1984, p. 2-1). As consumption dropped, so did production. As would be expected, the average wellhead price declined, albeit just by a penny, from late 1982 to mid–1983, but contrary to all logic the average delivered price to consumers rose by 14 percent (Energy and Commerce Committee, 1983e, p. 417).

Why did prices increase at all, anywhere? The answer lies in the contracts signed by pipelines. In the 1970's producers preferred to sell to the unregulated intrastate pipelines, which could pay higher prices than the regulated interstates. To obtain gas at all, many interstates agreed to purchase fixed quantities regardless of market demand. In these take-or-pay contracts, the pipelines would have to pay for gas even if they did not actually need it. The percentage of gas subject to these provisions rose from 60 before 1973 to 86 between 1973 and 1977 (Department of Energy, 1984, p. 3-2). The total amount of these obligations was estimated at the end of 1983 to be almost $5 billion (Energy and Commerce Committee, 1983d, pp. 33ff). Recent contracts often gave producers the right to deter-

---

[5] One reason for increasing costs is what has been called "category creep." When producers drill new wells to tap old oil fields or drill deeper into existing wells, they often reclassify it as new gas or deep gas. The former is currently regulated at higher prices than old gas while the latter is not subject to price controls. It is estimated that this reallocation of existing gas supplies has led to a $4 billion increase in the price to consumers (Hershey, 1981a).

mine the rate of flow of unregulated high-cost gas, making the pipelines captives.

Yet many pipelines incurred no costs, indeed even profited, from these provisions. The regulatory regime at FERC usually permits pipelines to pass along to consumers the costs of gas not sold. Many pipelines are also producers with access to their own deregulated gas, which they could substitute for low-cost old gas (Kumins et al., 1984, p. 11). While pipelines saw themselves as the victims of producers, most other actors viewed them as villains. Even as sales were declining, profit margins dramatically increased in the midst of the 1981–82 recession (Department of Energy, 1984).[6] Some pipelines with onerous long-term contracts were protected by "market-out" provisions that freed them from purchasing gas that could not be sold. Many could pass the burden on to local distributors through "minimum-bill" contracts that forced the utilities to buy all the gas provided by the transporters.

Not all pipelines were profiting handsomely. Some were confronted with severe take-or-pay problems and declining markets. One such pipeline, Columbia Gas, invoked *force majeure*, a legal provision under which a firm can opt out of contract obligations because "superior forces" make compliance infeasible, in 1983; several others followed suit (Berry, 1983a; Lueck, 1983b; Peterson, 1984). This was a strategy designed to induce cooperation by producers who could not otherwise sell the gas in a glutted market and who would be unwilling to pursue the lengthy legal procedures for enforcing contracts. Many producers did agree to reduce the burdens on pipelines.[7] But others responded in kind, seeking to portray the pipelines as the real villains of the gas crisis (cf. Tussing and Barlow, 1984, p. 175). Just a few years earlier the two groups had been allies in supporting full price decontrol.

The Scope of Conflict

Congress was confronted in 1983 with demands by consumers to recontrol natural gas, while producers insisted on immediate de-

[6]The interstates had the fourth highest average return on equity of all industries in the United States (*Congressional Record*, daily ed., 98th Cong., 1st sess., Nov. 2, 1983, p. S15223). See the comments of Rep. Thomas Corcoran (R–Ill.) in Energy and Commerce Committee, 1983a, p. 281, on the pipelines' profits from high-cost gas imported from Canada and Mexico.

[7]More than half the producers claimed to have reduced their take-or-pay obligations, and almost 75 percent were not receiving their full contract price (Department of Energy, 1984, p. 5-4; Olson and Associates, 1984).

control. It did neither and let the NGPA stand although very few actors, either inside or outside the Capital, had anything positive to say about the 1978 law. Although pricing remained the focus of attention, a host of subsidiary issues were brought to the fore by the NGPA. These conflicts could not be neatly separated into coalitions of the left and right (or anything similar), nor could they be separated from each other. The NGPA made the formation of a destructive coalition of minorities on future gas legislation inevitable.

The only issue to ignite public concern was pricing. Supporters of decontrol argued that producers would continue to "shut in" supplies until they could obtain a fair price and that the absence of a "market-clearing" price discouraged the search for new sources of gas (Arrow and Kalt, 1979). Opponents charged that old gas had been found and could still be produced at a very low cost, so that decontrol would mean little more than a boom in economic rents for producers (Energy and Natural Resources Committee, 1983a, pp. 245–46). Unlike the NGPA fight, however, the present conflict did not find the gas industry united in supporting regulatory relief. Even producers were split. The majors held 80 percent of the regulated old gas, while independents had produced 56 percent of the new gas, which was either unregulated or scheduled for decontrol under the NGPA (Energy and Natural Resources Committee, 1983a, p. 1525; 1983b, p. 239). Producers relying heavily on new gas feared that deregulated old gas would drive their prices down. The 27 categories of the NGPA meant that the effects of decontrol would not be uniform even among new gas producers. Since some independents produced mostly old gas, there were splits within this group as well.

User groups such as the National Association of Manufacturers, the Processed Gas Consumers, and the American Farm Bureau favored decontrol because (1) they generally supported reducing governmental regulations and (2) they believed that higher prices would lead to more secure supplies. Joining the chorus for price relief were butchers (National Cattlemen's Institute), bakers (Independent Bakers' Association), and candlestick makers (Chemical Manufacturing Association). Not all users were pro-decontrol, however, since some feared the effects of price increases on their own industry or on the economy in general (see Pressman, 1983). Consumer, labor, senior citizens, and community organizations led the charge against deregulation, joined by governmental organizations (for example, the National Governors' Association), public and private utilities, and some regulatory agencies. Governmental organizations in producing states such as New Mexico and Louisiana took the pro-decontrol posi-

TABLE 5.1

Group Representation Before Congress, 1983

Type of interest	Pro-decontrol	Anti-decontrol
Major oil/gas producers	15	0
Petrochemical industry	10	0
Intrastate pipelines	5	0
Industries associated with oil and gas	4	0
Oil and gas associations	8	1
Independent oil/gas producers	19	4
Royalty owners associations	3	1
Businesses	10	3
Professional and trade associations	3	2
Banking and investment	2	2
Private utilities	2	4
Interstate pipelines	4	12
Governments/governmental agencies	2	15
Public utilities	0	3
Citizens and labor organizations	0	60

tion. Pipelines had been united in 1978; they were badly split five years later. Interstates with access to old gas can average the price of those supplies with that of the new gas they purchase, providing themselves with leverage in bidding wars with intrastates over the more costly supplies. Although the battle lines were not always clearly drawn, interstates generally opposed decontrol while intrastates supported it. To see how few groups were united, I present the results of a spelunking expedition through Congressional hearings and debates and press accounts in Table 5.1. I make no claim that this sample is complete, random, or even indicative of any overall balance of group opinion on this issue. But the table does show how convoluted the conflict on pricing was, though the issue was by far the most straightforward one in the 1983–84 legislative battle.

The other issues in the conflict are best understood in the context of the two major bills considered in the Senate in 1983. The administration proposal, called the "Hodel bill" after Secretary of Energy Donald Hodel, was a modified decontrol bill, designed to bring all gas, even gas already freed from controls, under a system of price regulations that would be in force for three years. This provision was known as the *ramp-up, ramp-down* of old and new gas prices. It was subsidiary to another element, the *gas cap*, which would maintain for three years controls on any gas currently under contract by permitting periodic price increases not to exceed predetermined ceilings. When the gas cap expired in three years, the *removal of incremental price escalators* would be completed. Consumers strongly favored this provision. *Incremental pricing repeal* was an automatic by-product of a deregulated market, so large industrial users would not have to pay higher rates than residential and commercial customers.

The Hodel bill also provided for *pipeline accountability*: interstate pipelines would no longer be permitted to pass their increased costs on to consumers unless they could demonstrate to FERC that such actions represented prudent pipeline purchasing decisions. Distributors, who believed that the pipelines bore no risk in the marketplace and were protected by FERC, were one of the driving forces behind this provision. Intrastate pipelines, which were not subject to federal regulation, generally favored stronger oversight of their counterparts.

A proposal favored by producers and feared by interstate pipelines was *mandatory contract carriage*. This provision, offered as an amendment to the Hodel bill by Sen. Bill Bradley (D–N.J.), would permit users to purchase gas directly from producers and mandated that pipelines carry it for a fee. While pipelines had traditionally transported gas they did not own, and indeed were doing so increasingly (Interstate Natural Gas Association of America, 1984b), such activity is voluntary. Most gas shipped is owned by the pipelines. Mandatory carriage would require them to transport gas purchased by users on a space-available basis. Agricultural and industrial users as well as distributors believed that mandatory carriage would eliminate the problem of imprudent pipeline purchasing practices by permitting the purchasers to buy directly from the producers. Most intrastate pipelines opposed the provision since they were often already required by state regulations to serve as contract carriers and were reluctant to have federal provisions become stiffer than state laws. Some, however, were so irate at the interstates that they were willing to support the transportation proposal. The final provision designed to "punish" the interstates dealt with *equal access* for intrastates to old low-cost gas. The NGPA granted interstates exclusive rights to Outer Continental Shelf gas and prohibited intrastates from repurchasing gas for resale in interstate markets without becoming subject to FERC regulations. Intrastates pressed for repeal of this provision, and the Hodel bill promised them relief.

On the other hand, the administration's bill provided interstates with *take-or-pay* relief. Pipelines would be permitted to reduce their take-or-pay obligations from between 90 and 100 percent in existing contracts to 50 percent in the first year of the law's implementation, rising to 70 percent after three years. Most producers opposed this proposal, which to the interstates only indicated how intransigent the majors were. Even the administration was convinced that the market itself would not restore order to the gas markets (Energy and Commerce Committee, 1983f, p. 180; 1983c, pp. 22–23). Both industrial and non-industrial users supported this provision. Independent producers did not press their opposition because few had substantial take-or-pay contracts. Only the intrastates, most of them already with contracts providing for resolution of take-or-pay problems, stood in strong opposition. But they admitted that this issue could be used as a trading point with interstates on some other provision.

A related proposal allowed either the pipelines or the producers to *market out* of a contract that could not be completed or successfully renegotiated. Some producers accepted the provision as long as it was bilateral since this would permit them to opt out of long-term contracts for low-cost gas. On the other hand, a gas recontrol bill offered by Sen. Nancy Kassebaum (R–Kans.) and Rep. Richard A. Gephardt (D–Mo.) and supported by consumer organizations, provided for something more radical: unilateral *contract abrogation* by the pipelines. Producers were unalterably opposed, but distributors (who hoped that the provision would set a precedent for their own relationship with pipelines) and some non-industrial users supported the provision. Consumer groups were split, and even some interstates worried about the effects of such a proposal. The Kassebaum-Gephardt bill would roll back gas prices to their January 1982 level and maintain controls on old gas forever. New gas decontrol would be delayed from 1985 to 1987. This legislation had no provisions on equal access or incremental pricing repeal and set take-or-pay limitation at 50 percent rather than 70 percent as proposed in the Hodel bill. Only the Hodel bill would repeal the Fuel Use Act, thus terminating restrictions on gas use by utilities.

The administration proposal was presented as a compromise with something for everyone. Major producers received price decontrol, intrastate pipelines received equal access, and users believed that they would be assured future supplies. While aspects of the administration's bill were favorable to interstate pipelines, distributors, and even to consumers (the gas cap and ramping-up/down), these actors lined up behind the Kassebaum-Gephardt bill. Most independent producers so feared the effects of price decontrol that they formed an alliance with consumers. Yet this is not a story of a straight fight between two competing groups, one pro-decontrol and the other pro-regulation. The other issues in the legislative struggle, as detailed above, were of at least equal concern to the varous actors. The full range of concerns shows a far less straightforward pattern of conflict than is found on pricing. The ensuing battle pitted not just allies against foes, but allies against allies. Destructive coalitions of minorities were inevitable, and *both* bills, the only two of the more than 40 filed in the Congress to take an omnibus approach, were to go down to overwhelming defeat.

Both the House and the Senate held extensive hearings on the various proposals.[8] Even though the scope of conflict was wide and included groups that are not part of the gas community, the legislation was not the subject of action by multiple committees. The very scope of the jurisdiction of the Energy and Commerce Committee in the House belies any narrow construction of the scope of conflict in that chamber. In the House the battle was not confined just to the Fossil and Synthetic Fuels Subcommittee. There was substantial disagreement between the subcommittee and the full committee. In the Senate the issue was so explosive that nothing accomplished in committee was any guide to what would ultimately happen on the floor.

The Hodel bill barely survived an initial test in the Senate Energy and Commerce Committee in April 1983. An amendment to delete the decontrol provision was defeated by only 8–10 with two abstentions. A vote the next month to delete the bilateral market-out section lost on a 10–10 tie. The committee did include a mandatory carriage proposal in the bill. Several efforts were made to find some middle ground, all of which failed as the committee voted 11–8 (with one member voting present) to send the bill to the floor without a recommendation for its passage or defeat. Both Democrats and Republicans were badly split.

The House Fossil and Synthetic Fuels Subcommittee of Energy and Commerce was even more stymied. Rep. Billy Tauzin (D–La.) said that the body became known as the "Bo Derek subcommittee" because no proposal could get more than nine votes: "No one can get a majority. We're all looking for a 10″ (Maraniss, 1983a, p. A1). The subcommittee finally approved a compromise bill that full committee chair John Dingell (D–Mich.) declared would pass only "over my dead body." After his committee killed a recontrol bill, he banged his gavel and terminated the meeting before price deregulation legislation could be brought to a vote. A new compromise was reached in 1984; a majority of members petitioned the speaker to take action on the legislation, but O'Neill decided in September that the issue was "just too controversial" (Gettinger, 1984a).

The Senate had begun considering natural gas proposals in August 1983, but had to contend with a filibuster until November 3, when

[8] The sources for the chronicle of events in the next four paragraphs are Hershey, 1981d, 1983; Benjamin and Hoffman, 1983; Murray, 1983b,c; Nutting, 1983a–e; New York *Times*, 1983; Maraniss, 1983b; Washington *Post*, 1983; Davis, 1984b; and Gettinger, 1984a.

supporters of decontrol finally agreed to permit a vote on recontrol. On November 15, Senators defeated the Kassebaum-Gephardt proposal by a vote of 26–71. Minutes later it rejected the Hodel bill by the similar margin of 28–67. Only 9 Republicans voted for recontrol, while 45 voted against it. Democrats also failed to produce a majority for the proposal, 17–26. On decontrol, the Republicans split almost down the middle, 26 supporting it and 28 opposing it. Democrats, on the other hand, voted 2–39 against decontrol. What were the motivating forces behind the votes?

Finding Destructive Coalitions of Minorities

The battle over deregulation of energy prices has been portrayed as an ideological conflict spanning at least a decade. Virtually every roll call-study has reached this conclusion.[9] Is this the way the participants see the issue as well? To examine the question, I interviewed twelve key actors on the 1983–84 natural gas legislative battle. These actors represented ten distinct groups that participated in the struggle. Because some groups appeared from other evidence (press accounts and Congressional hearings) to be less cohesive than others, I deliberately oversampled them. The sample can hardly be called random, but it is representative of the key contenders in the legislative conflict. While each participant was guaranteed anonymity, all agreed that the others I had selected were the major participants in the debate.[10] Nevertheless, since many press reports (as well as the Congressional hearings) indicated that there was anything but unanimity within each group on many issues, I supplemented the interview data with information derived from public hearings and press accounts to determine

[9] Kalt (1981), Kalt and Zupan (1984), Mitchell (1979), Nivola (1980), Lopreato and Snoller (1978), Bernstein and Horn (1981), and Riddlesperber and King (1982) have all reached this conclusion. Only Kalt has found any independent effects for constituency variables, although Sanders (1981) persuasively argues that party and constituency factors generally coincide.

[10] The interviews were conducted between May and December 1984. They were conducted in the Washington area and lasted between 30 minutes and an hour and a half. Every lobbyist I contacted agreed to speak to me, and no one refused to answer any question. The varying length of the interviews reflected only the detail in which some lobbyists chose to answer each question. I interviewed lobbyists rather than legislators (or their staff aides) because I believed that the former would be more knowledgeable about the group conflicts on this issue. Many legislators (or staff members) would have contact only with select groups and thus might not see the full range of actors, while lobbyists would perceive the full panoply of players. There is some possibility that using interest groups might lead to different conclusions than interviewing legislators or staff. Salisbury and colleagues (1986, p. 10) indicate that energy interest groups do not see policy issues in as partisan terms as government officials. Nevertheless, I believe that the above reasons for preferring the views of lobbyists remain valid.

TABLE 5.2

Groups' Preferences on Issues in Natural Gas Debate

Group	Old gas decontrol	Take-or-pay	Contract abrogation	Market-out	Contract carriage	Equal access	Removal of indefinite price escalators	Elimination of incremental pricing	Gas cap	Ramp-up/down	Pipeline account-ability
Consumers	---	+++	+	++	+	×	+++	+++	×	×	+++
Regulators	-	+++	×	++	×	×	++	++	×	×	++
Distributors	---	+++	++	++	+++	++	++	×	--	--	+++
Trade associations	---	+++	++	--	---	+	++	+++	--	-	-
Interstate pipelines	-	+++	+	++	-	--	+++	+	+	+	---
Intrastate pipelines	+	+	t-	++	-	+++	t-	+++	+++	+	++
Industrial users	+	+	---	++	+++	++	++	+++	+	-	+++
Non-industrial users	+++	++	++	×	++	+	×	×	×	×	×
Independent producers	+	-	-	-	+++	t+	---	+	+	+	-
Major producers	+++	--	--	---	++	++	t-	++	+	-	+++

KEY:
+++ (---): Strongly favor (oppose).
++ (--): Favor (oppose).
+ (-): Mildly favor (oppose), or group split but majority favors (opposes).
t+ (t-): No strong position; favors (opposes) but willing to trade for other issues.
×: No position.

Interview Schedule for Natural Gas Lobbyists

---

1. Why did the administration plan fail?
2. Why did the recontrol bill fail?
3. Could any bill have passed?
4. With which groups did you work most successfully?
5. Which groups were your most formidable opponents?
6. Which groups, if any, were the most formidable?
7. Which groups, if any, were the least effective?
8. How would you describe the nature of the conflict on Capitol Hill?
9. I'd like to get your views on some of the issues involved in the administration's proposals, as well as some others. How important were these various issues and what stands did you take?
   a. immediate decontrol of all gas prices
   b. restrictions on take-or-pay contracts
   c. contract abrogation
   d. market-out provisions
   e. mandatory contract carriage
   f. equal access
   g. removal of indefinite price escalator provisions
   h. elimination of incremental pricing
   i. the gas cap
   j. ramp-up, ramp-down
   k. pipeline accountability

---

where each actor stood on the eleven key issues that came before the Congress.

The data on preferences are presented in Table 5.2. On each issue every actor was scored from +++ (strongly in favor of the proposal, which was very important to the group) to − − − (strongly opposed to the proposal, which was also very important to the group). Intermediate scores of ++ and − − indicated that the group favored (opposed) the position, but that it was not an item of the highest priority. The scores + and − indicate that an actor either mildly supported (opposed) a proposal or was internally divided, the sign representing the majority position (as best as I could determine it) within the group. Finally, t+ and t− indicate that the actor favored (opposed) the provision, but *volunteered* that the issue could be traded off for something more important. The full interview schedule is reproduced opposite Table 5.2.

Not surprisingly, no two groups had identical preferences across all the issues. This hardly rules out an ideological interpretation of the conflict. Some groups displayed a strong convergence of attitudes. Consumers, regulators, and distributors did not disagree on any issues. The major and independent producers took majority stands that were similar on all issues except pipeline accountability. For the

majors, to whom pipelines were almost as obnoxious as the most vocif-
erous consumer group (CLEC, the Citizen/Labor Energy Coalition),
accountability was a priority ranking just below price decontrol. But
the independents were split both internally and on various provisions
of the legislation affecting pipelines: "Some . . . we found no objec-
tions to. Others required sticking it in the ear of the producer. We
didn't want to get pipeline accountability just so people could shit on
the producers." Two parties who worked closely together, the majors
and the industrial users, nevertheless disagreed on three issues: indefinite price escalators, take-or-pay, and market-out. The majors
were closer to the non-industrial users, perhaps because the latter
group took positions on fewer than half the issues. Both the majors
and industrial users disagreed with the non-industrials only on contract abrogation. On the other hand, consumers and regulators agreed
with producers (both majors and independents) only on contract carriage and pipeline accountability.

The preference data point to considerable ideological coherence,
but they do not take into account intensities of opinion. A full demonstration of cyclical preferences cannot be attempted since respondents
were not asked to rank-order all eleven issues. However, most indicated the concerns that were paramount to them. Here we begin to see
some divergences from a straight ideological model that would posit a
conflict between the left (consumers and regulators) and the right
(producers and users). Most, but not all, consumer groups focused on
pricing. Some did not anticipate a price escalation when prices were
decontrolled, while others did not view the producers as the major
culprits. These groups were more concerned with pipeline accountability and, to a lesser extent, take-or-pay relief. (Some consumer representatives, like the distributors, were pessimistic about the political
prospects of recontrol legislation and thus put their major efforts into
items that might reverse the price spiral.) Distributors were also interested in these issues, but because their relationships with pipelines
were more adversarial than those of consumers or regulators, they
were at least as concerned with mandatory contract carriage.

Both interstate and intrastate pipelines were motivated by the accountability issue, but the former were concerned with take-or-pay
and the latter with equal access. Non-industrial users were energized
virtually exclusively by pricing, while industrials cared more about
contract carriage. The major trade associations pressed most strongly
for take-or-pay relief, the elimination of incremental pricing, and
blocking contract carriage. The pricing issue dwarfed all others (perhaps save pipeline accountability) for the larger producers, while in-

dependents were split on this issue. For them, the key concern was fighting repeal of indefinite price escalators.

While it is possible to classify many of the groups for whom decontrol was the central focus according to their position on a left-right continuum, doing so would belie the scope of conflict on the natural gas issue in 1983–84. First, the debate was not limited to these actors. Second, many of the groups that were the key participants were divided internally. Not all interstate pipelines had contract problems that producers would not renegotiate (Taylor, 1982). The independents admitted that they were badly split; one observer referred to their internal dissention as a Tower of Babel. Third, there were important divisions even among groups that were allied on many issues. Industrial users and the majors worked closely with each other on the decontrol legislation, but they parted company on pipeline relief. The non-industrial users even went so far as to support unilateral contract abrogation. These are only some of the more prominent examples of cross-cutting cleavages that marked the legislative struggle. The criss-crossing of issues was confounded, as pluralist theory would predict, by varying intensities of preferences.[11]

This account does not square well with an ideological model of the natural gas conflict. We would expect a roll-call analysis of the 1983 conflict to demonstrate considerably less support for an ideological interpretation than we have seen in previous studies. To examine this thesis, I have conducted a roll-call analysis of Senators' voting behavior on these two votes. In constructing the scale that will serve as the dependent variable in the analysis, I encountered strong evidence to support an ideological interpretation. If the two votes form a unidimensional scale, it would appear that there would be some coher-

[11] One analysis of the 1983 debate put the conflict this way (Jacoby and Wright, 1983, p. 136): "The combatants represent a mixture of competing interests that is exquisite in its complexity. There is the natural and traditional conflict between consumers—residential, commercial, agricultural, and small industrial users who receive an economic rent on price-controlled gas—and gas producers and royalty owners. This division also pits region against region, with the gas-producing southwestern states against the gas-using eastern and far western states. Furthermore, there is conflict between users of gas. Large industrial customers tend to support deregulation in principle; however, they have different views of the proper place, depending on the weight of gas cost in the firm's overall cost of production, on the relative ease of substituting other fuels, and on the firm's relative position on the priority list for curtailment [under the Fuel Use Act]. The distribution companies are anything but unified. As a group, the distributors see only trouble in wellhead price decontrol. But some are happy with the NGPA as it is, and others would prefer to extend controls beyond 1985, perhaps more than the NGPA now provides for. The intrastates feel disadvantaged, compared to the interstates, on new gas . . . and on deregulated . . . gas [by the interstates' bidding cushion]."

ence, most likely ideological coherence, to the voting patterns. The two votes correlate at only −.40, but there were no Senators among the 95 who cast ballots on both roll calls who supported both recontrol and decontrol. This may not be earthshaking in itself, since Senators can be expected to vote consistently—even on an issue as complex as natural gas. But for a fourfold table (yea–nay versus yea–nay), a single empty cell (such as yea on both recontrol and decontrol) is sufficient to yield a value of the Yule's Q coefficient of +1.00. A Q as low as +.70 is sufficient to constitute unidimensionality in the classic sense of a cumulative, or Guttman, scale (Clausen and Cheney, 1970). Is this a harbinger of results to follow?

To test this thesis, I gathered data on the party, ideology, reelection status, and gas consumption and production patterns of the states for each Senator who voted on both roll calls.[12] The party variable is straightforward enough. For ideology, I selected the scores of the conservative organization Americans for Constitutional Action (ACA). This is a preferable indicator to the more commonly employed Americans for Democratic Action (ADA) scores because ADA scores penalize legislators for absences while ACA values do not. Some Senators who faced reelection in 1984 were clearly worried that a stand favoring the producers might have adverse political consequences for them. I thus constructed a variable that was operationalized as a dummy set at one for Senators up for reelection in 1984 and zero otherwise.[13] The constituency variables employed are (1) proven reserves in trillion cubic feet, 1982, (2) the average wellhead price of natural gas per thousand cubic feet, 1982, (3) the average price delivered to consumers per thousand cubic feet, 1982, (4) the average percent change in consumer prices from 1981 to 1982, and (5) consumption per capita in dollars.

[12] The data sources are as follows. The roll-call votes are reported in *Congressional Quarterly Weekly Report*, Nov. 19, 1983, p. 2453. The subjective reelection variables were derived from various issues of *Congressional Quarterly Weekly Report* in 1983 and 1984 and from accounts in the New York *Times* and the Washington *Post*. Proven reserves, the average wellhead price of gas, the average price delivered to consumers, the percent change in price from 1981 to 1982, and dollar consumption were obtained from Energy Information Agency, 1983, pp. 15, 16, 10, 42–43. To convert consumption figures to a per capita basis, population figures were obtained from Department of Commerce, 1984, p. 11. The ACA scores are reported in *Congressional Quarterly Weekly Report*, July 14, 1984, p. 1695.

[13] An alternative specification of the reelection variable was tested as well. In this case, it was not simply a matter of whether a Senator had to face the voters in 1984, but whether the Senator was expected to have a difficult race. This subjective estimator was derived from reports in the New York *Times* and Washington *Post* and *Congressional Quarterly Weekly Reports* for 1983 and 1984. The coefficients and MLE/SE estimates did not change dramatically.

The scale for the two votes gives the highest values to support of recontrol and opposition to decontrol. Thus I expect proved reserves and the average wellhead price to have negative relationships with the voting scale and the average price delivered to consumers, the percent change in prices, and the level of consumption to have positive coefficients. The predicted relationship between the roll-call measure and ideology is negative, while those for the reelection and party variables are anticipated to be positive. This means that Senators facing reelection in 1984 would be expected to support recontrol and oppose decontrol, as would Democrats. Party is also a dummy variable, with Democrats coded as one, Republicans as zero. Since the scale is a trichotomy, regression analysis is inappropriate; the technique that should be used, and is employed here, is probit analysis (McKelvey and Zavoina, 1975). The results are presented in Table 5.3.

Since party and ideology were posited to be highly correlated with each other (and, indeed, are correlated at −.70), separate analyses were run employing each as a predictor of natural gas voting in the Senate. The analysis shows that ideology, party, and some constituency factors significantly affected roll-call behavior in the Senate. For Model I, in which ideology is employed as a predictor, it clearly has the strongest effect. Probit coefficients have no ready interpretation as regression coefficients do. But the maximum-likelihood estimates divided by their standard errors scores (similar to the t ratios in regression analysis), which indicate the probability that the observed value

TABLE 5.3

Probit Analyses of Natural Gas Votes in Senate

Predictor	Model I		Model II	
	Coefficient	MLE/SE	Coefficient	MLE/SE
Ideology	−.0349	−6.455**	—	—
Party	—	—	1.0468	4.075**
Reelection	−.0107	−.038	−.2543	−.952
Proven reserves	−.0558	−2.594**	−.0541	−2.487**
Avg. wellhead price	−.0013	−1.338*	−.0010	−1.042
Avg. price delivered to consumers	−.0024	−2.396	−.0048	−.522
Percent change in price	−.0024	−1.301	−.0024	−1.351
Per capita consumption	1.678	1.280*	1.771	1.378*
Constant	4.291	4.398**	.8521	1.133
$\hat{R}^2$		.540		.306
Rank order correlation		.669		.510
Percent predicted correctly		66.3		52.6

*p < .10. **p < .01.

of the probit coefficient could have occurred by chance, provide useful information on the relative importance of the predictors employed. Only ideology and proven reserves are significant at the .01 level. The average wellhead price fails to reach statistical significance in both models; per capita consumption (in dollars) is only significant in Model I. However, the other consumer-oriented consumption variables (average price delivered to consumers and percent change in price) have the wrong signs! Overall, the analyses presented in Table 5.3 suggest most strongly an ideological model similar to that of observers of previous deregulation battles. Specifically, the conflict appears to be similar to that of the NGPA battle of 1978 examined by Nivola (1980). Constituency effects are visible, but much more so for producer than consumer interests.[14]

I make no pretensions that this simple model captures the complexity of the voting decisions made by Senators. The analysis by Kalt (1981) is far more sophisticated. However, the results are very similar to Kalt's and there is no reason to presume that a more elaborate methodology would yield different conclusions. The issue I wish to raise, however, is considerably broader than that of determining precisely how important ideology (or any other predictor) is. It is whether roll calls can capture the underlying political dynamics of the conflict on Capitol Hill.

We are thus confronted with two very different perspectives on the natural gas battle of 1983 in the Senate. Which is the preferred account? To answer the question, I asked my lobbyist respondents how they perceived the structure of the conflict. Participants in the fight should have an understanding of the forces at work. Without suggesting that the conflict might involve an ideological battle or something else, I simply asked each to describe the nature of the conflict. Eight of the twelve representatives I spoke with specifically downplayed any ideological component to the legislation and spoke very much in terms of a destructive coalition of minorities. A consumer representative stated: "The seventies gridlock was a question of the titanic conflict between producers and consumers. The eighties were different. You had complexity and subtlety that bogs people down. People thought that contract carriage was simple and would only take three hours, but it took three weeks. You're dealing with a set of issues on

---

[14] Some constituency variables may have attenuated MLE/SEs because of collinearity among them. Per capita consumption was highly correlated with proved reserves (.77) and average price delivered to consumers (−.51). There were several other correlations in the range of .35–.42. However, none of the constituency variables for which insignificant probit coefficients were obtained had zero-order correlations with the voting scale greater than ±.12, compared to −.63 for ideology and .40 for party.

which legislation is complex." A spokesman for a major producer agreed with this perspective: "There are so many cross-cuts that it's hard to predict by philosophy or ideology how members will vote. . . . Unlike a number of issues in which special interests compete against each other, gas deregulation is more of a public issue. It brought in groups that were never before active. The stakes involved on natural gas are so near and dear to various interests that compromise is extremely difficult." A representative of an interest pipeline added: "Nobody could find a consensus on what the problem was because the problem was different for everyone. That's why we couldn't find a solution."

What about the four actors who did see an ideological battle? Two, I believe, had conflicting views of the way the issue played out. One, a regulator, called the conflict both regional and philosophical, but also gave some detailed explications in response to other questions about precisely why no majority coalition could be formed since "there's no consensus on what to do" and since "the numbers are so slippery as to what the impact is going to be." The second, a representative of majors, called the conflict ideological, but later said: "You had an effort to reconstruct the wheel with a block of stone. You came out with something that everyone wanted to disown because it was too controversial and too convoluted." The other two respondents more clearly saw the issue in terms of the old-fashioned left-right battle. One, who represented independents, stated: "Of all the economic issues, energy is the most ideological." He immediately added: "You really ought to see this fine little study by Mitchell of the American Enterprise Institute. Have you read it?" Earlier he had discussed the internal splits in his industry in great detail, as well as those in others, and offered the opinion that no bill could have passed. Finally, a non-industrial user called the battle one "between those who agree with the free-market system and those who don't." His organization concentrated almost exclusively on the pricing issue and did not take positions on most of the other questions that formed the basis of the debate.

The hearings and debates in Congress also belie the idea of an ideological conflict. Rep. William Dannemeyer (R–Calif.) argued: "Even if you're on the [Fossil and Synthetic Fuels] subcommittee, it gets to be a little mind-boggling just remembering who's supporting what position" (quoted in Pressman, 1983, p. 797). Finally, Johnston, together with Energy and Natural Resources Committee leader James McClure, the floor managers of the Hodel bill, admitted more than two weeks before the Senate voted: "There are not the votes on this floor to pass S. 1715. I would dare say that there are not the votes on this floor to pass anything. And I am certain that there are not votes on this floor to endorse the Natural Gas Policy Act, which is the law of the land today" (*Congressional Record*, daily ed., 98th Cong., 1st sess., Nov. 1, 1983, p. S15158).

Except for the two observers who insisted that the 1983 battle was a straight fight between the right and the left, all attributed the difference between this and past deregulation battles to the enactment of the NGPA. Thus, despite their limitations, previous roll-call studies were not necessarily incorrect in assessing the role of ideology. A respondent from an interstate pipeline noted: "In World War I you read about trench warfare with clear battle lines. That was the NGPA. You never heard anything about such things in Vietnam (or in last year's fight)." The contrast with the NGPA battle was expressed by virtually all observers as a distinction between a united industry in 1978 and a divided one in 1983–84. The situation changed because the act created 27 categories of gas, setting up a whole new web of conflicts. The revolt against the pipelines, leading to proposals for contract carriage and accountability, was sparked by provisions of the NGPA that induced the interstates to purchase high-cost gas. Instead of resolving the tension between the interstate and intrastate pipelines, as the NGPA was originally designed to do by eliminating the dual-tier market, the 1978 act only heightened them by making the gas industry even more factionalized.

Support for the NGPA, at least as revealed in the voting studies, was a liberal (and Democratic) party position. The issues in that legislation were not as complex as those in 1983. Pricing was the focal point; issues related to pipelines had yet to surface. In the end, however, only a very complex compromise could be attained, and most of those in the producing sector *opposed* this decontrol proposal. Once the legislation had been enacted and profits exceeded most people's hopes, "the natural gas industry was 'delighted' by the bill. Traditional coalitions were being rearranged in the pursuit of energy policy" (Katz, 1984, p. 113). Had the 1978 battle been a straight fight between the left and the right, however, there probably would have been no need for a bill with 27 categories of gas. If this characterization of the NGPA conflict is correct, then roll-call studies may consistently err.

Roll-call studies are biased in favor of ideological explanations and against constituency-based ones, as well as more complex frameworks. First, there is plenty of reason to fault the constituency variables I have selected. My best defense of the indicators I selected is that appropriate data are hard to come by. The conflict was not just one between consumers and producers. Many producers of gas that had already been decontrolled or was scheduled to be deregulated in January 1985 strongly opposed freeing old gas of price restraints. In some areas, such as the Midwest, prices for residential fuels had skyrocketed over the past few years, while in others increases were more moderate or even nonexistent. The percentage change in prices from 1981 to 1982 ranged from a high of 32.2 in Missouri to a low of -1.7 in Hawaii and 1.1 in Vermont. There was no single "producer" or "consumer" interest. To conduct a more sophisticated test of a model that pits ideology against constituency interests, one would need data on state-by-state production of different types of gas and the nature of pipeline contracts with producers. In the absence of such figures, any analysis would have to be considered tentative at best. Second, any roll-call vote necessarily involves a binary choice between yea and nay positions. The complex nature of cross-cutting cleavages cannot be determined readily when legislators are forced to make such choices. On the other hand, the overwhelming defeat of both the decontrol and the recontrol packages suggests that something other than a straight ideological fight was taking place.

The cross-cutting cleavages and splits within each group make a preference cycle likely. Without rank-ordered data I cannot demonstrate a pattern of cycles. However, we can get some clear indications of the multidimensionality on the gas issue. Consider first the prospect for a destructive coalition of minorities. Both major proposals went down to overwhelming defeat. What about the levels of support for each of the eleven subissues that shaped the debate? I have rearranged the data in Table 5.2 by issue and aggregated the responses to total figures for each position. The results are presented in Table 5.4. These data should be interpreted with some caution since the sample selected may not be exhaustive even though it contains all the key actors. Furthermore, simply counting the number of responses to each position does not take into account any differences in size, strength, or political acumen of any of the actors. Finally, the positions attributed to each actor are themselves imperfect indicators of their preferences. When all is said and done, however, the numbers in the final column of Table 5.4 indicate that there were clear-cut majority positions on most subissues. The lopsided "votes" recorded should allay most fears stemming from the less than perfect quality of the data.

Eight of the eleven issues have strong majorities supporting them. Only ramping-up or -down appears to have a plurality against it. There is a slim, and perhaps elusive, plurality supporting contract abrogation, while the pricing issue appears to result in a tie. With such

TABLE 5.4

The Structure of Conflict on Natural Gas Issues, 1983

Issue	+++	++	+	t+	×	t−	−	− −	− − −	Support − Oppose − No position
Old gas decontrol	2		3				2		3	5 − 5 − 0
Take-or-pay	5	1	2				1	1		8 − 2 − 0
Contract abrogation		3	2		1	1	1	1	1	5 − 4 − 1
Market-out		6			1		1	1	1	6 − 3 − 1
Contract carriage	3	2	1		1		1	1	1	6 − 3 − 1
Equal access	1	2	2	2	2					7 − 1 − 2
Indefinite price escalators	2	4			1	2			1	6 − 3 − 1
Removal of incremental pricing	3	3	2		2					8 − 0 − 2
Gas cap		3	2		3			2		5 − 2 − 3
Ramp-up/down			3		3		3	1		3 − 4 − 3
Pipeline accountability	5	1			1		2		1	6 − 3 − 1

NOTE: See Table 5.2 for key.

heavy support for the remaining issues, there appears to be little opportunity for groups to engage in vote trading across issues on which they care less. Ramping was of little concern to most actors. One respondent who strongly favored decontrol called it "a political compromise we supported because it was better than the status quo," while a respondent at the other extreme said that "it was political window dressing." Contract abrogation had no adherents who were willing to put up a fight for it. Even the interstates recognized that it was "politically impossible." This left decontrol. More than any issue other than pipeline accountability and possibly contract carriage, it involved intense positions at both extremes. No one volunteered that it might be an issue that could be traded for something else. Nor did any of the respondents indicate that their position was predicated on goodwill toward some other group. Of course, pricing was the lynchpin on which the entire debate rested. Pricing was dragged down with all the other proposals precisely because it was so controversial and produced no clear-cut majority position on either side.

Could any bill have passed? I asked this question of each lobbyist, and many offered some pet project of their own. But even those who had designed a bill they thought could command a majority reflected that this might well have been wishful thinking. A majority was pessimistic, at least on further consideration, that any legislation could have been enacted. The reasons given are instructive:

Everybody favored repeal of incremental pricing except CLEC. If you could have gotten all the various players in a room and got a pledge that each wouldn't have offered their own amendments to a clean bill in incremental pricing, it would have passed. But no one cared enough about that issue.

Up to the last minute it appeared that you'd get a quick fix on contracts and something on carriage. But nobody had much to gain by voting on just those issues, so you had to consider the whole bill. And that led to the whole thing collapsing.

There was too much blood on the floor. The head of the Natural Gas Supply Association told me, "I've gone through too much hell for the last two years to get only the Fuel Use Act repealed."

Even today you could get 300 votes in the House for contract carriage. Those of us who were strong advocates of contract carriage stuck to our guns that it had to be part of a package. We realized that there would be adverse things tacked onto a contract carriage bill. Those of us supporting contract carriage all stuck together. We all sunk but we wound up no worse off than we already were.

These are clearly tales of a destructive coalition of minorities. They also suggest how issues hang together. Every proposal had to have some component of take-or-pay relief, generally also with a market-out provision, because no one wanted to make the confrontation into one between pipelines and everybody else. The concerns that were controversial had to be balanced by giving the adversely affected group something. Less salient issues such as incremental pricing repeal and elimination of the Fuel Use Act were not considered worthy of the type of effort it takes to have anything passed by the Congress. Several respondents noted that both industrial and non-industrial users lent more moral support to the philosophical idea of decontrol than anything else because, as one put it, "they had other fish to fry. It was an important issue for them, but it gets a bit lost in the shuffle." Each group had its own agenda, but it was impossible to isolate a few actors and set them to work on a compromise. There was too much mistrust among the participants for this to occur: "Not even a bill to negate indefinite price escalator clauses would have passed. Each time any proposal was made, all the groups wanted to add their own items."

A more conclusive approach to demonstrating multidimensionality is found in Table 5.5. There I report the results of an unfolding analysis of the interest group actors' preferences on the subissues. Unfolding is a form of multidimensional scaling that places both the actors and the issues in the same space (Coombs, 1964). While methods of Guttman scaling can reveal unidimensionality, they cannot guarantee that the stricter conditions for avoiding a preference cycle are met. Only unfolding can do that (Niemi and Wright, 1987, pp. 174, 181).

The "best" unfolding analysis yields a three-dimensional solution with a "badness-of-fit" (or stress) measure of .053. The highest scale "loadings" for each entry are printed in bold type; where second values are almost as high, these are italicized. The names I have selected for the dimensions are based on the issue configurations. The first dimension reflects pipeline pricing issues. The marker items are both interstate and intrastate pipelines as well as industrial users, the pipeline accountability issue, and especially (and ironically) major producers. Take-or-pay and contract abrogation also have their highest scores on this dimension. As we shall see below, the interstate pipelines were seen as the villains by most other participants. On this dimension, they occupy a polar position in opposition to other actors (especially the majors, industrial users, and intrastates).

The second dimension is clearly related to gas pricing. At one pole we find consumers, regulators, and distributors (as well as trade associations to a lesser extent). Non-industrial users, who cared primarily about pricing, and independent producers (who were split on the

Unfolding Analysis of Energy Issues and Interest Groups

Category	Pipeline pricing	Pricing	Carriage and subsidiary issues
Issues			
Price control	.054	**−.676**	.524
Take-or-pay	−.514	.436	.368
Contract abrogation	−.565	−.485	−.308
Market-out	−.601	−.268	**−.644**
Contract carriage	.229	−.511	**.759**
Equal access	−.156	−.545	−.430
Indefinite price escalators	−.561	−.316	**−.583**
Incremental pricing	.078	−.370	**−.535**
Gas cap	−.464	**−.537**	−.327
Ramp-up/down	−.548	−.523	−.301
Pipeline accountability	**1.097**	.345	−.338
Actors			
Consumers	.051	**1.116**	.152
Regulators	−.131	**.953**	−.217
Distributors	−.301	**1.194**	.465
Trade associations	−.093	**.663**	.194
Interstate pipelines	**−1.105**	.528	.266
Intrastate pipelines	**.792**	.284	−.429
Industrial users	**1.085**	.417	−.366
Non-industrial users	−.080	−.626	**.860**
Independent producers	.389	−.617	**.887**
Major producers	**1.345**	−.461	.003

N O T E : See accompanying text for explanation of boldface and italics.

Stress = .053. Stress is approximately equal to the coefficient of alienation ($1 - R^2$). There are no formal criteria for judging how "bad" a stress value is, although a frequently used rule of thumb is that values above .15 are unacceptable. One examines a graph of the values of stress versus the number of dimensions and selects the value at which the rate of descent begins to taper off sharply. In this case, the slope approached zero at the fourth dimension (where stress = .010). However, the four-dimensional structure was considerably less interpretable than the three-dimensional one presented here. For one dimension, the type of result needed to establish an ideological straight fight, stress = .231.

issue) occupy the other extreme. Price control is the marker issue, but equal access was also important, as were, to a lesser extent, the two contract issues. Finally, contract carriage and market-out, as well as subsidiary issues such as indefinite price escalators and incremental pricing repeal, form the third dimension. However, this is not simply a conflict over pipeline issues. The two actors with the highest scores are non-industrial users and independent producers. They were the only actors (other than the distributors, who have a moderate score on the dimension) who strongly supported mandatory carriage.

The message of the unfolding analysis is twofold. First, the group conflict on the gas issues was hardly unidimensional. Second, and still more interesting, none of the three scales produced a sharp producer-consumer cleavage. The consumers and their allies (distributors and regulators) had their most extreme scores on pricing issues, but the major producers became caught up in pipeline pricing issues. The conflicts engendered by the NGPA were extremely complex. Even as the price regulation issue drove the demand for new legislation, the pipeline concerns ultimately overwhelmed even the major producers. Ironically, the independents—who were internally divided on the pricing issue—appeared to be concerned primarily with pricing issues if only because their contract problems with pipelines were more limited.

In arguing that the conflict on natural gas deregulation was multi-dimensional, I am assuming that the responses of the lobbyists reflect the same cleavage patterns as those among legislators. This assumption is not quite as bold as it might seem. First, the lobbyists were asked to describe the conflict in Congress, not among themselves. Given their centrality to the debate and their continuing activity in the natural gas policy community in Washington, it is unlikely that they would misperceive the nature of conflict. It strains credulity to claim that so many of them could find chaos in the midst of a straight ideological fight. Several comments by legislators, especially those by John-ston and Dannemeyer quoted above, also suggest a complex situation. The inability of the House Energy and Commerce Committee's Fossil and Synthetic Fuels Subcommittee to report *any* legislation at all points in the same direction. Finally, and perhaps most conclusively, as noted above, over 40 bills dealing with natural gas pricing were filed in 1983. If there were a piece of legislation that could command a majority in a straight fight, it is rather implausible that it would have failed to reach the Senate floor when two proposals so far from the median Senator's "ideal point" would be considered.

Strategies for Coalition Formation

In formulating a strategic scenario, I assume that the conflict in the Congress reflected the struggles among interest groups. Although there will not be a one-to-one correspondence between the interests of legislators and outside groups, the story of the conflict indicates that the coalition dynamics took place mostly among the outside groups. The complex nature of the cleavages also means that any representation of the strategic options open to the players must be dramatically simplified if we are to make any sense of it whatsoever. Unlike the pork barrel game presented in Chapter 2, this is a game in which the interests of the various actors cannot be reduced to two players. We thus have an n-person game. In such a situation, we should ideally have data on the values of the payoffs to each actor from alternative outcomes. Without any such data, my inferences must be more speculative.

I propose, then, a representation of the strategic situation that assumes that only one proposal could pass. Each actor does favor the enactment of such a bill, but recognizes that such legislation will provide not only benefits but also costs. The major producers, for example, clearly see benefits in legislation that decontrols gas prices, but also recognize that there will be costs involved in agreeing to provisions such as market-out and take-or-pay relief. Similarly, the interstate pipelines would benefit from the latter provisions, but accountability provisions would impose costs on them. Each actor, then, has to decide whether to join a coalition. Electing to do so will ensure that the actor's most salient issue will be included in the bill under consideration. Failure to join the coalition does not necessarily mean that the provisions will be excluded. Recall that some groups (e.g., major producers and non-industrial users) had similar preference structures and also cared most about the same issue (price decontrol). So even if an actor decided not to join a coalition, there is some probability that its most salient issue would be included in a bill anyhow. Since the number of actors available for coalition formation is somewhat restricted, this probability is likely to be quite large.

Why would an actor elect not to join a coalition? I assume that in addition to the costs and benefits involved in simple economic terms, there are also costs associated with coalition formation. The only acceptable legislation, according to virtually every interest group, would have been an omnibus that not only gave everybody something but also imposed some costs on each group. This meant that each actor had to accept the legitimacy of others' claims. The interstate pipelines doubted that major producers were willing to do so. One interstate representative said: "I slightly suspect producers and feel that they do need a little hit with a stick. It's easier for the producers to swallow hard and come to grips with the smaller pipelines. No producer wants to be the first to fully accommodate us." If the major producers were to enter the coalition bargaining process, they would be explicitly accepting the pipelines' arguments that contracts needed to be renegotiated. This would affect producers' bargaining power on contracts above and beyond any costs imposed on them by legislation that merely *forced* them to adjust contract terms. Agreeing to form coalitions thus indicated a willingness to engage in negotiations, not just on the pending legislation but also on the future of the gas industry. For every actor, this was costly.

The strategic calculation each actor had to make was whether to join a coalition or to refrain from doing so. The payoffs each would receive would depend not only on its own strategy choice, but those of other players. The critical variable here is whether a majority coalition forms.[15] In Table 5.6 and Figure 5.1 I outline the scenario facing each player. Group A might elect to join a coalition when a majority coalition does form. In this case, it gains with certainty the benefits associated with its most salient position. For major producers this would be the economic rents accruing from price decontrol. Group A would also bear the costs of policies it did not support but had to accept with the enactment of the law (e.g., adjustments in pipeline contracts). Furthermore, it would incur the costs of negotiations. Algebraically, we can express the payoff to Group A as $(B - C - N)$, where:

B = benefits accruing to the actors from the most salient issue;

C = costs imposed upon the actor from policies he/she must accept in the legislation;

N = costs of negotiation, as described above.

C will vary depending on which majority coalition is formed. It is at a maximum when only a minimum winning coalition is formed, since that bloc contains the fewest possible members and hence represents a less inclusive bill than under other majority scenarios. The less inclusive the bill, the fewer the costs imposed on Group A. In Figure 5.1 I represent these costs as C_m, which can be considered to be the group's evaluation of either the average cost of any minimal winning coalition or, if the actor is very risk-averse, the largest cost. In Table 5.6 and in the text I do not consider such complications and I simply refer to costs as C. Similarly, B will vary as the size of the coalition increases. The addition of some other actors to a coalition will impose costs on Group A, but there will also be spillover benefits: producers would benefit from equal access given intrastate pipelines, consumers from distributors' concern for pipeline accountability. Overall, however, I assume that the costs of including additional coalition members will outweigh the benefits. B_m in Figure 5.1 represents the benefits obtained when a simple majority coalition forms; like C_m, it represents either average or minimum gains accruing to Group A. Note then, in

[15] I use the term "majority" in a loose sense here. The game among interest groups was not a simple majority rule game where half plus one of these actors could form a winning coalition, since group strength does not correspond one-to-one to legislative votes. Instead of majority, a "sufficient number" of groups is needed to form a winning coalition. However, this number is not likely to vary widely from the majority principle and the term "majority" is more familiar in coalition formation contexts.

TABLE 5.6

The N-Actor Gas Prisoners' Dilemma

Actors' preferences:	Coalition forms, Group A doesn't join
	Coalition forms, Group A joins
	No coalition forms, Group A doesn't join
	No coalition forms, Group A joins
Strategic options:	Join coalition:
	Most salient issue included in bill with probability 1.0.
	Don't join coalition:
	Most salient issue included in bill with probability p_i

Strategic scenarios:	*Payoffs to Group A:*
A doesn't join coalition, majority coalition forms	$p_i B - C$
A joins coalition, majority coalition forms	$B - C - N$
A doesn't join coalition, no majority coalition forms	0
A joins coalition, no majority coalition forms	$-N$

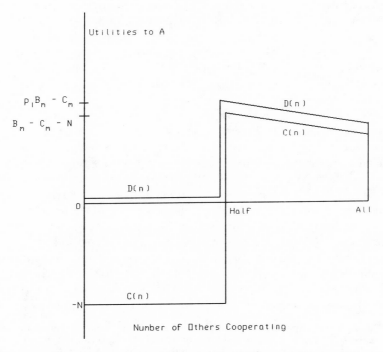

Fig. 5.1. Payoffs to Group A in Natural Gas Prisoners' Dilemma. $C(n)$ = payoff to A for cooperating based on n other cooperators; $D(n)$ = payoff to A for defecting based on n cooperators.

Figure 5.1, that payoffs to Group A are highest (whether A cooperates or defects) when a minimal winning coalition forms. In the text I also omit subscripts on B.

If Group A agrees to join a coalition, but that bloc does not achieve majority status, its payoff will simply be $-N$. No benefits are gained nor are any costs imposed if the legislation does not pass. Similarly, if the actor decides not to join a coalition and none achieves majority status, the payoff is zero (0). No benefits or costs result, nor are there any negotiation costs. This zero payoff represents the situation under the NGPA, around which other figures are normalized. If Group A decides not to join a coalition, but a majority bloc forms anyway, (1) the group will not incur any negotiation costs, but (2) policy costs will be imposed. On the other hand, it is probable that benefits will accrue to the actor because other groups are likely to have similar demands. Some actors (major producers, consumers, distributors, users, intrastate pipelines) had more allies than others (interstate pipelines); however, the critical issue for one group was generally very salient for at least one other (see Table 5.2 above), so even the least advantaged actor had a good chance of getting its way on an important issue. If p_i represents the probability that group i will obtain the benefits from its most salient issue, then its payoff from a majority coalition that it does not join is $p_iB - C$.

Every actor is presumed to have these payoffs (which may, however, vary from one to another in terms of the precise figures). First, note that refusal to join a coalition (the defection strategy) dominates becoming a member (cooperating) when no majority bloc forms. This is straightforward since $0 > -N$. What happens when a winning coalition does form? It suffices to say that defection dominates cooperation when negotiations costs will be significantly less than the benefits that might be obtained from the legislation.[16] This assumption is eminently reasonable since net benefits are presumed to be greater than net costs for each group, lest the entire problem be degenerate. Thus defection dominates cooperation for Group A regardless of whether a majority coalition forms. The preferences for each actor are as follows: (1) do not join when a majority bloc is formed; (2) join when a

[16] Formally the problem of what happens when a winning coalition does not form is expressed as follows. Is it the case that $p_i B - C > (B - C - N)$? Clearly if p_i is close to 1.0, it does not pay to join a coalition. If the costs of negotiation fall within a particular range, then it also does not pay to join a coalition even if p_i does not approach 1.0. For (1) to hold, all that is required is that $N > B(1 - p_i)$. Or, the costs of negotiation must be less than the benefits foregone if one is not a member of a winning coalition times the probability that one will not be in that bloc. As noted in the text, this means simply that negotiations costs will be significantly less than the benefits obtained if the coalition forms.

majority bloc is formed; (3) do not join when no majority bloc is formed; and (4) join when no majority bloc is formed. These preferences correspond, in terms of cooperation and defection, to the temptation, reward, punishment, and sucker's payoffs respectively. Since the game is presumed to be symmetrical for all players, we have an n-person Prisoners' Dilemma and the predicted outcome is all-defect. Figure 5.1 shows how the defect strategy for a generic group, A, dominates the cooperate strategy no matter how many other actors cooperate.

We could imagine a similar scenario for the 1978 conflict in which some accommodation was reached. Why was there no resolution of the PD in 1983? The answer is that the scope of conflict increased dramatically. The 1978 battle revolved around gas pricing; five years later a whole host of subsidiary issues had emerged. Not only had the scope of conflict expanded, but the cross-cutting nature of the cleavages led to a series of shifting alliances that sharply reduced trust among the players. Not only had the level of conflict increased, but so had the intensity of the struggle. Many of the actors in 1978, including both types of pipelines and distributors, could support deregulation of prices because they would not be radically affected by the legislation. By 1983, however, the costs that would be imposed on these groups by others' proposals on subsidiary issues came to the fore. Whatever fiscal illusion had existed for such actors in 1978 was shattered. Because so many groups faced large losses of economic rents, they were unwilling to make such compromises. Furthermore, a willingness to cooperate in 1983 would indicate to others that the player had been crying wolf in insisting on a "clean" bill. These are the negotiations costs I have discussed above; they were largely absent in 1978 when the industry was not torn by internal conflicts and trust was much greater. The cross-cutting nature of the cleavages further reduced the bargaining room, increasing the level of conflict of interest. The negotiations process broke down because each actor saw it as imperative to push for a restrictive bill. Most admitted in the interviews that they could live with the Hodel bill. In this sense it was a prominent solution to the game. But each thought that it could do better. Everyone thus did worse.

Beyond Issue Networks

An ideological conflict, I argued in Chapter 3, would have loud voices with a clear message. The natural gas issue had many voluble participants, but was more like a Tower of Babel. On the other hand, in an iron triangle relationship, one would expect that the patterns of communication and the attributions of power would be rather sharply delineated. This is the picture of traditional pork barrel politics. The shale barrel, which is different from both, would be marked by a more fluid set of actors and a high pitch. Both Heclo (1978) and Gais et al. (1984) have argued that contemporary U.S. interest group politics is characterized by more adversarial relationships than the traditional pork barrel. However, neither study attempts to tackle the point at which coherence breaks down and iron triangles are dislodged by issue networks. I suggest that neither model applies to the sort of political battles one finds on a shale barrel issue such as natural gas. What we have, instead, is such a loose network that a destructive coalition of minorities becomes virtually inevitable. It is not a "policy community" in Heclo's sense, because there is no agreement on what the stakes are and who the important actors are. Nor is there a consensus on who has power and who does not.

To examine the extent to which the various actors perceived the legislative and group conflict in similar terms, I asked my lobbyist respondents to name (1) the most and least powerful actors on the natural gas issue in 1983–84 and (2) the groups they worked most effectively with and were their most formidable allies. In either an iron triangle or an issue network with clearly defined adversaries, one would expect to find substantial agreement on who was powerful and who was not. For a triangle, there should be considerably more allies than enemies. For an issue network with clearly defined adversaries, there should be a large number of both positive and negative linkages, but one would expect them to be reciprocal. Know thy enemies is a clarion call of adversarial politics.

The responses of the lobbyists are tallied and reported in Table 5.7. Looking first at attributions of power, one is struck by the dispersion of mentions for both those with influence and those without. About the only thing close to a consensus (and even here we find a lone dissenter) is the argument that interstate pipelines are not overly imbued with political muscle. Five respondents felt that the majors were the most powerful, while three put them at the other extreme. For consumer groups, the results were 5–4. Consider the divergent responses on the power of the Citizen/Labor Energy Coalition:

CLEC has changed the arithmetic. A focused national campaign can really change the balance. They scared the shit out of a lot of members of Congress.

[CLEC was] worthless. They're the most overrated group in the country. They're only good at rallying the left. Their studies on gas prices were worthless.

TABLE 5.7

Attributions of Power and Alliance Formation in the Natural Gas Struggle, 1983

Actors	Power		Alliance formation	
	Most	Least	Worked with	Worked against
Major producers	5	3	2	4
Consumers	5	4	1	2
Distributors	2	0	1	2
Interstates	1	4	1	5
Intrastates	0	1	2	1
Users	1	2	2	3
Independents	2	0	1	3
Trade associations	1	2	0	1
TOTAL	17	16	10	21

NOTE: Some lobbyists gave multiple answers to questions of power, while others simply stated, "Nobody was powerful." In creating this table, I eliminated all self-mentions. Similarly, for alliance formation, mentions of other actors within the same group were excluded from the tallies.

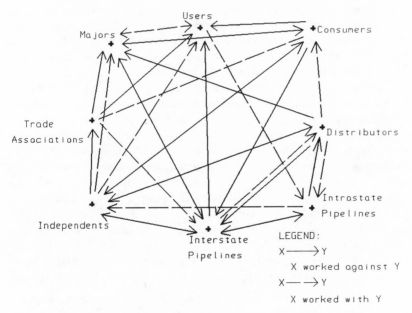

Fig. 5.2. Alliance Formation Patterns on Natural Gas Issues, 1983.

Altogether there were 33 mentions of who was powerful and who was not. The major producers and consumers together had just 17 of these nominations. To be sure, this pair of actors did fare somewhat better among those listed as most powerful, with 10 of the 17 mentions. But this hardly constituted a monolith. There was little agreement on whether the tactics of the consumers helped or hurt them. Even the trade association was said to be influential by one observer, but very weak by two others. In either an adversarial or an iron triangle situation, one would expect far more coherence.

With whom did the lobbyists interact? In Figure 5.2 I present a diagrammatic exposition of the network of alliances, both positive (dotted lines) and negative (straight lines), a total of 31 linkages. Comparing the figure with Table 5.7, we see that the pattern of alliances is even more fragmented than that for power attributions. Of the 31 linkages cited, no group received more than 6 (or 20 percent of all mentions) and only one (trade association) accounted for fewer than 10 percent of the mentions. Only 6 linkages were reciprocal, accounting for a total of 12 (or 40 percent) of the 30, hardly indicative of a coherent issue network and almost diametrically opposed to the strongly cohesive pattern one would expect in an iron triangle. This figure is slightly greater than the 29 percent found by Knoke and Laumann (1983) for coal and gas "information publics" in their study of communications patterns in federal energy politics. The differences are most likely attributable to sampling frames and the greater focusing that occurs in the midst of a heated battle.[17]

Only 2 of the 6 reciprocal linkages involved mutual cooperation. These were between majors and users on the one hand, and independents and users on the other. Independents claimed to have worked with the majors, but neither representative of the larger producers with whom I spoke cited an alliance with independents. There is thus some evidence of a community among the strongest decontrol advocates, but it is not as cohesive as one might anticipate. The four reciprocal linkages among adversaries demonstrate even less connectedness. The interstate pipelines were adversaries of the intrastates and both the major and the independent producers; these relationships

[17] Similarly, the amount of coherence on natural gas politics is undoubtedly greater than on the energy issue in general (which has an even wider scope of conflict). Laumann et al. (1986) report that the energy policy community is marked by highly unstable patterns of group participation across bills considered by Congress. This means that energy is no longer marked by sectoral politics (see Chapter 1), but that the pattern of group participation is essentially random. Furthermore, there is no consistent pattern of agreement or disagreement across groups on legislation. Both findings stand in stark contrast to the agricultural, health, and particularly labor policy domains, all of which are either clearly polarized or more clearly divided into sectors.

were mutual. So were the conflicts between the major producers and the consumers. These linkages merely point to the extent of the interstates' isolation. The intrastate pipelines claimed to have worked with the independents, but this relationship was not reciprocated. The energy policy community was not united into clearly opposing camps, because the grievances of each segment against the others were different. What made the situation so unstable was the lack of a common language that led to an inability to reach a compromise. Indeed, four of the actors claimed not to have worked with anyone outside their own groups. One pipeline representative said, "We made an effort to work with producers, distributions companies, and intrastates, but no one wanted to work with us." An independent producer said, "Toward the end we didn't even meet together. Everyone was doing their own thing." [18]

The respondents' failure to agree on who had power and even on whom one interacted with suggests, as does the Knoke and Laumann study, a language breakdown that inhibits communication. This sets the energy lobbies apart from what Heclo (1978) considers to be a key element in an issue network. On ideologically charged issues such as race, there is a common language. High stakes and clearly perceived costs inhibit cooperation, but the ideological anchor that socializes conflict guarantees that there will be some majority position. On shale barrel issues, language breakdown makes even problem definition difficult. In comparison with agriculture (marked by a relatively nar-

[18] What the Reagan administration could not achieve through legislation, it sought to implement through regulatory fiat. In October 1985 the Federal Energy Regulatory Commission enacted rules that would require pipelines agreeing to participate in the program to deliver whatever cheap gas was available to customers and to permit utilities to back out of 25 percent of their contracts for high-cost gas per year. In addition, producers would be precluded from "blending" the prices of old and new gas. The industry was reportedly upset with these policies, and most pipelines refused to join the FERC program, instead seeking legislative relief from Congress (Osterlund, 1985). As natural gas prices declined 33 percent in 1985 and an additional 34 percent in the first five months of 1986 (Hayes, 1986), FERC issued another regulation in late May 1986 permitting the price of price-controlled old gas to rise above current market-clearing levels to $2.57/mcf, even as some spot market supplies were selling for $.95/mcf. Pipeline officials threatened to hold up the proposed regulation in the courts for years (Associated Press, 1986). The gas glut seems to have changed the economic situation rather than the political one among the key participants. The politics of abundance, however, has removed the issue from the public limelight, thus reducing the scope of conflict. Because of the depressed market, it is unlikely that people will experience any direct costs of the FERC regulations, so the major political confrontation will have to await the next crisis. Even in a period of lower prices, the decontrol issue still generates much conflict. In 1987 the Congress finally repealed the Fuel Use Act. However, in the process of disposing of the equally uncontroversial (by this time) "incremental pricing" provision, Rep. Phillip Sharp (D-Ind.) of the House Energy and Power Subcommittee on Energy had to resort to a complex parliamentary procedure to prevent a vote on wellhead price decontrol that might have derailed the entire package (Davis, 1987).

row scope of conflict), health (marked by stable ideological coalitions), and labor (highly partisan), energy politics is relatively unstable in coalitional terms, has a considerably broader range of participation, a higher level of visibility, and a greater intensity of conflict (Salisbury et al., 1986, pp. 8–10).

Once a proposal has been placed on the public agenda, it is a ready target for destructive coalitions of minorities, particularly if it is (or is *claimed to be*) a prominent solution to a policy problem. Unlike most energy issues, gas legislation was not derailed by "jungle warfare" among congressional committees, so it is unlikely that a committee acting as a monopoly agenda-setter could have functioned in a more coherent manner. In the next chapter, we shall see how an attempt to impose such an agenda-setting body appeared to be a prominent solution to coordination on energy policy-making. For that very reason, as we would expect, it was killed by a destructive coalition of minorities just as the various natural gas provisions were.

Jungle Warfare over Jurisdictions

He were an iron-hearted fellow, in my judgment,
that would not credit him upon this volley of oaths.

(*Everyman Out of His Humor*, IV. vii, p. 377)

T HE CASE studies of synthetic fuels and natural gas point
to the difficulties of forming an energy policy in Congress. However, failure to enact any specific proposal or even a series of bills does
not mean that stalemate is inevitable. The leadership in the House of
Representatives took this optimistic approach in mid-1979, amidst the
energy shortages of that summer. Something had to be done so that
something could be done.

Despite two major energy crises in the 1970's, Congress had not
enacted a comprehensive energy policy. The leadership, especially
House Speaker Thomas P. O'Neill, was frustrated with the lack of
Congressional action. This chapter is a tale of how the Speaker sought
to disentangle jurisdictional squabbles in the House (cf. Chapter 3).
The leadership decided to press for the creation of a monopoly
agenda-setter on energy policy by means of a standing committee on
energy that would have exclusive jurisdiction over that policy area.
The reform proposal failed. I shall argue that this happened because
the energy issue generated a destructive coalition of minorities, none
of whom were willing to sacrifice effective veto power over alternative
"comprehensive" policies, particularly given the uncertainty of who
might be the agenda-setter. Tinkering with legislative structure, then,
cannot be divorced from the possible policy implications that such reforms might have. In this sense, structure is endogenous. The conflicts on substantive issues spill over to jurisdictional questions. In the
fight over an energy committee, we see how the preference patterns
of destructive coalitions of minorities are mirrored in the debate over
institutional design of committee systems. In the next chapter I consider the relationship between preferences and structures at the level
of the constitutional order.

The House leadership in 1979 had two options to consider in its
quest for greater coordination on energy policy. The first involved

manipulating preferences to induce cooperation. By expanding the scope of interests involved in decision-making, the leadership could hope to involve more legislators in shaping legislation. This in turn would give more members a stake in seeing that the bill actually was enacted. As the Speaker argued, "Give me a frustrated guy and I'll give him a job to do and he becomes a Tip O'Neill man" (quoted in Sinclair, 1981, p. 409). The strategy worked marvelously in the House on Carter's omnibus energy legislation in 1977–78 as O'Neill established an advisory Task Force and a broad 50-member *Ad Hoc* Select Committee on Energy to work out compromises on the package (see Sinclair, 1981). In effect, this strategy is the one traditionally found on pork barrel politics. Distributive coalitions of the whole depend on widespread participation of affected legislators. However, they are also based on the fundamental assumption that the amount of conflict of interest among actors is sufficiently low to permit accords to be reached. In 1977–78 agreement was possible on Carter's energy bill (at least in the House) because fuel supplies were adequate. By 1979, when the Iranian revolution led to another disruption of supplies, the Speaker had to take to the well of the House to plead (unsuccessfully) for support of the President's first standby gasoline rationing plan of 1979. He ultimately chastised his fellow legislators: "We want to think of parochialism, we want to take the easy way out" (quoted in *Congressional Records,* daily ed., 96th Cong., 1st sess., May 10, 1979, p. H3017).

If you cannot remove the cause of faction, Madison wrote in the Tenth Federalist paper, then you should try to control the effects. The way to accomplish this was to tinker with the constitutional order. In other words, the Speaker would attempt to create a structure-induced equilibrium. That is, he would push for reform of the Congressional committee system. When tensions run high, cooptive strategies such as task forces are not likely to be useful in resolving conflicts. Indeed, the Energy Task Force established in 1977 existed only on paper two years later. The leadership traced much of its troubles to Rep. John Dingell (D-Mich.), who chaired the Energy and Power Subcommittee of Interstate and Foreign Commerce. In the more open Congress of the 1970's, following the reforms of 1970–75, it was a rare committee or subcommittee leader who dominated an issue area. But Dingell was himself an anomaly. He was more comfortable with the older style of Capitol Hill politics of strong committee leadership independent of party pressure. Dingell had often feuded with O'Neill, particularly over energy issues. It was likely that these conflicts would intensify since he was in line to chair the entire Interstate and Foreign Commerce Committee in 1981 upon the announced retirement of Harley Staggers (D-W.Va.).

The Speaker supported a proposal that would create a single Energy Committee in the House of Representatives to be chaired by another veteran legislator with close ties to labor, Rep. Thomas L. (Lud) Ashley (D-Ohio). Ashley, however, was much closer to the party leadership and was willing to serve as a mouthpiece for O'Neill. Furthermore, the proposal also called for restricting multiple referrals, so that other committees (including, but not limited to, Dingell's Commerce panel) could no longer obstruct energy bills favored by the party leadership. As noted in Chapter 3, multiply referred bills were significantly more likely to be amended on the floor and to lead to legislative stalemate. Furthermore, energy bills were far more likely to be referred to more than one committee than almost any other legislation. The leadership proposal clearly attempted to create order out of chaos through a structure-induced equilibrium. Where there were multiple actors, the plan called for a single monopoly agenda-setter. While preferences across committees with energy jurisdiction spanned the entire domain within the Congress, the new committee would clearly reflect the priorities of the party leadership and, by implication, the Democratic President.

The House had tried twice since 1946 to effect a major restructuring of its committee system. A Select Committee on Committees chaired by Richard Bolling (D-Mo.) in 1973–74 and a Commission on Administrative Review chaired by David Obey (D-Wis.) were both attempts by the party leadership to impose some order on a chaotic House. The latter completely failed; the former did produce some changes, but its story was more one of a destructive coalition of minorities—and it too had proposed realignment of energy jurisdictions. In the Bolling reform effort the principal opposition to an Energy and Environment Committee came from environmentalists who feared that such a body would be captured by producers (Davidson and Oleszek, 1977, pp. 193–97). These groups formed but one part of the opposition to the 1979–80 Select Committee's Energy Committee proposal, indicating how much wider the scope of conflict on this issue had become in less than a decade.

The remainder of this chapter is a narrative and analysis of how a destructive coalition of minorities developed to defeat the Energy Committee proposal by a large margin in 1980. After a discussion of the internal politics of this proposal in the House, I shall argue that this destructive coalition of minorities involved cyclical group preferences and a strategic Prisoners' Dilemma. There was a "prominent" solution to the energy jurisdiction game—and it was precisely the one proposed by the Select Committee. However, for that very reason, it was defeated. The stakes on the energy issue were simply too great for any legislator to permit a structure-induced equilibrium. The lesson of this reform effort, when compared with the Bolling reorganization plan and a seemingly more successful Senate effort, is that institutional structure reflects the underlying pattern of preferences on substantive issues in the Congress. Expecting greater policy coordination on energy by rearranging committee jurisdictions is reasoning in reverse gear.

The New Select Committee on Committees

The 1979 reform effort, like that of 1973, began with a single target. The Bolling panel focused on reducing the power of Wilbur Mills, who chaired the Ways and Means Committee. The new committee took aim at Dingell: "The Michigan congressman has a reputation for a volatile temper and has been portrayed by some House members as ruthless in the conduct of his jurisdictional authority" (Arieff, 1979, p. 2486). Indeed, his obstructionism was reportedly the basis of the Speaker's decision to establish the *Ad Hoc* Select Committee on Energy in 1977, and Dingell also reportedly once blocked a synthetic fuels bill because it originated in a different committee (Weaver, 1979).

Even with such an unlovable target, members did not flock to join the new Select Committee on Committees. The two most recent reform efforts in the House were chaired by widely respected members close to the leadership: Bolling and Obey. In contrast, the new panel was headed by third-term Rep. Jerry Patterson (D-Calif.). He was certainly not viewed as either a legislative activist or a voice of the leadership. The nine other Democrats on the panel were also predominantly junior (see Table 6.1); none had served more than six terms. Furthermore, the three majority members who had been identified with the energy issue (John Breaux, Mike McCormack, and Peter Kostmayer) were not that close to the party leadership. The five Republicans were more broadly representative of both their party and its power centers. The two most senior members had approximately the same combined seniority as the four Democrats who had served the longest.

The Select Committee was well primed to launch an attack on Interstate and Foreign Commerce. None of its members served on that committee. Other bodies with energy jurisdictions, however, were well represented. The two major committees were Interior, on which Patterson and Kostmayer served, and Science and Technology, repre-

TABLE 6.1

Members, House Select Committee on Committees, 1979–80

Member/state	Terms served[a]	Remarks/energy-related committee assignments
	DEMOCRATS	
Jerry Patterson (Calif.)	3	Chairman; junior moderate-liberal on Interior and Banking
William Clay (Mo.)	6	Liberal; no energy committee position
Mike McCormack (Wash.)	5	Moderate; chairs Science and Technology subsubcommittee on Energy and Production; Public Works
John Breaux (La.)	4+	Conservative; chairs Merchant Marine subcommittee on Fish and Wildlife; Public Works
Bob Traxler (Mich.)	3+	Moderate-liberal on Appropriations
Patricia Schroeder (Colo.)	3	Moderate-liberal on Armed Services
Butler Derrick (S.C.)	3	Moderate on Rules; strong supporter of procedural reforms
Joseph Fisher (Va.)	3	Liberal on Ways and Means
Peter Kostmayer (Pa.)	2	Liberal environmentalist on Interior
Charles Whitley (N.C.)	1	Moderate-conservative on Armed Services and Agriculture
	REPUBLICANS	
James Cleveland (N.H.)	9	Conservative ranking minority member; second-ranking on Public Works
Frank Horton (N.Y.)	9	Moderate; ranking minority member on Government Operations
Bill Frenzel (Minn.)	5	Moderate on Ways and Means
Jim Leach (Iowa)	2	Moderate on Banking; advocate of procedural reform
Gerald Soloman (N.Y.)	1	Conservative on Public Works

[a] Breaux and Traxler were first elected in special elections.

sented by McCormack. Four members served on Public Works (which funds hydroelectric dams) and two each on Ways and Means (taxation authority), Banking (federal financing, including synthetic fuels), and Armed Services (the Strategic Petroleum Reserve and offshore oil). Other bodies with energy jurisdictions represented on the Select Committee were Merchant Marine and Fisheries, Agriculture (gasohol), and Government Operations (oversight). One member of Commerce, freshman Republican Thomas Loeffler (Tex.), had been named to the committee, but he declined to serve. The very fact that such a junior member, and one from the minority party, was the only member of Commerce named suggests that the leadership sought to restructure energy jurisdictions by focusing on a single source of difficulty. Making Dingell the center of attention restricted the scope of conflict. Concentrating on his difficult personality made it possible to downplay the spillover effects on the energy jurisdictions of other committees. Yet Dingell could argue that the attack on him only presaged an effort by the Speaker to punish chairs who did not hew the leadership line. Furthermore, the scope of the energy issue is so broad that jurisdictional battles could not be avoided.

In the attempt to build a base of support for the assault on Dingell, the Select Committee staff initially posed as many as eight possible alternative plans for reform. These were quickly narrowed to three that constituted what the Select Committee (and also the Speaker) would accept as a bottom line, would tolerate as a compromise, and hoped to achieve. These options were (1) reform of the multiple referral system, (2) the establishment of a permanent Select Committee on Energy, patterned after the *Ad Hoc* Select Committee in the previous Congress, coupled with referral reform, and (3) the creation of a new standing Committee on Energy along with multiple referral changes.

The leadership had good reason to assume that the first option would be achievable from the Select Committee's early hearings. While most of the chairs who testified preferred multiple referrals because they permitted many different ideas to compete with each other and also encouraged the development of staff expertise in the many different areas of energy policy, all saw the major energy problems in terms of their own (sub-)committee. Yet the major actors from committees such as Commerce, Interior, Science and Technology, and Ways and Means all favored some mechanisms to prevent "irrelevant" committees (such as Education and Labor, Judiciary, Post Office, and the like) from seizing jurisdiction from the major bodies.

The proposal on referral reform would permit the Speaker to designate for any multiply referred bill (not just energy legislation) a committee of primary jurisdiction; all other chambers to which the bill was referred were designated as secondary committees. The Speaker would then set time limits on secondary referrals, after which the secondary bodies would be relieved of jurisdiction had any failed to act. Both primary and secondary committees could seek rules for floor consideration after the deadline had passed, although it was widely felt that the primary committee would prevail most of the time by favorable consideration of the leadership-dominated Rules Committee. While the existing rules allowed the Speaker to set time limits, this was a very risky strategy and would remain so until such deadlines

were mandated. The leadership was also concerned that referral reform would be insufficient without altering energy jurisdictions, and
it sought to highlight the latter on the ground that it not only would
be a greater victory for the Speaker and the Select Committee but also
constituted the more difficult political battle.

The second option would establish a permanent version of the ad
hoc committee of two years earlier, a body with no original legislative
jurisdiction but with the power to coordinate energy policy-making in
the House. Whatever the attraction of this alternative as a fallback
position, the leadership quickly had to abandon it when *opponents* of a
new energy committee proposed this very solution at the January 30,
1980, meeting of the Democratic Caucus Committee on Organizations, Study and Review, a body created by the caucus to oversee the
Select Committee to try to ensure that its efforts would not be defeated in the caucus as were many of the key Bolling proposals in
1974. Responding to them, Ashley commented: "An ad hoc committee should be reserved for limited periods of time for specific purposes and not established on a permanent basis" (unpublished Rules
Committee transcript).[1] The issue of the desirability of a permanent
Select Committee had been joined, and the leadership could no longer
avoid even the minimal public political commitment that would have
allowed it to claim victory were this option chosen by the full House.

The first option also disappeared as an acceptable outcome less
than a month later when Dingell and others lent their support to a
resolution before the Democratic caucus by Jonathan Bingham (D-
N.Y.) that would have joined the two issues by considering referral reform first. Bolling, who now chaired the Rules Committee, spoke for
the leadership and demanded that the Democratic caucus follow the
"regular order" of permitting Rules to consider the Select Committee's recommendation before the full party body acted. The Patterson
committee had already sent to Rules its proposal for the third option,
a standing Energy Committee.[2] The precariousness of the Select
Committee's standing was demonstrated by the parliamentary tactic
Bolling had to employ—a purposeful "vanishing quorum"—to prevent the adoption of the Dingell plan.

[1] While the ensuing narrative does not always adhere to the strict sequence of events,
the strategic situation is emphasized so that the elimination of various options is presented logically rather than chronologically.

[2] While the leadership did not play up the anti-Dingell aspects of the reorganization
drive (so as not to engender additional opposition), the implications for the Michigan
member were clear. The third option, as referred to Rules, was called "the Ashley
proposal." See Select Committee on Committees, 1980c, p. 8. That proposal had been
drafted by the Select Committee itself.

The Select Committee, by a strong majority, had presented an Energy Committee proposal to Rules on December 20. Its package took jurisdiction away from Science and Technology (commercialization, production, and regulation over nuclear, solar, geothermal, hydroelectric, and fossil fuels), Public Works (production of hydroelectric power), and Interior (mining on public lands), and would give these areas to the new committee. Each chamber would retain some energy concerns (research and demonstration for Science and Technology, the construction of dams for Public Works, and regulation of the Nuclear Regulatory Commission [NRC] for Interior). Even within the Select Committee, however, were the seeds of future problems. Rep. Bill Frenzel (R-Minn.) proposed an amendment to transfer control over the NRC to the new Energy Committee. It initially passed on an 8–7 vote, but a reconsideration motion led Breaux to change his vote, yielding a majority in favor of Interior. Rep. Patricia Schroeder (D-Colo.) thereupon insisted that if Interior were to lose jurisdiction over the NRC, she would propose an amendment taking research and development out of Science and Technology and giving it to the new committee (Select Committee on Committees, 1980c).[3]

The Conflict Intensifies: The Outcome

The Frenzel amendment set the stage for the creation of the destructive coalition of minorities on the Select Committee's proposal, H. Res. 549. Environmentalists had been active in opposing the creation of an energy committee in 1974, again because the nuclear regulatory jurisdiction of Interior was to be ceded (Davidson and Oleszek, 1977, pp. 173–77). Interior chair Udall, who had been viewed as a quiet supporter of energy jurisdiction reform, joined forces with his traditional archenemy Dingell at the February 27 meeting of the Rules Committee. Once the alliance, which Udall himself parodied by hugging the member he admitted was an unusual compatriot, was sealed, so was the fate of the Select Committee's proposal. Udall turned down an offer to share jurisdiction over the Nuclear Regulatory Commission with the proposed panel.

Udall, Dingell, and Science and Technology chair Don Fuqua joined forces to support a substitute offered by Bingham. This proposal essentially took H. Res. 549, without the Frenzel amendment, and gave all its jurisdiction to Interstate and Foreign Commerce—which was to

---

[3] The strategic importance of these amendments clearly lay in the fight over environmentalist support. The Rules Committee did not make either in order on the House floor, arguing that only full-fledged substitutes ought to be permitted.

be renamed Energy and Commerce. Interior's jurisdiction over nuclear power would remain intact. No other committee would lose jurisdiction, although some committees might have to share control with Energy and Commerce. The proposal drew support from members of the affected committees, as well as Merchant Marine and Fisheries, environmentalists, and anti-nuclear activists. Other opponents of the reorganization—conservative Representatives Phil Gramm (D-Tex.), Clarence Brown (R-Ohio), and James Broyhill (R-N.C.)—proposed a substitute that would have combined virtually all energy jurisdiction in the House into a single committee. Gramm stated at Rules that the Patterson plan simply did not do enough: "The Bingham proposal takes the Patterson proposal as it is and gores the minimum number of oxen. My proposal gores every ox in the Congress" (unpublished Rules Committee transcript). Clearly, the Gramm proposal was offered as a foil for Bingham, and even Broyhill admitted that he preferred the Bingham substitute to his own. Gramm, Brown, and Broyhill wanted their proposal to be made immediately following Bingham's in the hope that should the first strategy fail, the House might vote symbolically for a comprehensive energy panel and then kill the entire resolution.

The Frenzel amendment had expanded the scope of conflict. The Rules Committee tried to restrict it by presenting on March 13 a modified closed rule that permitted votes only on the Gramm and Bingham substitutes and one recommittal motion. The Gramm motion was to be voted upon first, contrary to the wishes of its sponsor (and Bingham). Were it to be adopted, it would effectively kill the Bingham amendment. This is precisely what Select Committee supporters wanted: narrow the scope by constricting the range of alternatives (cf. Arrow, 1951). By making the single other possible outcome one that almost no one in Congress wanted (the Gramm proposal), Bolling hoped to induce support for H. Res. 549. The recommittal motion would permit Cleveland to offer a Republican substitute, essentially the Select Committee proposal with Frenzel's original amendment plus a new one he had proposed.[4]

Select Committee leaders worried that opponents might attempt to defeat the rule. Yet neither Dingell nor any other opponent de-

[4] As the actors chose up sides, at least some viewed the battle as so fraught with conflict that further expanding the scope would not matter. Frenzel thus proposed (at the Rules meeting) another amendment, which would give the proposed Energy Committee even more turf. It would gain jurisdiction of the Select Committee on the Outer Continental Shelf (OCS) and would share power over most energy matters left in Interior. The latter proposal was later dropped and the former was viewed by many as unnecessarily provocative since the OCS body was scheduled to expire in June.

manded a roll call as the rule was adopted on March 18 by voice vote. Six days later, the day before the resolution reached the floor, Gramm announced that he was withdrawing his substitute and urged support for the Bingham amendment instead (Hon. Phil Gramm, "Dear Colleague" letter, Mar. 24, 1980). These two events lulled the Select Committee into a false sense of confidence. It began issuing "Dear Colleague" letters specifically attacking Dingell. Democrats and Republicans on the body had agreed to support the GOP recommittal motion.

However, the Frenzel amendments mobilized the chairs of other committees with energy jurisdiction. On the morning of the vote (March 25), O'Neill was quoted in the Washington *Post* as saying that the recommittal strategy might yield the most desirable outcome, but "he as Speaker couldn't support it [but] wouldn't mind if other Democrats did" (Lyons, 1980a). This was widely interpreted as the Speaker's attempt to cut his losses. Later that morning the Speaker received a letter from 117 Representatives, including all but two members of Commerce, urging support for the Bingham substitute. During the debate neither O'Neill (who did not even take the floor) nor Ashley spoke. Select Committee members were stunned when Bingham announced during the debate that the chairs of the major committees and subcommittees dealing with energy had worked out a set of referral procedures among themselves to expedite energy policy-making in the House (see *Congressional Record,* daily ed., 96th Cong., 2d sess., Mar. 25, 1980, pp. H2140–43). Only a small number of Democrats, not including Majority Leader Jim Wright, stood fast in opposing the Bingham amendment, which the House adopted 300–111. The recommittal motion failed 125–282 and the amended resolution passed 274–134. The most malleable of institutions, rules for the consideration of legislation, did not serve to protect the Select Committee's proposal. When faced with the prospect of a structure-induced outcome by the Rules Committee, the allies of Dingell simply withdrew the Gramm substitute to prevent the Patterson body from testing its strength in the House (and thereby possibly trying to mobilize greater support).

The wide margins of defeat for the Select Committee reflected the Speaker's abandonment of the reform battle. Only two Select Committee members (Peter Kostmayer and Robert Traxler) defected on the Bingham amendment, although ten of the 23 original co-sponsors did. There was little partisan or ideological coherence in the voting. A better predictor is committee membership. For the committee most directly threatened by H. Res. 549, only 2 of the 39 members of Commerce, 6 of 40 members of Interior (including Patterson himself), and 5 of 42 members of Science and Technology (including Mike McCormack) voted against Bingham. The other committees in the compact were Foreign Affairs (where 5 of 35 members voted against Bingham), Armed Services (11 of 43), and Public Works (11, including 4 members of the Select Committee, of 48). Only 2 committee chairs (Bolling and Henry Reuss of Banking, on which Ashley was second-ranking) and just 24 (17 percent) of the subcommittee leaders voted against the substitute.

The compact was tested twice in 1980. Immediately after March 25 attention shifted to referral reform. The compact leaders squabbled over time limit proposals and McCormack demanded that Science and Technology become the lead committee on the Department of Energy authorization as the price of his support. Weary, the Select Committee disbanded a month later. By June the compact, completely unraveled as an overwhelming destructive coalition of minorities led by Dingell, defeated the Energy Mobilization Board (see Chapter 4). The 1980 elections brought about another irony: Udall lost his anti-nuclear majority on the Interior Committee. Neither compacts nor committee lines, and certainly not committee reorganization, can induce legislators to adopt policies when they are determined not to do so. Legislators' preferences underlie the stalemate in Congress on energy policy; promises to cooperate in the future are, the Prisoners' Dilemma tells us, unreliable guides to behavior. Rearranging outcomes by changing committee jurisdictions is unlikely to succeed, simply because the legislators will resist the reorganization. Electoral change is far more likely to lead to policy change than committee realignment.

Energy, Power, and Leadership

What resulted in the defeat of the Patterson committee proposals? Outside groups lobbied heavily on committee jurisdictions that directly affected their interests in the Bolling reform battle, but the Patterson committee faced a wide array of groups not all of which were readily identified with energy. But the level of group activity in the 1979–80 committee was substantially less than that observed six years earlier. Fewer groups saw the stakes in the energy reorganization in as bold terms as they did in the broader reform of the Bolling committee. Agriculture and veterans' organizations, among others, were not involved. The oil companies, not surprisingly, paid a great deal of attention to the hearings but did not take a public stand, either individually or collectively.[5] Labor (the AFL-CIO, Communications Workers of America, Teamsters, Machinists, and United Auto Workers) and environmentalists (Congress Watch, Sierra Club, Environmental Policy Center, Natural Resources Development Council, National Audubon Society, Consumer Energy Council of America, Consumer Federation of America, and League of Women Voters) had worked together in fighting an energy committee during the Bolling reforms because they feared that it would be captive to the producers. In 1979–80, on the other hand, they were unusual allies. The environmentalists were myopic over the nuclear issue, but the auto workers were primarily concerned that a new energy committee might stress *conservation* and insist on stricter automobile mileage standards— against which Dingell had worked to protect them. Other unions joined the auto workers in a show of solidarity for Dingell, who was one of labor's champions in the Congress. Only Common Cause, with a single full-time lobbyist, supported the Patterson committee proposal.

The external environment showed that committee reform on energy had little support, but considering the wide scope of the energy issue, surprisingly few groups actively participated in the struggle. First, the Select Committee had attempted to restrict the scope of conflict by not targeting all energy jurisdictions. Gasohol would be left in Agriculture, dams in Public Works, and so on. Second, members themselves were sufficiently concerned about retaining their turf that there was little need for outside groups to prod them into action

Jurisdictional Power Games

The strategic scenario of the energy jurisdictions of House committees was portrayed by Gramm, who taught economics before his election to Congress, as "a zero-sum game. In order for somebody to win, somebody has to lose" (*Congressional Record*, daily ed., 96th Cong., 2d sess., Mar. 25, 1980, p. H2149). But the mere fact that there are winners and losers does not mean that a game is zero-sum. Only if there is

[5] There was some effort on their part to support the creation of a new committee, but it was neither well publicized nor widespread. The industry may have taken such steps on behalf of Breaux, who probably would have become an important figure on the Energy Committee; more likely, however, because the committee would become the center of energy activity, would be an attempt to build up support in the event that the new committee was established without regard to specific personalities. An equally plausible explanation is that many oil companies also had investments in nuclear energy and supported the proposed committee because they agreed with the Republican position that a single committee should have jurisdiction over nonmilitary energy.

a monopoly agenda-setter will realignment of jurisdictions mean that what one committee gains, another loses.

The Select Committee on Committee's hearings clearly establish that the sole priority of most members was the protection of their own turf. Each key actor on energy proposed, not forming a new committee, but rather strengthening the energy authorities of their own panels. Thus we have the making of a cyclical majority with each bloc of actors in support of making it the lead energy committee in the House. Multiple referral reform was not discussed in the hearings, but it is safe to assume that members of Science and Technology (Commerce, Interior, Public Works, and perhaps others) would prefer that other committees not have primary and equal jurisdiction over energy issues. But each of these panels has different policy priorities. Science and Technology is strongly pro-nuclear, Interior is more pro-environment, Public Works strongly supports hydropower, and Commerce (now Energy and Commerce) is deeply entrenched in coal and natural gas. Oil is represented in other committees (notably Ways and Means), as are synfuels (Banking).

The jurisdictional reform battle occurred in the middle of the second energy crisis of the 1970's. At the time, it appeared that disorder in energy markets would be a fact of life for the indefinite future and that prices would continue to increase dramatically. Thus legislators representing each energy sector (and the associated committees representing the fuels) worried about how government action would affect them. Clearly, some sectors would be favored at the expense of others. Each wanted to maximize its role in shaping the nation's energy future. The existing jurisdictional maze doled out power to every sector. In effect, each had a veto over the course of future policies. But none was favored. Since large price increases for energy meant high stakes, every interest (fuels, environmentalists, consumers) sought to change the jurisdictional boundaries in the House to its advantage. Merely being one player among equals (in the sense of having a veto power) was not sufficient. The days of separate policy subsystems on energy had passed; now each sector was competing against all the others.

The hearings before the Select Committee demonstrate that each committee with energy jurisdiction recognized these stakes. The chairs of the affected committees (except Dingell, who declined to appear) testified that their bodies were uniquely situated to be the lead committee on energy. Everyone seemed to accept multiple referral reform, since it would provide a key point of leverage for a favored committee. On the other hand, virtually every committee also had a last choice to be monopoly agenda-setter. Science and Technology, for instance, feared the intrusiveness of Interior. Banking wanted to cede as little as possible to Science and Technology, since synfuels and nuclear compete for funds and each needs large grants for its programs to be sustained. This likely yields a cyclical majority, at least among the affected committees. An Energy Committee with monopoly agenda-setting power is no one's first choice, since it would disrupt existing relationships (which give everyone at least a veto power now). The policy predispositions of such a chamber are unknown. While many in the House feared that the Speaker would appoint Democratic members with a consumerist orientation, the quiet support by some sectors of the petroleum industry for jurisdictional reform indicates that the conflict was not strictly ideological. Without referral reform, an Energy Committee would be just another actor in the jungle warfare of energy jurisdictions in the House, an outcome few were willing to entertain seriously.

The preferences of each (committee) actor could thus be ordered as follows: (1) establishing one's own committee as the lead, coupled with referral reform; (2) the creation of an Energy Committee with monopoly agenda-setting power; (3) the status quo; and (4) the vesting of lead status with some other body. Referral reform without the establishment of an agenda-setter is logically contradictory. These issues are thus nonseparable. For each committee, attaining agenda-setter status is clearly a temptation payoff. This would effectively mean that the fuel (or other interest) in question would set the tone of the debate in the House for years to come. The creation of a single lead Energy Committee would be preferable to the existing jurisdictional maze, at least in 1979–80, because most legislators saw some pressing need to take action on this very salient issue. Even if they could not agree on what to do immediately, and even if they believed that a solution currently on the Congressional agenda (synfuels) would go a long way toward resolving some of the nation's problems, they realized that the energy issue would be with them for years to come. A lead committee that was open to capture by any interest would be preferable to prolonged stalemate, which is what the status quo promised. Thus the establishment of such a committee can be properly labeled the reward payoff, and continuation of the status quo (which is effectively what the renaming of the Interstate and Commerce Committee was) the punishment payoff. Temptation was establishing one's own committee as the agenda-setter, while the sucker's payoff would obtain if one's key opponent obtained that status.

TABLE 6.2

The Generic Energy Committee Prisoners' Dilemma

		COMMITTEE B	
		Cooperate	Defect
COMMITTEE A	Cooperate	Both vote to cede power. Outcome: new Energy Committee formed.	Committee A votes to cede power, Committee B votes not to cede power. Outcome: Committee B becomes lead committee.
	Defect	Committee A votes not to cede power; Committee B votes to cede power. Outcome: Committee A becomes lead committee.	Both vote not to cede power. Outcome: status quo, no lead committee.

ACTORS' PREFERENCES:

Committee A: Committee A as lead, new Energy Committee, status quo, Committee B as lead.
Committee B: Committee B as lead, new Energy Committee, status quo, Committee A as lead.

The n-actor PD is depicted in Table 6.2 in generic form (committee A versus committee B), since at least the four actors that could lay some claim to becoming a monopoly agenda-setter were the key players. Strategically, this meant that each committee would vote either to cede power or not to do so. If both committees agreed to relinquish power, a new Energy Committee would be formed. If neither did so, the status quo of no monopoly agenda-setter would obtain. If one committee elected to cede power and the other did not, the non-cooperator would become the lead committee. The outcomes, of course, depended on the votes of members of the House, not on these committees. However, the central role of committees in the legislative process ensures that the outcome in the House would reflect the agreements (or lack of them) among the four major actors.

If, as I have maintained, there was more support for the creation of an Energy Committee than for the existing jurisdictional arrangements, why did the Select Committee proposal fail? The answer lies in the reluctance of committee members to agree to referral reform. If there was substantial support for the idea of some committee being the monopoly agenda-setter, there was little agreement on which body that should be. While, in the Prisoners' Dilemma outlined above, only a majority of the committees need to have cooperated, there is little incentive for *any* to do so unless it is sure that majority support will be forthcoming. This is the classical dilemma of collective action in an n-person PD (Olson, 1965).

Déjà Vu?

What are the lessons of the Energy Committee reform? Is committee reform simply too difficult to accomplish, as the Bolling committee comparison might suggest? Or is there something else at work, as indicated by the Senate's formation of an Energy and Environment Committee in 1977 as part of a more general committee reorganization? I suggest that neither is the case, despite surface similarities. The scenarios of the 1973–74 and 1979–80 reform efforts are strikingly similar: (1) committee reform was sponsored by the leadership; (2) significant opposition developed both within the Congress and from outside groups; (3) environmental groups provided the strongest basis of opposition to proposals for energy committees; (4) (sub-)committee chairs not directly affected by the proposals joined with their fellow leaders who would lose power in the successful attempts to defeat the proposals; (5) the bulk of the opposition came from within the Democratic party; and (6) the final outcome in each case was a reinforcing of the status quo in the name of reform.

The Patterson committee did not repeat the mistakes that Davidson and Oleszek (1977, pp. 262–63) call the "lessons of hindsight" of the Bolling panel. First, it did not concentrate its attack on full committees when power had passed to subcommittees. The Patterson Select Committee took aim at Dingell, who then chaired only a Commerce subcommittee. Second, the Patterson body realized that legislators and staffs of the affected committees would mobilize outside groups to protect jurisdictions. It sought to limit the scope of conflict to a considerable degree and win in a fight that would focus almost exclusively on Dingell. Third, if the Bolling committee members were too close to the leadership, the Democrats on the Patterson committee were perceived as too far removed from any real center of power in the House.

Having learned these lessons, the Patterson committee and the party leadership could do little to change the outcome of the 1979–80 battle. The level of the struggle, be it focused on committees or subcommittees, was of little consequence. The relations of the Select Committee members to the party leadership were also of little consequence. Few in the House doubted that Bolling rather than Patterson was the key strategic actor in the 1979–80 battle. Establishing a body with a membership not deemed to be close to the leadership was carefully planned by the Speaker. First, it would avoid the problems faced by the earlier reform effort. Second, it could provide the leadership with a way out if, as it must have feared after the defeats of the Bolling and Obey proposals, the House was not about to accept another committee reorganization effort.

Recognizing that committee members and staff might attempt to
organize outside support in the turf fight did not save the Patterson
committee from defeat. Where it erred was in believing that the battle
would be easier because it was confined to a single issue. Energy is not
a neatly segmented issue like agriculture or merchant marine affairs.
The very need for reorganization of energy jurisdictions suggests
how intractable the problem is. Attempting to focus on a single subcommittee (or its leader) is only an exercise in self-deception. Once
the question of jurisdictions has been opened, the conflict cannot be
socialized, because most energy issues cannot be separated from each
other. Where the Bolling committee's proposal was defeated by disparate groups with little in common, the Patterson plan lost to a destructive coalition of minorities formed by people with a common interest
but divergent preferences. The interest these actors shared made
coordination to *defeat* the plan even easier to achieve than in the Bolling fight.

The success of the Senate reorganization in 1977 (Parris, 1979) and
the creation of an Energy and Environment Committee shows that
committee reform is not impossible. But it also highlights the limitations of structural tinkering. The major focus of the Stevenson committee was relief from too many subcommittee assignments. Some full
committee reorganization became inevitable. Even as a chamber designed to handle both energy and the environment was fashioned out
of one that formerly handled only the latter, no committee had to
cede any jurisdictional claims over the former. There was no attempt
at referral reform. And since the Senate is a much less committee-
centered body than the House, with individual members often not respecting boundaries in offering amendments or even legislation, the
impact of turf changes on the policy process is considerably less. The
Senate reform succeeded because it merely reshuffled jurisdictions
rather than realigned them.

Senate committee reform was thus marked by a narrow scope of
conflict, few clearly visible costs, and very little conflict of interest. The
major concern of most Senators was to reduce the number of subcommittee assignments each had. This issue engendered little concern
outside of the Capitol and was widely popular inside the upper house
because workloads had become unmanageable. Only a handful of
Senators were forced to give up subcommittee slots they cherished.
This does not mean that the Stevenson plan was adopted without a
fight. Few jurisdictional realignments ever are. It does mean that the

issues could be compromised, but also that the effects of the reorganization would hardly be remembered as changing the nature of Senate policy-making.

In contrast, the Patterson committee was fraught with conflict of interest. The compact that ultimately formed among the committees with the most important energy jurisdictions was, like the initial alliance between Dingell and Udall, an alliance between actors who fundamentally distrusted each other. However distasteful the status quo was, it remained preferable to a situation in which the policy outcome was unknown and not subject to the veto power of any of the previous actors. This fear of the unknown was so pervasive that Udall rejected a leadership offer (made shortly after the Rules meeting) to chair an environmental committee of the proposed Energy Committee and presumably to be second in seniority on the entire body. Yet, perversely, members of committees with energy jurisdictions would rather face a new body than permit some other committee to become a monopoly agenda-setter.

The all-pervasiveness of the energy issue made expansion of the scope of conflict inevitable. The question of Dingell's allegiance to the leadership was never very salient to most members of the House, who themselves viewed party loyalty with varying degrees of enthusiasm. By not focusing on committees with subsidiary energy interests, the Patterson panel hoped to restrict the scope of conflict. However, it made a strategic miscalculation. Agriculture and Banking were peripheral actors on energy; there was simply no way to exclude other committees from seeking to protect their jurisdictions. The nonseparability of referral reform from committee reorganization ensured that the scope of conflict would be wide. Shifting turf responsibilities would be meaningless without the establishment of a monopoly agenda-setter. Once these issues were joined, all actors with major energy jurisdictions were automatically brought into the fray. The battle over power was thus marked by costs that every player clearly perceived. If energy could be neatly segmented into a single committee, the entire problem would not have arisen.

It is ironic that the proposal for an energy committee as a monopoly agenda-setter might be a prominent solution to the problem of energy decision-making. If a single committee could send legislation to the House floor (ideally under a rule prohibiting amendments), a perceived need to take some action to resolve an energy crisis might lead to the bill's adoption. While this is unlikely, many members of the House feared that such a committee, particularly if it became a tool of the party leadership, *just might* succeed in pushing legislation through the House. The memories of the Speaker's success in enacting Carter's 1977 package were vivid for many members of the House, even if that victory was attributable to rather unusual circumstances (see Chapter 8).

For the very reasons that the Patterson committee proposal seemed to be a prominent solution and that stakes appeared to be so high, the package was doomed to be defeated by a destructive coalition of minorities. Had there been less conflict of interest among House committees, an accord would have been possible. Had the cleavages been more reinforcing, and thus indicative of a clear-cut ideological and partisan battle, a prominent solution could have been adopted by majority rule.[6] However, the lines of division were cross-cutting rather than overlapping. Policy coordination becomes extremely difficult, if not impossible when preferences are so arranged and the stakes are so high. Every possible outcome in substantive energy policy imposes costs on some legislators. Thus the reelection motive dictates that no proposal be adopted. This holds equally for any jurisdictional reorganization that threatens to impose some substantive outcome. Risk-averse legislators fear the worst and, particularly when they do not know which proposal will be adopted, they pursue their reelection strategies by doing nothing. This corresponds, in the electoral game, to everyone cooperating with everyone else, the reward payoff, but to defection, the punishment payoff, in the policy game.

The failure of the Select Committee's proposal can thus be traced to the same set of dilemmas that confronts the Congress on substantive energy policy. As a former Presidential press secretary once told a group of political scientists (quoted in Price, 1972, p. 11): "You people have this congressional reform business all wrong. What's wrong with Congress is not the rules, seniority, and all those things. What's wrong with Congress is the *people* in it. You're not going to change anything until you change that" (emphasis in original). What he meant by "the people in the Congress" was not the specific individuals. More than a decade and a half has passed since the comment was made, and most of the members then serving have been replaced. Indeed, the institutional structure has been drastically transformed into a more decentralized system. Even the new breed of more independent, more policy-oriented members (Uslaner, 1978b) has not transformed Congress into an institution that comes to grips with the great issues of

---

[6]This assumes that the electoral mechanism functions so as to put into a majority position in the legislature (and executive) supporters of the prominent solution. However, if the solution appears prominent to the electorate, this is rather a minimal demand on an electoral system.

our time. What has not changed, and what the press secretary was clearly alluding to, is the reelection motive.

The system of democratic elections, even with single-member districts, is not the demon that prevents coordinated policy formation. What is determinative is *how* preferences are structured within the electoral system. In the United States, Representatives and Senators each campaign for reelection on their own. There are few partisan or ideological anchors on which a legislator can rely. Political parties do not take coherent policy positions, particularly on very divisive issues (as the natural gas example in Chapter 5 demonstrates). There is no sense of collective accountability. Each legislator is thus a hostage to the constituency interests that might be hurt by a particular policy proposal. The entire effort to establish an Energy Committee in the House was based on the false presumption that institutional structure will have an exogenous effect on preferences. It was an attempt to put the genie back in the bottle by replacing noncooperative (sub)committee leaders with legislators close to the Speaker. Indeed, the Democratic leadership demonstrated precisely how much it believed that this was the case by proposing a modified closed rule on the Select Committee proposal in the attempt to restrict the scope of conflict. The failure of the rule to induce the favored outcome and the ultimate defeat of the Select Committee's proposal indicate just how fragile institutional solutions are.

Efforts at institutional reform begin with the assumption that structures are malleable. To act otherwise would be to act perversely. Yet the reformers are often mistaken about why their clientele—the members of Congress, in this case—are expected to want to reform. When the agenda has changed and the old institutional structures work to inhibit policy changes, the situation may be ripe for reform (Dodd, 1986; Uslaner, 1978b). Predicting when this occurs is often difficult, since institutions are more than simply "congealed tastes." Yet they are hardly etched in stone either, and the resilience of the existing power structure on energy in the House of Representatives in 1979–80 tells us more about the nature of preferences on energy than about the staying power of institutions in general. In this sense, preferences were clearly endogenous to policy preferences at the level of legislative committees. If we could have achieved institutional reform on energy jurisdictions in the House, we most likely wouldn't have needed it in the first place.

SEVEN

Oh, Canada!

> Why are you not merry then? There are but two of
> us in all the world, and if we should not be comforts
> one to another, God help us.
>
> (*Everyman Out of His Humour*, IV. i, p. 359)

IN THE United States during the Ford and Carter administrations, proposed energy legislation was known as the National Energy Policy, or NEP. The NEP in the Ford administration was never
enacted into law, but Carter's NEP was finally passed in 1978, albeit in
emasculated form (see Chapter 2). Yet most Americans would not recognize the acronym NEP even in a nation where government programs are often referred to as "alphabet soup." In Canada, on the
other hand, the legislation promulgated by the Liberal party government of Prime Minister Pierre Elliot Trudeau, is known far and wide
as the NEP, or National Energy Program.

The Progressive Conservative (PC) government of Prime Minister
Joe Clark fell in December 1979 on the defeat of the administration's
budget in the House of Commons. The major issue in the defeat of
the budget was a proposal to increase the excise tax on gasoline by 18
cents a gallon.[1] Most observers regarded the ensuing federal elections
in February 1980 as a referendum on the minority PC government's
energy policy. Indeed, it has been called the "18 cent election" (Doern
and Toner, 1985, p. 5). Soon thereafter the reinstated Liberal government enacted the most wide-ranging energy policy the North American continent has ever witnessed.

This chapter is about why Canada was able to adopt a national energy policy while the United States has not been able to do so, except
in name. It is not a brief for adopting a Canadian-style energy policy
in the United States. Rather I am concerned with the conditions for
cooperation among actors with diverse preferences. Explicating the
Canadian case, which in terms of energy resources is the most similar
in the world to the U.S. case, will highlight the political and cultural
differences between the two nations. Specifically, Canada was able to

---

[1] Unless otherwise noted, all figures reported in this chapter are in Canadian dollars.

overcome a potential crisis in energy decision-making in a federal system because the preferences of its citizens and its legislators are marked by partisan, ideological, and constituency cleavages that overlap and reinforce each other. The strategic scenario was not marked by cyclical preferences leading to an n-person Prisoners' Dilemma, but rather by a two-party game, which I trace to an ideological politics at least on the energy issue.

I also argue that the differences in institutional structure between Canada and the United States do *not* suffice to explain why the former is marked by a strong party system on energy and the latter is not. The Westminster system found in Canada is generally believed to be virtually a prerequisite for party government, while the Congressional system in the United States is held to be inimical to it (see Sundquist, 1986). Yet an institutionalist account is deficient on two counts. First, the differing institutional structures in the two countries reflect long-standing cultural distinctions between them. Thus constitutional forms are endogenous to deep-seated values. Second, Canadian politics is marked by cohesive legislative parties, but not innovative ones.

The structuralist account fails to explain why a bold initiative on energy was possible in 1980. The answer lies in how preferences are structured on energy as opposed to other issues. Preferences over outcomes, especially when they are clearly related to conflicts over more deep-seated values, can readily overwhelm institutional forces. The clear-cut message of this chapter is that attempts at institutional reforms to foster party solidarity on energy in the United States are unlikely to be successful (cf. Chapter 8). This lesson is particularly interesting because a comparison of Canada and the United States is as close as one can get to a laboratory test of two similar countries with different policy outcomes on energy, and because Canadian political history has been marked by countless calls (many even sponsored by the federal government) for structural (Constitutional) reforms to resolve underlying tensions within the country.

Here is a brief outline of what is to come. First, I show that comparing the two nations is justifiable. Then I examine some of the more fundamental differences between them: the sense of nationhood, different political cultures, variations in the nature of federal systems, patterns of regionalism, the party systems, and differences in institutional structures. The idea of a Canadian national identity is central to the analysis. All the other conflicts—partisan, ideological, regional, economic, and institutional—revolve around this issue, making the battle over energy policy a straight fight between two contending interests as opposed to the jungle warfare of each against all that we find in the United States. A brief historical analysis of Canadian energy policy will set the stage for a discussion of the NEP, which in turn will permit comparisons with the United States.

Canada and the United States

Canada and the United States are inextricably linked by patterns of life-style and reciprocal trade. Each is the other's largest trading partner by far. Yet there are two major distinctions: (1) the United States has almost ten times the population of Canada, and (2) the United States is a net energy importer while Canada is a net exporter (Doran, 1984, p. 213). On a per capita basis, proven oil and gas reserves are two to four times greater in Canada (computed from International Energy Agency, 1982, p. 264). We should not make too much of the issue of population, which appears to be unrelated to the cultural factors that will loom large in our explanation; it is important only insofar as it affects the energy resource bases of the two countries. While there are important differences between the United States and Canada on energy resources, the two countries are more similar to each other than to any other major industrial democracy. The data in Table 7.1 indicate that only in petroleum production per capita is any other such nation closer to the United States than Canada; furthermore, Canada had become a net importer of petroleum by 1975 (Chandler and Chandler, 1979, p. 266).

TABLE 7.1

Energy Comparisons Among Industrialized Nations, 1980

Country	Total primary energy use per capita[a]	Petroleum consumption per capita[b]	Avg. no. of minutes needed to work for liter of gasoline[c]	Retail price for U.S. gallon premium gasoline[d]	Petroleum production per capita[e]
Canada	9.78	3,663	2.1	0.89	2.941
United States	9.20	2,928	2.7	1.31	1.863
United Kingdom	4.02	1,472	6.4	2.65	1.411
West Germany	5.03	1,622	5.3	2.57	.001
Norway	5.76	1,802	—	2.93	6.009
France	—	2,121	9.5	3.17	.022
Italy	—	1,640	9.4	3.15	.082
Japan	3.91	1,890	8.5	2.89	.004

[a]Helliwell, 1979, p. 182; figures are estimates derived by the Organization for Economic Cooperation and Development.
[b]United Nations, 1984; quantities are in thousand metric tons.
[c]Dobson, 1981, p. 48.
[d]United Nations, 1984; prices are in U.S. dollars.
[e]United Nations, 1984; quantities are in metric tons.

The United States and Canada are united by a similarity of life-styles: fashions, fads, technology, radio and television waves, and even some political movements (see Richards and Pratt, 1979, pp. 49–58) freely cross the border. For all that binds us together, there is much that sets us apart. The United States stresses the idea of being a melting pot of many groups and religions, a country with a common set of values expressed in the idea of "one out of many." Canada, on the other hand, is regarded as a mosaic of many groups retaining their own cultural and linguistic identities from their countries of origin. There are few Canadian institutions or myths; Canadian provinces, unlike U.S. states, can and do impose tariffs on each other's goods (Malcolm, 1981; Esman, 1984, p. 27). Perhaps the most telling distinction is the use of language: Canadians generally refer to their country as the "confederation." One rarely reads or hears the word "nation" as one does in the United States. Most Canadians identify more with their home province than with the country (Clarke et al., 1984, p. 41).

The struggle over what this identity should be overshadows all other issues, with the result that Canada has less class-based voting than any other Anglo-American democracy (Alford, 1963, p. 257; Pammett, 1986). The British values inherited by Canada include an acceptance of heterogeneity, a belief in the importance of the group rather than the individual (in contrast to the U.S. experience, as noted by Hofstadter, 1955, ch. 1), and a commitment to settling disputes by cooperation rather than conflict (Doran, 1984, p. 88; Presthus, 1973, p. 21). The Canadian society was in need of some sort of centralizing authority to hold the country together: this vehicle is a strong state, which provides a cultural and economic defense against domination from outside and also serves to resolve internal conflicts.

The weak sense of nationhood has led to a conflict over where the powers of the state should be exercised. This is what has shaped the Canadian federal system. Until 1982 Canada had no constitution in the U.S. sense; its legal superstructure was set forth in the British North America (BNA) Act of 1867. The BNA Act often failed to draw clear lines between federal and provincial authority. In contrast to its U.S. counterpart, the federal government "arrogrates to itself any powers not specified to the provinces" (Wren, 1985). Much of Canadian policy formation, including the battles over the National Energy Program, centers on resolving the constitutional ambiguity over where power ought to lie: the provinces have become involved in a range of activities (welfare services, transportation, resource development) that elsewhere in the industrialized world belong to central governments (Stevenson, 1977, p. 72).

The best-known example of tension between the federal and provincial governments is the drive of Quebec in the 1970's for independence or at least "sovereignty-association." Equally critical, however, is the alienation felt by Westerners against the "Toronto-Montreal" axis, historically the repository of both wealth and political power in Canada. Westerners feel neglected by an Eastern-dominated federal government, which depends for its political support on Quebec and particularly Ontario (Clarke et al., 1980, p. 45; Reistrup, 1980). Western grievances are encapsulated by the Liberal party's program to impose a consumer-oriented energy policy on the producer provinces of the West, a bastion of Progressive Conservative party support. But it was more than that: it was a drive, together with the movement for a national constitution, to assert the predominance of the federal government over the provinces.

Since their admission into the confederation as provinces in 1905, Alberta and Saskatchewan have had disagreements with Ottawa over resource development. Not until 1930 did Alberta and Saskatchewan gain title to their mineral resources, although every other province had such control. Alberta, which has historically been almost totally dependent on minerals and agriculture, has 85 percent of the established oil and gas reserves of Canada, and 85 percent of these reserves are on provincially controlled land (Harrison, 1981, pp. 66–67). Albertans thus regard energy resources as a "special birthright" (Richards and Pratt, 1979, pp. 62, 161). Conservative governments in Alberta have taken large royalty payments from the private development of provincially owned oil and gas fields; in 1976, the province established the Alberta Heritage Savings Trust Funds (AHSTF) as a development bank to pave the way to a more diversified economy once energy resources were depleted (Norrie, 1981, p. 145).

The battle over control of energy resources was a partisan as well as regional conflict, but it cannot be encapsulated solely in terms of the two major parties. The Liberals are a shade to the left of the Democrats in the United States, as are the PCs relative to the Republicans. There is a third force as well, the NDP (New Democrats), a mildly socialist party with close ties to Canadian labor. Its base is even stronger in the agricultural heartland of Canada, and its roots are in the tradition of farmer-labor movements in the United States. The extent of alienation in the West is best characterized by the fate of the two national parties: from 1921 to 1957 they failed to capture even a majority of the Western seats in the federal House of Commons (Smith, 1981, pp. 41–42). From 1911 to 1979 the region never elected a provincial government of the party that controlled the federal government. The very success of the Liberals in dominating control of the federal government made success in the West unattainable (LeDuc, 1984, p. 424). The disjunction between federal and provincial politics in Canada, as the provincial contests in Quebec largely exclude the PCs while those in the West exclude the Liberals, actually exacerbates party conflict in Parliament by asserting the hegemony of each party within its own regional base.

The energy battles of 1979–81 were fought on precisely the lines of West versus East. Ontario and the federal government in Ottawa feared being dominated by "blue-eyed sheikhs" of the West. Western energy-producing provinces had for some time been seeking a movement toward world prices for their resources. Income was, in a reversal of historical trends, flowing from East to West. The NEP was an initiative by a Liberal federal government to implement an energy policy against the wishes of Tory governments in the prairie provinces. Unlike the United States, where the legislative and executive branches have independent powers and separate electoral bases, with a legislature further split into two equal branches, Canada is governed by a Parliamentary system with a single dominant chamber (the House of Commons). In a legislature patterned after the Westminster (Parliamentary) model, an alienated minority thus has few opportunities to obstruct. The federal structure becomes particularly important because it is the only power base the minority has.[2]

The National Energy Program

Prior to 1973, U.S. and Canadian energy policies were very similar (Richards and Pratt, 1979, p. 21; Doern and Toner, 1985, p. 67). Both countries based their energy policies on expanding supply and protecting price stability for both producers and consumers, to ensure orderly markets amidst abundance. U.S. energy policy paralysis began after the Yom Kippur War, which had less of an effect in Canada (Fischer and Keith, 1977, p. 107). Canada, like the United States, imposed price controls on oil. In 1975 a Liberal government established a national oil company, Petro-Canada. A year earlier, in a key depar-

[2] Two specific devices have been employed to reduce conflict. First, beginning in 1927 the federal government began making special payments to the (Atlantic) Maritime provinces, and in 1957 it introduced the present system of equalization payments designed to reduce income inequalities among the provinces (Stevenson, 1979, p. 147). Second, the Prime Minister and the provincial premiers meet periodically to negotiate solutions to the problems facing the country. Both mechanisms are extra-constitutional, and each is predicated upon some understanding by all the provincial actors that accommodation is in everyone's interest. When the stakes are sufficiently high, however, the incentives for cooperation break down.

ture from the traditional policy of negotiating energy revenue agreements with the provinces, the federal government disallowed the deduction of provincial royalties from federal income taxes. Ottawa was responding to bills enacted in Alberta in 1973 that empowered the provincial government to set oil and gas prices within the province and to determine production levels (Toner and Bregha, 1981, pp. 4–5).

The 1979 round of price increases had a more pronounced effect on Canada, particularly in the redistribution of wealth. The AHSTF, from an initial endowment of $1.5 billion, was projected to reach ten times that level by 1990, with almost 30 percent of the revenues coming from residents of Ontario. That province, historically viewed as the richest, had begun to receive equalization payments in 1975 (Doern and Toner, 1985, p. 101; Simeon, 1980, p. 183; Norrie, 1981, p. 147).

The Tory government of Prime Minister Joe Clark, elected in 1979, proposed selling Petro-Canada and imposing an 18 cent per gallon increase in gasoline prices at the pump to encourage conservation. Clark also proposed pegging domestic energy prices to 85 percent of the world market, but insisted on a windfall profits tax of 50 percent on increases over $2.00 per barrel of oil or over 30 cents per thousand cubic feet of natural gas. The energy pricing agreement with Alberta was to expire in July 1980, and a new accord had to be reached. However, Alberta PC Premier Peter Lougheed rejected the proposal and no accord had been reached when the minority federal government fell on December 11, 1979, over the issue of the 18 cent tax. Reeling from the defeat on the budget and other assorted problems that tarnished Clark's image, the Tories were soundly defeated in the February 1980 elections. The Liberals returned to power, once again led by Pierre Elliot Trudeau. Trudeau proposed the National Energy Program to Parliament on October 28, 1980. Canada's dependence on imported oil and on multinational (read "U.S.") oil companies was to be sharply reduced in favor of "made-in-Canada" petroleum produced by Canadian companies and sold at (governmentally set) Canadian prices.

The major provisions of the program are as follows (Energy, Mines, and Resources Canada, 1980; Palmer, 1981; Pratt, 1982, pp. 35–36).

1. A new "blended" price system for oil would be introduced to average the costs of domestic and foreign oil from both conventional and unconventional sources, leading to modest increases in prices to consumers, a reduction of the role of the federal government in subsidizing energy costs, and a cap on producers' prices. Oil prices were to rise $1.00 a barrel at the wellhead on January 1, 1981, and by a similar amount every six months until the end of 1983. The rate of

increase would then more than double until 1986, when it would rise again at a fixed rate until 1990, when a more rapid set of price hikes would be considered. Government subsidies would continue until the blended system was fully implemented. However, the new price would never exceed 85 percent of the world price or the average price of oil in the United States, whichever was lower.

2. Natural gas prices would be frozen for a year and afterwards rise more slowly than oil prices.

3. A Petroleum Compensation Charge was levied on all refined petroleum products to cover the costs of import subsidies. This charge would also increase gradually over time.

4. A Natural Gas and Gas Liquids Tax was imposed on all gas either for domestic consumption or for export. (The Alberta government challenged this tax in court.)

5. A Petroleum and Gas Revenue Tax, set at 8 percent, was established on net operating revenues, including royalty interests.

6. Depletion allowances for oil and gas exploration were to be phased out of the federal tax system and replaced by a set of grants based on the extent of Canadian ownership of energy companies. Companies that were at least 65 percent Canadian-owned (rising gradually to 75 percent by 1986) would be eligible for Petroleum Incentive Program (PIP) grants that would cover as much as 80 percent of exploration costs on federally owned land, 35 percent for provincial land, and stipends covering up to 20 percent of development expenditures for domestic exploration and development.

7. The Canada Oil and Gas Act would provide that companies seeking to develop the "Canada Lands" in the northern territories and offshore must be at least 50 percent domestically owned. Furthermore, the Crown reserved to itself an automatic 25 percent interest in any such developments, including those already in progress, as well as the right to determine the rate of development and other issues.

8. A goal of 50 percent Canadian ownership of all oil and gas production by 1990 was established, a goal to be accomplished in part by Petro-Canada's purchase of one or more foreign-owned firms. A tax on oil and gas consumption would finance these purchases.

9. The role of oil as a contributor to Canada's primary energy needs was to be reduced from 43 percent to 27 percent by 1990. Gas, hydroelectricity, and renewable resources were targeted for increased use, and incentives for conversion from oil were proposed, including an extension of the gas pipeline from Montreal to Quebec City and ultimately to the Maritimes and the establishment of a gas bank for small Canadian producers.

10. The federal government's share of petroleum rents was to increase from 10 to 24 percent by 1983, while the provincial share would fall from 45 to 43 percent and the industry's from 45 to 33 percent.

The government report (Energy, Mines, and Resources Canada, 1980) cited four central goals of the NEP: (1) greater energy self-sufficiency, (2) conservation, (3) nation-building, and (4) increased Canadian control of the energy industry. The first goal would be met by a combination of pricing and production schemes. The former would establish a made-in-Canada price that would gradually rise but never reach world levels. There would be increased use of natural gas, which Canada has in abundance, and the price would be guaranteed to be below that of oil. The federal government granted itself a 25 percent share in the largely undeveloped areas of the northern territories and offshore Newfoundland, claiming that it would ultimately bear more than 90 percent of the costs of exploration by way of incentive grants (Doern and Toner, 1985, p. 51). These same strategies would give Ottawa more of a role in conservation.

The nation-building goal was intimately connected with that of increasing Canadian control of the energy industry. New taxes on oil and gas would help the federal government capture some of the economic rents of the domestic energy boom. These revenues would be shared among all Canadians, with none being able to claim any revenue as a "special birthright." Nation-building would also be pursued by the made-in-Canada prices for oil and gas and by the policy of the "Canadianization" of energy firms.[3]

The NEP: Never-Ending Politics

Predictably, the NEP was not favorably received in the Canadian West. The pricing accord between the federal government and the province of Alberta had not been resolved by the Tories, and stale-

[3] Canadians have always feared being overwhelmed by the United States. The domestic oil and gas industry was 75 percent owned by foreigners, and 80 percent of foreign ownership was U.S. The Canadianization proposal was popular among Canadians of every age group and *in every region* (Foster, 1982, p. 32; Toner, 1984, p. 241). In the next two years Canadian firms went on a spending spree purchasing foreign energy interests as the domestically owned share of revenues increased from 28 to 35 percent in just one year (New York *Times*, 1982b; Giniger, 1981). The centrality of the energy industry in the Canadian economy—it accounts for 40 percent of corporate profits in the resource sector as compared to 26 percent in the United States—further helps account for the salience of the Canadianization program (Malcolm, 1982b). Yet, as Tory critics pointed out, Canadianization and price caps worked to scare away foreign firms and within a year they resulted in a 50 percent cut in the number of oil rigs operating in Canada (Dobson, 1981; *Oil and Gas Journal*, 1982c).

mate persisted past the July 1980 expiration date. The provincial government in Edmonton immediately responded to the NEP by announcing a unilateral price increase for oil—in accord with the NEP's provisions but several months earlier. Ottawa did not challenge the move, but the provincial government's reaction was merely the first shot in a protracted battle.

As Doern (1983, p. 223) argues, "the NEP . . . is patently about far more than just energy policy. It also embraces national identity, regional policy, economic policy, social policy, foreign policy, transportation policy and the like. . . . Revenue was a genuine issue but it was also a surrogate for many of the normative concerns that are inherent not only in energy policy but in Canadian politics in general: different views of federalism, the role of Western Canada, the control of resources, regional disparities, growing budgetary deficits, and Canadian ownership of the economy." The conflict, then, was over whether the federal or provincial government would determine how energy resources would be distributed. In the midst of a drive by Trudeau for a Canadian Constitution, the NEP was just as much about the future of Canada.

The overall political strategy of the NEP, and the strategy underlying the proposed Constitution, was to establish political dominance by the Liberals and to shift economic power back to the East and the consumers of energy (Pratt, 1982, pp. 34, 43). The government, to be sure, did not flaunt its political goals. It sought to portray its policy as beneficial to the West as well, arguing that provincial energy revenues would more than double in the next four years and that Alberta's economic rents compared very favorably with those of any subnational authority in the world (Energy, Mines, and Resources Canada, 1980, p. 109). The NEP focused on large-scale developments, called megaprojects in Canada when they involve expenditures of more than $100 million (Doern, 1983, p. 219), and some observers thought the Liberals were trying to use pork barrel politics to attract NDP supporters in Western constituencies.[4] On the other hand, the program needed no boost to win popularity in Ontario. Nation-building was a popular issue there. The left-leaning provincial Tory government even purchased 25 percent of U.S.-owned Suncor to express its solidarity with the goals of the NEP. Polls indicated that a majority of Canadians, and especially those in Ontario, believed the government

---

[4]The NEP itself marked a departure from the capitalist politics of the Liberals and may have been designed to preempt a more radical proposal from the NDP itself. One neo-Marxist critic called the NEP "a program of public works for the Canadian bourgeoisie" (Pratt, 1982, p. 57; cf. Doern and Toner, 1985, p. 33).

had an important role to play in setting energy prices (Marmorek, 1981; Foster and Jacobs, 1980, p. 66). In Ontario, the provisions of the NEP did not divide the rank-and-file consumers from the business community as natural gas issues did in the United States (Chapter 5). Businesses were attracted to the NEP because they believed that lower energy prices would help them compete in the world market and they believed that Canadianization would stimulate domestic economic growth (Doran, 1984, p. 227).

Ontario and Alberta were the major provincial actors on the NEP. Among other energy-producing provinces, Saskatchewan and British Columbia did support Alberta's demand for more generous prices, but partisan differences (Saskatchewan was governed by the NDP and British Columbia by the right-wing Social Credit party) led to different economic strategies. Newfoundland and Nova Scotia had disagreements with Ottawa over offshore oil resources and were less interested in East-West issues. Manitoba, New Brunswick, and Prince Edward Island took no position on the NEP. Quebec felt cross-pressured: as a consuming province, it stood with Ontario, but it was vitally concerned with the issue of provincial rights (Doern and Toner, 1985, pp. 181–82, 281–83).

All the other issues were subordinate to this provincial-federal conflict (Smiley, 1980, p. 201). The issue of the environment, so important in the United States, was hardly raised. Even though many Canadians do see the environment as an important issue, political organization of environmentalists tends to be strong only in Ontario (Doran, 1984, p. 205), where support for the NEP was also strongest. Many Canadians seem to regard the problem as one of foreign policy—acid rain coming from the United States (Lanouette, 1982). It is not that regionalism overwhelmed all other issues. Rather, the energy issue encompasses all the tendentious agenda items in Canadian politics: regional, ideological, producer-consumer, and partisan conflicts overlap (Toner and Bregha, 1981, p. 3; McKinsey, 1981, p. 24).

The reinforcing of partisan and regional cleavages is not as strong in the United States as in Canada. In Table 7.2 I compare the regional patterns of representation in the federal and state/provincial legislatures in the western regions of the two countries following the 1980 elections. The Democrats maintained a healthy minority of all positions even at this, their low point in recent years, and they even had a slim majority of Governorships. In contrast, the Canadian Liberals were reduced to but a single member of the Federal Parliament and to a lone seat in the provincial Legislative Assemblies. Both legislators represented the easternmost Western province, Manitoba. The Tory

TABLE 7.2

Democratic and Liberal Party Representation in the West After the 1980 Elections

Office	Democratic/Liberal party representation		
	Party seats	Total seats	Party percentage
United States			
U.S. Senate	12	34	35.3
U.S. House of Representatives	42	89	48.3
Governorships	9	17	53.0
State Upper Houses[a]	251	560	44.8
State Lower Houses	538	1,212	44.4
Canada			
Federal Parliament	1	77	1.3
Provincial Legislative Assemblies	1	259	0.0

NOTE: For the United States, the West is defined as all states west of the Mississippi River except Texas and Oklahoma (which are traditionally Democratic). For Canada, the West is defined as the provinces of Manitoba, Saskatchewan, Alberta, and British Columbia.
[a] Nebraska's nonpartisan unicameral legislature is excluded from these calculations.

hegemony was so complete in Alberta that the party controlled 75 of the 79 seats in the provincial legislature. The ensuing battle over the NEP thus stands in sharp contrast to the multiple preference cycles on energy issues in the United States.

The War Between the Provinces

If the lines of cleavage were clearly defined, the issues themselves were anything but clear-cut. In a Parliamentary system of government, the majority rules. Thus we would expect a simple, straightforward fight that Ottawa would win and that would resolve the issue once and for all. However, Canada is not patterned precisely on the Westminster model. It is a federal system, and the document that established the confederation is excruciatingly detailed about the rights and obligations of the federal government and the provinces. If anything, it is too detailed because many of these provisions contradict each other.

Alberta viewed the NEP, and particularly its taxation provision, as violating the federal bargain expressed in the British North America Act. Under Sections 92 and 109 of the Act, all lands, mines, minerals, and royalties within a province's borders are the property of the province. Section 92 further gives the provinces the power to tax these lands, whether public or private (Toner and Bregha, 1981, p. 4). Section 125 further stipulates that no lands or property belonging either to Canada or to a province may be subject to taxation. Thus Alberta saw the Trudeau push for country-building as a direct threat to constitutional provisions and to the historical role of the federal government and the provinces in energy development. Ottawa marshaled legal arguments of its own, to be sure. Section 91(2) of the BNA Act gives Parliament the power to regulate all aspects of both international and interprovincial trade. Furthermore, section 92(10)(c) reserves to the federal government control over provincial works that it "declares" to be "for the general advantage of Canada" or "of two or more of the provinces," a power that had been previously used by Ottawa to secure control of the atomic energy industry (Toner and Bregha, 1981, p. 4). Was Ottawa intervening in provincial affairs or was it simply following the BNA Act and providing for good government and the regulation of intraprovincial commerce?[5]

Alberta Premier Peter Lougheed viewed the introduction of the NEP as an abrogation of the unwritten contract that would settle federal-provincial disputes by negotiation rather than by unilateral action; he took to provincial television to tell his audience that Ottawa's promulgation of the NEP was like "having strangers take over the living room" (quoted in Foster, 1982, p. 166). Alberta was to challenge the natural gas tax in court, winning a favorable ruling in the provincial Court of Appeals. The province believed it had strategic advantages over other provinces through loans made by the AHSTF and over the federal government because local cooperation was needed if the development of the Cold Lake and Alsands tar sands plants was to proceed (Doern and Toner, 1985, pp. 44, 190).

Two days after the NEP was introduced, Lougheed announced a delay in the two plants, as well as a cutback of 60,000 barrels a day in oil production, or 5 percent of the oil that was pumped daily in the province. He promised periodic further reductions of 5 percent until 15 percent was reached or an accord had been signed with Ottawa. Lougheed put forth his own proposals calling for no new taxes, a faster movement toward world prices, lower royalties on synthetic fuels plants, a sharply restricted and entirely Alberta-based program

[5] Insofar as constitutions are living documents, the argument of Stevenson (1977, pp. 76–77) is convincing: "In 1867, Section 109 seemed relatively unimportant. Mining was almost nonexistent, except in Nova Scotia where coal royalties provided about 5 percent of the colonial government's revenues just prior to Confederation. Forestry was important only in New Brunswick, since the accessible forests of Ontario and Quebec had been almost completely cut down and shipped to the United States. . . . The technological developments that gave economic significance to sprucewood pulp, nickel, hydro-electric power, oil, and natural gas lay in the future. Most of the land suitable for agriculture in the original provinces had already passed into private ownership."

of Canadianization, and no increase in the federal share of economic rents (see Dobson, 1981, pp. 7–8, for a comparison of the plans).

For almost a year Ottawa and Edmonton traded charges and retaliatory acts. The 15 percent cutback was reached on June 1, 1981, and Ottawa was forced to import more crude oil than usual, raising consumer prices through its "Lougheed levy" to make up the difference in cost. There was pressure on both sides to reach a compromise: Alberta's oil industry was hurting from the cutbacks, as was the service industry. The smaller companies in particular were urging some solution (Doern and Toner, 1985, p. 273). Alberta, later joined by British Columbia, withheld payments of the natural gas tax. Saskatchewan threatened similar action (Giniger, 1981). Energy Minister Marc Lalonde threatened to invoke the Petroleum Administration Act of 1974, which permitted Ottawa to take strong measures in times of national crisis.

The two parties began negotiating seriously in late August and on September 1 reached an accord that provided for the following: (1) the wellhead price of oil would immediately increase by $2.50 a barrel, which would amount to 65 cents a barrel once the temporary import levy was removed; (2) there would be a further increase of $4.50 a barrel in 1982 with annual adjustments of $8.00 a barrel through 1986, finally reaching a price of $57.75 a barrel, excluding federal taxes; (3) the federal government would retain the natural gas tax, but set its rate at zero percent; (4) Ottawa's share of economic rents would rise to 29 percent, the province's to 34 percent, and industry's share would drop to 37 percent; (5) new oil would immediately be priced at 85 percent of the world price; (6) Alberta promised expeditious approval for the two delayed tar sands plants; (7) industry would be permitted to claim a 25 percent resource allowance on the petroleum and gas taxes to resolve Alberta's charges that the levies were wellhead taxes; (8) the tax rate would be increased from 8 percent to 12 percent and there would be a new windfall profits tax of 50 percent of the additional revenues obtained under the agreement; (9) industry would be permitted to deduct royalties from the windfall profits tax; (10) Alberta would impose a lower royalty rate on tar sands projects once they began making payments to their sponsors; and (11) the Canadianization features of the NEP would remain in force (Lewington, 1981).

Who won in this protracted conflict? Rusk (1981) argues that Alberta received most of what it was seeking in terms of prices. Alberta was also said to have claimed victory simply by forcing Ottawa to resolve the issue by negotiations rather than unilateral action (Norrie,

1984, p. 89). In contrast, the Liberal government believed that it won a political victory in two senses. First, it had consolidated support in central Canada. Second, it had established its authority to regulate energy within Canada (Doran, 1984, p. 249). Doern and Toner (1985, p. 313) view most of the issues as draws except for that of federal revenue shares, on which Ottawa won; Pratt (1982, p. 56) even sees the pricing accord as "consistent with the Liberal objectives." Less than two months after the agreement with Alberta was reached, an accord was signed between Ottawa and Saskatchewan that was clearly in Ottawa's favor.[6]

Who Really Won?

Did either side prevail in the battle between Ottawa and Alberta? One of the signs of a good compromise is that both sides can claim victory. Indeed, it appears that this was true of the September accord. Unfortunately, there is no agreement on what either side viewed as the more important issue in the conflict. Some observers (Helliwell and McRae, 1981; Rusk, 1981) saw the dispute entirely in terms of the economic stakes. Others (Dobson, 1981, p. 46; McKinsey, 1981, pp. 17–18; Doran, 1984, p. 238) consider the constitutional principles and the political problems of prolonging the stalemate to be of at least equal salience. Fortunately, both scenarios can be modeled and either scenario leads to the same expected outcome.

The strategic scenario is of course quite complex. However, some reasonable simplifying assumptions can be made. First, since the other provinces opted out of the battle between Ottawa and Alberta, we can represent the conflict as one between Alberta and the rest of Canada, with the government in Ottawa acting on behalf of the latter. Clearly, the standstill arising from Alberta's actions imposed costs on all the other provinces; furthermore, the heavy concentration of energy resources in Alberta pitted that province against the others, including those with their own energy supplies. The reluctance of other provinces to support Alberta effectively put them in alliance with Ottawa. Second, the politics of the energy wars indicates a dynamic bargaining scenario. Yet the very uncertainty of what stakes were central to each side makes any attempt at dynamic analysis unrealistic. A static representation of the game is the only possible approach.

---

[6]The federal government would fund and administer the Petroleum Incentives Program in the province, but it would also set the new oil reference price. Both the federal government and the province would contribute $15 million for synthetic fuels research development, while the province would reduce its royalty take and its tax rate (Energy, Mines, and Resources Canada, 1982, p. 8).

TABLE 7.3

Economic Rents Under Four Alternative Scenarios

(in thousands of 1980 dollars per capita)

Scenario	Albertans	Canadians outside Alberta
NEP	94	13.2
Alberta proposal	112	10.3
Stalemate	85	11.9
Compromise	98	13.1

SOURCE: Helliwell and McRae, 1981, p. 20.

In the scenario based on dollars alone, we begin with estimates by Helliwell and McRae (1981) of the economic rents accruing to Albertans and to the rest of Canada under four possible scenarios: the NEP, Alberta's counterproposal, the stalemate (assuming the stalling of the tar sands plants and the 15 percent production cutback), and a compromise solution that approximates the one actually reached.[7] The rents accruing to these actors are presented in Table 7.3.

For Canadians outside Alberta, the economic gains would have been highest under the NEP and lowest under Alberta's proposals. For Alberta, on the other hand, the best scenario would have been the province's own proposal—by a substantial margin—and the worst scenario the stalemate that threatened to continue indefinitely. Clearly, it was in Alberta's interest to avoid its worst outcome, the stalemate. Indeed, it appears from a strictly economic perspective, to have been more crucial for Alberta to avoid this outcome than it was for Ottawa to do so. Albertans would even fare better under the NEP, and by a considerable margin, than if no accord were reached.

Let us see how this confrontation can be modeled. The cooperative solution, as we recall from the Prisoners' Dilemma, is R (reward). In this case, it is clearly the compromise. If both actors defect, we have the punishment (P) payoff, which here is readily seen to be stalemate. The optimal outcome for each player is the temptation payoff (T). For Alberta this is the province's own proposal, while for the rest of Canada it is the NEP. This means that the sucker's payoff (S) is the NEP

[7] The close approximation to the actual results is the interpretation of John F. Helliwell (personal communications). The assumptions underlying the compromise offered by Helliwell and McRae (1981) were a $2.00/barrel a year increase, with similar rises for natural gas, from 1981 through 1983, with later increases following the NEP. If anything, then, the Canadian living outside Alberta might be slightly worse off under the accord actually reached than under the proposal reported herein. The authors also report rents for Quebec and Ontario, but ordinarily they do not differ from those for Canadians outside Alberta.

for Alberta and the Alberta proposal for other Canadians (henceforth labeled "Canada"). From Table 7.3, we see that for Canada the traditional inequalities of the PD hold:

$$T > R > P > S.$$

For Alberta, on the other hand, we have:

$$T > R > S > P.$$

This preference order does not conform to the PD, but to another game often discussed in conjunction with it, Chicken. The story of Chicken is a familiar one. Two young hot-rodders agree to a race, starting at opposite ends of the road and facing each other. If both stay in the center of the road, they both will die in a car crash (P). If both swerve, neither "wins" the race but neither dies either (R). If one driver swerves and the other doesn't, the latter wins (T) and the former loses face and the race (S). Clearly, each player's preference order is that found for Alberta in the economic rent data. A representation of the game of Chicken with hypothetical payoffs is presented in Table 7.4.

What makes the PD so interesting is that there is an undominated solution that is not stable—both players defect. Furthermore, there is an alternative solution that *both* players prefer to this undominated solution. In Chicken the problem is more complicated. There is not one undominated solution, but two: the strategies involved are (defect, cooperate) and (cooperate, defect). In terms of payoffs, we have (T,S) and (S,T). That is, the players take turns being the victor. Thus the outcome that is worst for both players is avoided and the actors do not have to compromise on a non-optimal outcome (R). What happens when the preferences of one actor conform to the PD and the other to Chicken? The economic rents of Table 7.3 are rearranged in a payoff matrix in Table 7.5. Viewing the game as a noncooperative one, we note that the only condition under which the compromise would be reached is one where at least one player is ignorant of the payoffs for the opponent(s). Alberta has no dominant strategy, but Canada does: to defect (since its payoffs are higher regardless of what

TABLE 7.4

Payoffs in the Game of Chicken

		PLAYER 2	
		Cooperate	Defect
PLAYER 1	Cooperate	(0, 0)	(−5, 5)
	Defect	(5, −5)	(−10, −10)

TABLE 7.5

Payoffs to Canada and Alberta in Game Form

| | | ALBERTA | |
		Cooperate	Defect
CANADA	Cooperate	(13.1, 98)	(10.3, 112)
	Defect	(13.2, 94)	(11.9, 85)

Alberta does). Alberta's conditionally best strategy, given Canada's, is to cooperate—leading to the predicted outcome of the NEP (cf. Rapoport and Orwant, 1962). However, Alberta did not simply capitulate. This perspective on the confrontation misses the mark because the game is more fruitfully viewed as involving bargaining. Certainly the two parties spent many hours behind closed doors working out a compromise.

Perhaps the best-known negotiations model is the "Nash bargaining set," in which we begin with a status quo point and normalize the payoffs to both players at that outcome to zero. Then, each player may propose a trade to some other point in a bargaining space and we compute the value of that trade by the product of the payoffs to each player. The highest value of the product of the payoffs is the solution to the bargaining problem (Luce and Raiffa, 1957, pp. 124–26). How do we choose the status quo point? We have no data on economic rents before the NEP was proposed, so we must select an outcome that appears to be closest to that unobserved set of points. We can rule out immediately the NEP (which proposed a radical realignment of economic rents) and the compromise (which accepted many provisions of the NEP). On the other hand, Alberta's proposal was equally disruptive of historical arrangements, transferring both dollars and constitutional principles away from Ottawa. This leaves only the stalemate as a choice for the status quo. When we normalize the payoffs in Table 7.3 to zero, the products of the four outcomes, as listed in the table, are 11.7 (NEP), −43.2 (Alberta proposal), 0 (status quo), and 15.6 (compromise). Thus the compromise is the Nash solution to the bargaining problem.

The alternative perspective, focusing on constitutional and political issues as well as economic rents, implies that money was not the only concern of the two players. The Liberal government in Ottawa was greatly concerned about the constitutional power to tax what Alberta (and other provinces) claimed were provincial resources. It viewed the NEP as a clear test case. Furthermore, the NEP was part of a larger strategy for establishing a sense of nationhood in Canada. The repatriation of the Constitution was of even greater importance, but a defeat on the NEP would weaken the Liberals in their longer-term efforts. Prolonging the stalemate itself would be costly (Dobson, 1981, p. 46; Doran, 1984, p. 238). Despite the cute name of the "Lougheed levy," the import tax was becoming a political burden for the Liberal government. So was the growing perception that Ottawa had lost interest in the consumers of central Canada simply for the sake of pursuing a partisan battle with Lougheed. Furthermore, the stalemate did nothing to resolve the constitutional issue. Thus a good case can be made that this outcome represented the worst of both worlds for Trudeau: on the one hand, the struggle over federal power was no closer to resolution than under Alberta's proposal; on the other, the political costs threatened to outweigh the differences in economic rents between Canada's two least preferred alternatives. If this interpretation is correct, then the stalemate may have been a worse outcome for Ottawa than even the Alberta proposals. This would yield a payoff configuration of Chicken for Ottawa. There is no reason to expect Alberta's payoffs to change under this alternative scenario. Thus we have, in this interpretation, a game of Chicken for both sides. In the absence of cardinal-level data on the stakes for each side, we cannot examine a bargaining game model.

Even representing the game as a noncooperative one, we find that the compromise is likely in single-play games of Chicken, especially—as in the case of the NEP—when the benefits of defection are small relative to those of cooperation (Rapoport, Guyer, and Gordon, 1976, pp. 228–31). Ottawa and Alberta each kept trying to stare the other down, but both certainly realized that some accommodation was necessary. That the conflict may even have had a prominent solution is suggested by the fact that the Helliwell and McRae article was written considerably earlier than the compromise was actually announced. Their proposal may have even influenced the agreement ultimately reached.

On either interpretation there is less straightforward evidence that there was a clear-cut winner. Ottawa had some key advantages in prevailing on the constitutional issue, particularly the power of the federal government to regulate interprovincial commerce on energy resources. Furthermore, in the Nash model the lowest payoff to Ottawa was zero (the stalemate) while the payoff to Alberta on the NEP was sharply negative. However, Alberta won on the immediate pricing issue and may have been advantaged politically in embarrassing the federal government into increasing energy prices through the temporary import taxes. Both sides obviously benefited from the compromise.

Whichever interpretation is correct, a key difference between energy politics in the United States and Canada is that in the latter we can readily model events as a two-person (two-party) game. Cleavages reinforce each other so that the bargaining model is easier to depict. This leads to a more fundamental question: Why is the conflict so neatly structured in Canada and so loosely configured in the United States?

Westminster in Ottawa: Clue to the Puzzle?

According to most students of Canadian politics, the Canadian system performs as it does because of the country's Parliamentary system, which is held to produce sharper conflicts than one finds in the United States. Indeed, as U.S. reformers who find insufficient coordination in the policy process pine for a Parliamentary system, not a few analysts of the Canadian House of Commons think that the high level of polarization in that chamber might be tempered if Canada were to adopt a Congressional system (Weaver, 1984). This constitutionalist perspective offers the hope that structural reform might lead to the enactment of controversial policies such as energy in the United States. If this thesis were correct, then the way out of the dilemma of collective action on energy would be to change the institutional structure of the American government. As noted in Chaper 1, the general overall similarities between the United States and Canada permit a quasi-experimental test of the institutionalist/constitutionalist perspective.

The argument is more complex than the claim that the Westminster system depends on a cohesive parliamentary party, lest the government fall—although it includes this claim. It begins with the electoral system. The most sophisticated version of it, which has become almost folklore in the study of Canadian politics, has been formulated by Cairns (1968). First, single-member district plurality electoral systems reward the largest parties or those minor parties with highly concentrated bases of support (cf. Rae, 1967). A party such as the Liberals may consistently poll a quarter of the votes in the Prairie provinces but receive at most a handful of seats. Thus the West becomes more Tory than its votes warrant, Quebec more Liberal than the party "deserves." Sectional conflicts are exaggerated as Liberal governments represent primarily Ontario and Quebec, and Westerners become alienated and turn to minor parties as the only alternative to the Tories (Smiley, 1984, p. 55). The Westminster system, with its emphasis on party discipline, compounds the problem by denying legislators the opportunity to respond to constituency and interest group pressures (Esman, 1984, p. 29). The two major parties thus become captives of their major electoral bases of support and cannot pursue conciliation and "national consensus" (Lemco and Regenstrief, 1984, p. 110).

The electoral system cannot be the culprit by itself since the United States has a similar method of electing members of the House of Representatives, yet the Democrats do quite well in electing legislators in the West (see Table 7.2). Yet those who are enamored of the "Westminster Canada" argument urge that the Liberals would do better in the West under a Congressional system because Liberal members of Parliament would be free to buck party discipline and curry the favor of constituents and interest groups (Weaver, 1984; Smiley, 1984). This argument puts the cart before the horse. It seems hard to fathom that a country reputed to have a very weak sense of nationhood and so many groups that still identify with the "old country" can expect to be transformed into a little United States simply by changing the form of its legislative and executive institutions. One has only to note the tremendous struggle involved in patriating the Constitution from Great Britain, which finally succeeded in 1982, to realize how difficult institutional change is. Furthermore, the Constitution Act did not fundamentally change the Canadian system of government; it did establish a formal Charter of Rights, but it did not propose tampering with constitutional provisions that affect anything as near and dear to so many interests as energy (cf. Toner and Bregha, 1984, p. 109). One need only imagine how difficult it would be to enact a change in the way the entire government is organized.

What this means is that institutional structures are not exogenous. It is no accident that the United States has a Congressional system and that Canada has a parliamentary one. As Richards and Pratt (1979, p. 282) argue, "it is usually a mistake to portray legal institutions as autonomous agents capable of bringing about major social change independently of more fundamental political and economic forces." The heart of the problem is that any reform of the electoral system would still not produce many Liberal seats in the West (Wilson, 1983, pp. 173–74). Nor would a change in the Westminster model necessarily lead to a Liberal renaissance on the Prairies without more long-term changes in attitudes on the part of the Canadian voter or in the nature of the party's appeals. Provincial Liberal parties have attempted to divorce their policy positions from the national party under the existing constitutional arrangement, but this has not prevented their decline in the Prairies (Smith, 1975, pp. 331–32). Ontario is central to Liberal party strategy precisely because it is a swing province. Attitudes toward parties *and* what they ought to do are deeply ingrained in people's minds. Restructuring institutions will not transform these values; rather, value change must precede any success in architectonics. Canada inherited more than a form of government from the British; it also received an *approach* to government. If, as Lemco and Regenstrief (1984, p. 110) admit, Canada is marked by an "absence of cross-cutting cleavages," why would changing the forum in which political discourse takes place fundamentally change the way people structure their preferences?

How Preferences Are Important

What makes Canadian energy politics so different from U.S. energy politics? If not energy resources, constitutions, or institutions, then what? The answer, I believe, is simple: preference patterns are different. What needs explication is not simply the fact that cleavages reinforce each other in Canada. That much should be evident by now. What is important is how these overlapping cleavages shape differences in policy formation. What does this tell us about the political party system and the role of elections in setting public policy?

Perhaps few things are as paradoxical in Canadian politics as the role of political parties. On the one hand, the Westminster model is generally thought to be coterminous with political parties that are ideologically distinct from other parties, internally cohesive, and program-oriented—in short, responsible. This is the essence of majority rule government (Ranney, 1962, pp. 12, 160). On the other hand, Canadian parties are generally described as "brokerage parties" characterized by "an unusually large variety of politically important cleavages" (Clarke et al., 1984, p. 11). Such parties are ideological potpourris and are particularly weak at policy innovation (Clarke et al., 1984, pp. 13–15). In short, Canadian parties and the portrait of the voters who support them appear to be very much like U.S. parties and their electorate. Another conundrum is how a society in which cleavages are said to be overlapping can be governed by two brokerage parties responding to an electorate that does *not* consistently cast ballots along any of the following lines: class, education, religion, sex, age, occupation, issues, or even (in comparison to Americans) the strength of partisan attachments (cf. Clarke et al., 1980, 1984). The very weakness of partisanship in Canada points to the distinctiveness of the energy issue. While Canadian brokerage parties do not divide neatly along many issues, they do on energy, and perhaps on energy alone, because the conflicts are reinforcing (Toner and Bregha, 1981, pp. 3, 21) rather than cross-cutting as they are in the United States.

A key test of difference in the Canadian and U.S. political environments is the place of issues in national elections. Miller and Stokes (n.d., pp. 32–33) argue that the principal requirement of party government is that voters cast ballots for political parties on the basis of the parties' perceived positions on issues. In particular, electors must have accurate perceptions of how the parties have performed in the past and what they are likely to do in the future. Markus (1982) reported that in the U.S. Presidential election of 1980, voters' evaluations of the competence of the two major party candidates and of the performance of Carter as President, together with the more long-standing effects of partisan identification, had much stronger effects than issue proximity. Was the "18 cent" election different, or was it as much a referendum on Clark's competence as the U.S. contest was on Carter's (Clarke et al., 1984, esp. p. 170)?

Table 7.6 reports results from a variety of surveys on the relative importance of issues either for the vote or for the nation's agenda. Energy clearly ranks high on the list of problems of concern to Canadians. But did it lead to gains for the Liberals? Irvine (1981), reporting on a Toronto *Star* poll, shows a 3–2 advantage for the Liberals as the

TABLE 7.6

Public Concerns on Election Issues, Various Polls, 1980

Issue	Gallup, most important[a]	Total mentions	Toronto *Star*, most important[b]	Government survey, how serious?[c]	Election study reason for vote[d]
Inflation	50	83	36	95	8
Unemployment	18	65	18	82	5
Environment/ pollution	11	33	–	72	–
Energy	8	42	27	–	29
(Cost of energy)	–	–	–	82	–
(Energy shortage)	–	–	–	66	–
Provincial-federal relations/national unity	7	38	–	71	11
Budget	–	–	5	–	15
Leaders, leadership	–	–	–	–	30
Political parties	–	–	–	–	23
General economic issues	–	–	–	–	15

[a] Most important problem facing country (LeDuc and Murray, 1983, p. 289).
[b] Most important problem facing country (Irvine, 1981, p. 374).
[c] Perception of problem as serious or very serious (McDougall and Keller, 1981, p. 17).
[d] Reason for vote choice in 1980 (Pammett, 1984, p. 273).

TABLE 7.7

Probit Estimates of Vote Choice in 1980 Federal Elections

Predictor	Liberal voters	Tory voters	Switchers
Party identification	.433***	.359***	.122*
	(15.750)	(11.604)	(2.194)
Thermometer difference	.011***	−.016***	.019***
	(5.325)	(−6.760)	(4.238)
Energy salience	.245***	.253***	.159
	(4.124)	(3.932)	(1.541)
Budget disapproval	.307***	−.553***	.704***
	(3.332)	(−4.697)	(3.424)
Pro-Canada sentiments	.178	.246	−.746
	(.478)	(.591)	(−.922)
Region	−.491**	.389*	−.796***
	(−2.459)	(2.082)	(−2.284)
Quebec residence	.225	.028	−.398
	(1.232)	(.135)	(−1.163)
Education	−.053**	.032	−.059
	(−2.449)	(1.410)	(−1.419)
Age	−.004	.012**	.299
	(−.946)	(2.456)	(.320)
Constant	−.270	.113	−.754
	(−.559)	(.217)	(−.795)
Estimated R^2	.823	.832	.692
−2 log likelihood ratio	1034.7213	1007.1056	130.3936
% correctly predicted			
Probit	92.6	93.6	86.7
Null	54.7	63.7	59.5
N	1,051	1,051	195

*p < .05.　**p < .01.　***p < .001.

party better able to handle energy, while Clarke and colleagues (1984, p. 169) find no such partisan advantage even among voters who considered this the most important issue in the campaign.

How can we reconcile these findings? One major problem with both analyses is that neither provides a multivariate model for considering the impact of the energy issue on the voting decision. I thus reexamine the data from the Canadian National Election Study's 1974–1979–1980 panel considered by Clarke and colleagues in such a context. The results of a probit analysis of the voting decision of 1,051 Canadian voters are presented in Table 7.7. As is traditional in studies of the Canadian electorate, separate analyses are conducted for Liberal and Conservative voting. The first dependent variable separates Liberal voters from all others who cast ballots in 1980; the second does likewise for the Tories (cf. Clarke et al., 1980, 1984). While examining vote choice is instructive, it is even more useful to consider the motives of the 195 voters who switched parties between 1979 and 1980 (see Uslaner and Conway, 1985). Fortuitously, the 1974–79–80 Canadian National Election Study provided a panel that makes inferences about switching possible.

The predictor variables include two measures of the effects of the energy issue. The first, encompassing prospective issue voting, is called energy salience and is a summary index of (1) whether the voter considered energy to be one of the two most important issues in the campaign, (2) how important the issue was to the voter, and (3) the partisan direction of the voter's issue preference (cf. Fiorina, 1981a, p. 70). In keeping with the dependent variable, separate measures were computed for the Liberals and Tories. The second, encompassing retrospective evaluations, is an ordinal measure of disapproval of the government's budget.[8] In addition, I constructed separate measures of party identification for the Liberals and Tories.[9] In the analysis of switchers, the Liberal measures of energy salience and partisan affiliation are used.

Clarke and colleagues (1984, ch. 5) have argued that, above all, the 1980 federal elections constituted a referendum on party leaders. Thus an index of leadership evaluations was constructed by subtracting the value of the Clark feeling thermometer for each respondent from that of the Trudeau thermometer. In addition, two controls for region were employed. First, a dummy variable for East/West was constructed, where the West included the three Prairie provinces and British Columbia. Second, a dichotomous variable for Quebec residence was employed. Region is more than simply a place of residence in Canada. Attitudes toward one's home province encompass views about what Canada ought to be. A measure of pro-Canada sentiments is constructed by subtracting a respondent's thermometer evaluation

[8] For a more detailed examination of the operationalization of all variables examined, as well as much broader discussion of the data analysis, see Uslaner, 1989. The budget disapproval measure was asked of only half the sample, yielding just 499 cases for analysis for all variables. To overcome this difficulty, I estimated an instrumental variable for budget disapproval based on demographic traits and PC party identification. This instrument was employed for the half-sample for which values on budget disapproval were not available; the actual values were used for the other half-sample. A series of tests showed no significant differences between the two half-sample estimates for coefficients in the vote choice equations (see Uslaner, 1987b, 1989).

[9] Liberal identification is scored from +4 to −4. Positive values represent very strong, strong, and not very strong identifiers, and non-identifiers who lean toward the Liberals, negative scores represent identifiers of varying degrees of strength (and leaners) with *all other parties*; and scores of zero represent non-identifiers. A similar measure is constructed for Tory identification.

of his/her home province from that for Canada. Finally, two demographic variables shown to affect vote choice in previous studies are age and education (cf. Clarke et al., 1980, 1984).

The probit equations do extremely well in predicting vote choice, especially for Liberal and Tory voters. In each equation the estimated R^2 values are above .80, and over 90 percent of the individual vote choices are correctly predicted. Most of the control variables either do not reach statistical significance or do so in only one equation. Region is the sole exception. I shall concentrate on the variables that are more central to the immediate concerns of this chapter (for an analysis of the others, see Uslaner, 1989). Party identification and the thermometer differences are clearly critical to an understanding of the 1980 vote choices, but so are the two energy variables. However, probit coefficients cannot be directly interpreted. There is, however, a technique for transforming the predicted values for each case into probabilities and one can assess the marginal impact of a particular predictor by (1) holding it "constant" at its highest and lowest values while permitting the other predictors to vary freely, and (2) subtracting the probability of voting Liberal (Tory) at the lowest value of the predictor from the probability obtained at the highest value.[10] The results of this analysis for some of the most theoretically important variables in the analysis are presented in Table 7.8.

Again we concentrate on the findings that bear most directly on the concerns of this chapter. Clearly, for the full sample of voters party identification has the strongest effects. For Tory voting, leadership evaluations rank second. But for Liberal voters, the thermometer difference has a marginal impact of approximately the same magnitude as the energy salience measure: a voter who strongly preferred Trudeau to Clark would be 32 percent more likely to vote for the Liberals than one who had more favorable ratings for the PC leader. Similarly, a voter who considered energy to be among the two most important issues and to be very important in making a voting decision, and who favored the Liberals, would be 32 percent more likely to vote for that

[10] Specifically, the predicted values for the dependent variable in a probit analysis are z (standardized) scores. Thus each score can be placed on the cumulative normal distribution and associated with a probability value. The technique operates by assigning to the predictor in question its minimum value and estimating a mean probability for the sample from an equation in which all other variables vary freely. Then the same procedure is followed for the maximum value taken by that predictor. The mean probability for the variable at its minimum is subtracted from that for the predictor's maximum to give the marginal impact of the variable. The procedure is discussed by Wolfinger and Rosenstone (1981), and the specific algorithm for computing the probabilities was graciously provided by Steven J. Rosenstone.

TABLE 7.8

Probability Estimates for Vote Choice Predictors

Predictor	Liberal voters	Tory voters	Switchers
Party identification	.709/.069/.640	.841/.148/.693	.658/.428/.229
Thermometer difference	.594/.275/.319	.159/.624/−.465	.920/.169/.750
Energy salience (adjusted)	.578/.256/.322	.576/.258/.318	.666/.466/.200
Budget disapproval	.507/.400/.107	.257/.456/.200	.809/.315/.494
Pro-Canada sentiments	.467/.437/.031	.379/.340/.038	.475/.673/−.198
Region	.407/.463/−.055	.394/.354/.040	.476/.598/−.173
Quebec residence	.474/.449/.025	.364/.362/.003	.540/.616/−.077
Education	.391/.527/−.136	.397/.324/.073	.438/.683/−.245
Age	.430/.466/−.036	.426/.332/.094	.594/.556/.038

NOTE: Entries are estimated probabilities of Liberal voting, Tory voting, and switching to the Liberals. First entries are evaluated at the maximum value of the predictor, the second at the minimum values. The third entries (in italics) are differences between the maximum and minimum values.

party than a similar respondent who favored the Tories on energy.[11] The energy salience measure has approximately the same effect for the Tories. The retrospective evaluations showed more modest impacts. A voter who disapproved of the Tory budget was just 10 percent more likely to vote for the Liberals, though 20 percent more likely to cast a ballot against the Tories, than one who strongly favored the budget. Since voters had other options—especially voting for the New Democrats—it is hardly surprising that the effects of retrospective voting would be stronger on the governing party than on the opposition.

The pattern of results for switchers is somewhat different. As expected, these are voters who are less predictable from contest to contest. Thus they are less well predicted: the estimated R^2 is lower, but the percentage predicted correctly is still quite respectable. Of greater interest are the far weaker effects of party identification and energy salience. The latter does not reach statistical significance at all, while the former does so only at the .05 level. The marginal impact of party identification for switchers is less than half that for either Liberal or Tory voters; that for energy salience is only two-thirds of that for the full sample. On the other hand, switchers were motivated by *both* party leader evaluations *and* budget disapproval to a greater extent

[11] In each case there were very few voters at the extreme (+6, −6) values for energy salience. The boundaries were thus adjusted to reflect cases with more than just one or two voters at these extremes. The relevant boundaries become (−6, 4) for the Liberals, (−4, 6) for the Tories, and (−3, 3) for switchers.

than the full samples. The marginal impacts were .750 and .494 for these variables respectively.

This pattern of results *suggests* that voting followed an elite-led model of issue effects. The full sample yielded strong effects for both prospective and retrospective evaluations, but the switchers only voted retrospectively. It thus appears likely that prospective voting occurred primarily among the voters who were strong partisans and who followed politics more closely. Less interested voters, including switchers, took their cues from this electoral elite and cast their ballots on the basis of the information most immediately available to them: their evaluations of past performance by the Tory government. To test this claim, I examined vote choice among the 338 voters who said they followed politics either very or fairly closely, perhaps the best available surrogate for opinion leaders. In this analysis (data not shown), the Tory measure showed *both* prospective and retrospective voting, with marginal impacts of .198 and −.137 respectively. For the Liberal measure, *only* prospective voting mattered: the net impacts of the two energy variables were −.009 and .177. Thus the data do seem to indicate a top-down model of issue effects in 1980, in addition to a more general concern for leadership qualities.

Clarke and colleagues (1984, ch. 6) do argue that issues affected individual vote choice in the 1980 elections, although they do not discuss the energy issue specifically. Yet their major conclusion was that resource concerns did not lead to a gain for the Liberals. They contend that the Liberals had only a 36 to 34 percent advantage among voters who considered energy the most important issue (Clarke et al., 1984, p. 90). My somewhat different coding scheme showed a similar slight Liberal advantage over the Tories of 42 to 40 percent. This hardly explains the Liberal rebound in 1980. Indeed, voters who considered energy to be among the two most important issues in the campaign *were* sufficiently energized to vote on the basis of these concerns, but they largely canceled each other out.

Instead, the Liberals gained largely on the basis of retrospective evaluations. To be sure, the out-party did not benefit because the electorate found the budget unpopular: 54.4 percent of the sample *favored* the budget. However, the effects of approval and disapproval were asymmetric. Over 90 percent of voters who strongly approved the budget cast Tory ballots. A similar percentage of ardent opponents voted for opposition parties. Yet while 94 percent of moderate opponents also supported the opposition, just 55 percent of lukewarm supporters backed the Tories.

Overall, 33.8 percent of the sample both approved of the budget and voted for the Tories, while 43.2 percent disapproved of the budget and voted for opposition parties. Fewer people (31.5 percent of the sample) opposed the budget and supported the Liberals than favored the plan and backed the Tories. The Progressive Conservatives lost because voters who opposed the budget cast ballots en bloc either for the Liberals or for the New Democrats. There was a retrospective policy mandate on energy in 1980, but the Liberals may have won the elections because of the geography of electoral support. Thus the Liberal government that fashioned the NEP deviated from its more traditional capitalist policies to woo supporters of the NDP who preferred a more direct role for government (see n. 4 above).

The results for the mass electorate are strongly reinforced by the conditions for cohesive and ideologically distinct political parties documented by Brady (1978) for the United States in the 1890's. When parties are strong, the support bases of the parties are clearly distinguishable. Specifically, each party derives its support from a relatively homogenous group of voters. The demographic bases of the party in the electorate can be neatly segmented according to the two contending groups of office seekers. Empirically, this means that there are clear-cut regional and income/occupational groups with party representations in the legislature. As for in the contemporary Canadian and U.S. contexts, we noted from Table 7.2 that party representation in both national and subnational legislatures has a much stronger geographic base in Canada than in the United States. The more extensive two-party system throughout the United States reflects the heterogeneity of ideologies and support coalitions for each party. In turn, this makes party cohesion on policy formation more difficult.

The distinct demographic bases of support for the two Canadian parties account for much of the cohesion in the parliamentary parties. The lack of effective two-party competition throughout the country, particularly in provincial elections, limits the role of parties in governing. If a legislative race is between, say, a PC candidate and an NDP candidate, the Tory has little to gain in concentrating fire on the Liberals' position on some policy issue. Canadian parties fit the brokerage model in large part because they do not fully compete with each other for control of the national agenda. It is thus not surprising that they differ from their counterparts in Westminster systems in having weak national organizations with limited powers to discipline errant members (Williams, 1981). Without concerted elite leadership, the Canadian electorate, very much like its U.S. brethren, does not generally divide along issue lines (Clarke et al., 1984, p. 11).

This in sum is the distinctive nature of the Canadian hybrid. While regional and partisan ties overlap, the support base for the two parties is otherwise heterogenous. On energy, constituency groups (even if we do not find a perfect fit with income and occupation) do correspond with regional and partisan ties in Canada, making party government possible. Canadian parties can be brokerage institutions *and* responsible parties at the same time if we pay attention to how conflict is structured on different issues.

The entire country was aroused over the energy issue in 1980. There clearly was no fiscal illusion for citizens faced with the possibility of a sharp increase in gasoline prices. The scope of conflict was expanded over periods when the energy issue did not occupy such a central place in the country's political debate. What distinguished the Canadian situation from that in the United States, however, was that the clear-cut lines of division "socialized" the conflict, in Schattschneider's (1960) sense. The boundaries of the fight were clearly demarcated—at the lines of division of the two parties. The reinforcing pattern of cleavages at the elite level, as indicated in the regional divisions of federal party representation in the House of Commons, provided a sufficient condition for strong party splits on the energy issue. In contrast to the wide range of interest group interests on the energy issue (see especially Chapter 5), group conflict in Canada was primarily restricted to consumer and producer groups during both energy crises (Berry, 1974; Toner and Doern, 1986). These divisions were mirrored among many members of the electorate. In the United States, on the other hand, there was no majority response to the events of 1979–80 simply because no position commanded a majority.

The energy battle would have been resolved fairly simply if the game being played were purely a majority-rule game. However, the control of Alberta over its resources meant that bargaining would have to take place. The two sides were very far apart in their policy goals. Alberta's capacity to restrict oil flows and to stall the development of synthetic fuels projects meant that the provincial Tories were something more than the "loyal opposition" in a Parliamentary system confined to carping at the unchecked decisions of the majority party. In this sense, the federal system played an important role in structuring the conflict. But that system is not endogenous. It reflects the weak sense of nationhood in Canada. Yet there was a common language in the Canadian energy dispute. This shared frame of reference made it imperative to avoid the joint disaster outcome in a game of Chicken. It also highlighted the prominence of the solution eventually reached; in September 1981 the two parties ended 22 months of haggling over a pricing accord and resolved the key issues in one

week of intensive bargaining (Doran, 1984, p. 238). The other recalcitrant Western provinces came on line quickly.

A Canadian Success Story?

Lest we conclude too quickly that Canada lived happily ever after
with its comprehensive energy policy, we must recognize (1) that some
of the economic assumptions of the NEP proved to be very wrong indeed and the program had to be considerably revised just two years
later, and (2) that the NEP was effectively dismantled by the new Progressive Conservative government of Prime Minister Brian Mulroney
in 1985. I shall discuss each of these developments in turn.[12]

The NEP was based on the assumption of continually increasing prices for natural gas and particularly for oil. Instead, oil prices
tumbled in the midst of a supply glut and a recession gripping the
industrialized world in 1981–82. By April 1982 Alberta had to provide \$5.4 billion in incentive grants to the petroleum industry. A
month later the Trudeau government announced an "update" of the
NEP, which included \$2 billion in exploration incentives, a reduction
of the rate of the petroleum and natural gas revenue tax from 12 to
11 percent, suspension until May 1983 of implementation of the incremental oil revenue tax, lowering of the tax rate on oil sands plants
over the next two years from 12 to 8 percent, an increase in the price
of oil discovered since 1973 to 75 percent of the world price, other
economic incentives particularly aimed at smaller producers, and a
relaxation of export restrictions on petroleum particularly to the U.S.
market (Energy, Mines, and Resources Canada, 1982, pp. 56–73;

[12] Synthetic fuel problems are similar to those in the United States. These projects
are concentrated in Alberta; estimates of the potential reserves of these alternative fuels
range all the way to 250 billion barrel equivalents, dwarfing the supplies of conventional crude oil in the country (Pratt, 1976, p. 34). Synthetic fuels development had
been planned for more than a decade before the 1973 oil embargo. The Syncrude
megaproject had to be rescued in 1974 by a consortium of three governmental (Ottawa,
Alberta, and Ontario) and three U.S. oil companies. Production began in 1978 with a
capacity of 12,000 barrels a day (Malcolm, 1982c). The Alsands project, a joint venture
of five private companies and Petro-Canada, collapsed the day before Exxon's Colony
project failed in the United States. The Cold Lake project, which had a projected yield
of 140,000 barrels a day, collapsed in 1981, but was resuscitated in September 1983
when the government of Alberta agreed to reduce royalty payments. By 1985 the government assistance program had worked: Syncrude had consistently increased production levels and was studying a further rise to more than 200,000 barrels a day. By 1985
the largest producers were ahead of schedule and several smaller ones were consistently increasing their yields (Martin 1984, 1985). While synfuels development faced
many of the same problems in Canada as in the United States, the Canadian governments did not simply cut their losses as the U.S. Congress ultimately did. The role of
the governments in both state- and province-building constitutes the difference in
outcomes.

Foster, 1982, p. 206). Canadianization was also restricted in scope: Canadian companies could put limits on purchases of future stock offerings by foreigners, but shareholders outside Canada would no longer be required to sell their holdings (Malcolm, 1982d). As oil prices continued to decline, the Memorandum of Agreement with Alberta had to be renegotiated in 1983. This occurred without substantial conflict since the environment of the 1980–81 conflicts, spiraling costs and economic rents for the West, no longer held (Toner and Bregha, 1984, p. 121). The prices of most oil and natural gas were frozen for eighteen months, and a series of price increases slated to go into effect were rescinded (Martin, 1983).

Canadian energy policy was not without its setbacks. The resuscitated synfuels industry was nevertheless considerably pared down. The NEP was revised several times. The biggest changes occurred after the 1984 elections, which the Tories swept in one of the biggest landslides in Canadian history. With Tory dominance even in Ontario and Quebec, some observers (Doern and Toner, 1985, pp. 469–70) believed that the NEP had been institutionalized and still retained a base of support within the Progressive Conservative party. However, the new government announced in November that it would terminate the subsidies on oil prices, amounting to a 9 percent increase in consumer prices as domestic costs rose to world levels. In March 1985 most of the NEP was effectively repealed: oil prices were to be deregulated on June 1 and gas prices five months later. The Petroleum Incentive Program was to be gradually eliminated and the gas and oil taxes were to be repealed for new wells in April and reduced on a sliding scale to zero by 1989 for old gas and oil. These moves were estimated to cost the government $500 million in revenues by 1986 and $3 billion by 1990.[13] In late October, Tory Energy Minister Pat Carney announced that "the final nails [had been driven] into the coffin of the National Energy Program," as the government deregulated the export and domestic prices of natural gas, a less generous incentive program replaced the PIP immediately, royalty payments for offshore wells would be transferred to the provincial governments, Ottawa ceded its power to purchase retroactively 25 percent of any oil or gas discovery, and Petro-Canada would no longer be accorded special status (Stewart-Patterson, 1985a,b).

The Mulroney government recognized that it was constrained on

---

[13] The description of the changes in the NEP and the estimates of budget impacts (made by the University of British Columbia economist John Helliwell) were obtained from a broadcast of the Canadian Broadcasting Company's "Sunday Morning" radio program, March 31, 1985.

one aspect of the NEP: the highly popular Canadianization program could not be abolished. Indeed, in August, Petro-Canada paid U.S. $650 million for Gulf Canada, making it the largest service station operator in the country (Whittington, 1985). But the October announcement did acknowledge that enforcement provisions of Canadianization would be relaxed; the industry had virtually reached 50 percent Canadian ownership anyway (Stewart-Patterson, 1985b,a). In April 1987 the first major crack in the Canadianization program occurred when Dome Petroleum accepted a takeover bid from Amoco, a U.S. integrated petroleum company, and the Tory government refused to block the sale. Otherwise, the message of the election was clear: even though the energy issue did not figure in the contest at all, the two parties were still very much divided over resource questions. The large Eastern bloc in the Tory party, indeed even the election of a Prime Minister from Quebec, did not change this.

Given the very large Canadian budget deficits, it would have been perfectly understandable for the federal government to seek to maintain as much in economic rents as possible (Doern and Toner, 1985, p. 470). Indeed, in August 1986, after agreeing to phase out the Petroleum and Gas Revenue Tax by 2 percent a year until it reached a rate of zero by 1989 at a cost to federal revenues estimated at $11.1 billion (Helliwell et al., 1986, p. 348), the Mulroney government refused to accede to Alberta's demand that the tax be lifted immediately. It insisted that the province reduce its own royalty rate and that industry provide more funding for exploration. New Alberta provincial Premier Don Petty, apparently believing that the royalty holiday and phased reduction in rates announced in 1985 were insufficient concessions (Helliwell et al, 1986, p. 344), rejected Ottawa's demand out of hand. That it chose to forgo this income suggests just how central to the two parties the energy issue was—and just how important the Western base remains to the Tories. A transformation in government energy policy is precisely what one would predict from a strong party system. The distinctiveness of the energy issue in Canada is highlighted by the fact that the Mulroney government took up its mandate to institute bold new policy directions in almost no other policy area (cf. Gibbins, 1988).

Are there lessons for the United States in the Canadian energy story? If one is searching for a way to adopt something labeled a comprehensive energy policy, I think not. If one wants to understand why the United States has failed to do so, then we can be more positive. The key to policy success in Canada is the reinforcing partisan, ideological, regional, and constituency cleavages on energy. This produces a responsible party system. Yet we cannot induce more party cohesion simply by changing to a Parliamentary system. The members of Congress could not agree to produce more policy cohesion by the much less sweeping proposal to reshuffle committee jurisdictions. The Canadian example once again indicates that structures are endogenous. Preferences matter more.

The outcomes in the two countries differ because the games are not the same. The Canadian situation is marked, not by the crazy-quilt pattern of cleavages on energy found among the many energy constituencies in the United States, but by a more straightforward ideological battle between two principal actors. Yet the cultural patterns of Canadian politics, particularly the weak sense of nationhood, have complicated the battle.[14] Instead of a simple majority game, the actors faced a potential stalemate that required either bargaining or at least pre-negotiation coordination. The game of Chicken is not a straight ideological fight. Rather, it differs from a Prisoners' Dilemma in having a noncooperative outcome that both players wish to avoid.

In a country fraught with identity problems, stalemate on a highly salient issue could lead to a constitutional crisis. Thus some outcome must be sought other than the one most preferred by either actor. That the reward payoff corresponded more closely to the Liberal position than to the Tory preference does indicate that some component of majority rule (or Westminster) politics is also very much part of Canadian political life. The Canadian party system *is* stronger than the U.S. In turn, interest groups are weaker. There is an absence of models of universalism in domestic policy formation in Canada.

The Canadian case has several implications for the institutionalist and macropolitical frameworks—and for U.S. energy policy. First, the institutionalist account of party government in Canada places far too much emphasis on the Westminster system. The constitutional structure has its roots in Canadian culture, but so does the web of conflicting principles in the BNA Act on federal versus provincial rights over natural resources. This confusing set of "rights" has its roots in the ambivalent notions of what federalism means in Canada—or what the idea of Canada is. In order to get Quebec to sign the Constitution patriated in 1982, Mulroney had to give *every* province a veto over Constitutional—and other—issues (Burns, 1987). This "many-out-of-

[14] While the intervention of Canadian governments in the synthetic fuels collapse is a heartening model of how not to cut and run (assuming that synfuels development itself is desirable), the strong role for the state in Canada is less a sign of resolve than of the need to hold the country (province) together.

one" solution to the problem of coordination and cooperation provides a sharp contrast to the ideal of a single nation that underlay Trudeau's political strategy. The "Emperor's New Clothes" of an accord merely ratified the sharp divisions in the confederation rather than resolved them. Constitutional politics reflects the most deeply felt value conflicts within a society.

Because constitutional structures are not very malleable, they are unlikely candidates as the causes of policy innovation. The Westminster system would lead us to expect strongly united parties. The federal system, especially with patterns of party cleavage that differ from one level to another, would herald weak parties. So would the lack of effective enforcement mechanisms that deny Parliamentary candidates renomination. Yet the very fact that Canadian legislators so rarely violate party discipline in the Commons again suggests that we should find strong parties.

We may be posing the wrong questions if we simply focus on what to expect from differing institutional mechanisms. In the case of Canadian energy politics, the pattern of reinforcing cleavages that correspond to the most critical underlying tensions in Canadian society (Constitutional reform, what the nation should be, how to distribute the country's wealth) made the energy issue different. The preferences overwhelmed the institutional lethargy of the brokerage parties, which otherwise bury divisive issues deep in the recesses of party caucuses.[15] They exaggerated the conflicts between the Westminster and federal systems, setting up a confrontation that ultimately threatened to disrupt the confederation. Had Alberta prevailed on the energy issue, Trudeau would certainly have failed on Constitutional reform.

Thus institutions were endogenous to preferences in both senses given in Chapter 1. The structure of cleavages determined the policy outcomes that the "system" produces. The federal system made compromise necessary, but the popularity of the Liberals' energy program throughout most of the country—as abetted by the Westminster system—made it inevitable that Trudeau would win. The strategy of majoritarianism dictated that when the Tories returned to power,

---

[15] The brokerage party system points to the importance of the electoral motive among Canadian members of the House of Commons. There is no need to presume that a cohesive party system must subjugate the reelection drive. Especially in the case of the politics of the NEP—which Liberals believed would be politically quite beneficial both in NDP constituencies and in swing ridings in Ontario—there is no conflict between party loyalty in the Commons and a desire to get reelected. Tories from Central and Eastern Canada were more cross-pressured. The "Red Tory" government of Ottawa Premier Bill Davis even purchased 25 percent of the shares of U.S.-owned Suncor to express solidarity with the goals of the NEP.

they would repeal the NEP. The message for the United States is that this nation cannot have a clear-cut energy policy without other lines of division separating us from each other. When we work under the assumption that resources are unlimited and that universalism is the preferred political solution, we shudder at such ideas.

EIGHT

Cooperation and Conflict Reconsidered

> Faith, I cannot tell, sister, but if a man had any true
> melancholy in him, it would make him melancholy
> to see his yeomanly father cut his neighbours'
> throats to make his son a gentleman: and yet when
> he has cut 'em, he will see his son's throat cut too, ere
> he make him a true gentleman indeed, before death
> cut his own throat.
>
> (*Everyman Out of His Humour*, IV.i, p. 359)

PERHAPS the best time to think about energy policy is when prices are steady or declining. In 1981–82 the Congress enacted an emergency gasoline rationing plan as prices began to decline, only for President Reagan to veto the legislation. In 1977–78, when the rate of price increases began to level off, the House enacted Jimmy Carter's national energy plan with many of the key provisions either intact or with modifications the President could accept. The Senate was later to cannibalize it. When the energy issue was more pressing, however, the Congress and the President pushed for a poorly planned Energy Security Act (see Chapter 4), gasoline rationing and price decontrol were soundly rejected, and the nation was still left without a strategy for coping with the next supply interruption or price spiral. In this final chapter I shall consider the conditions under which coordinated action such as the House passage of the 1977 energy bill took place, why this was unusual and is unlikely to be repeated, some strategies for Congressional leadership that have been proposed as likely to increase cooperation on energy issues, and the prospects for finding and adopting a "prominent" solution to energy problems.

Several factors were working in tandem to permit quick action on Carter's 1977 bill. Energy prices had moderated and the issue had faded from public attention. A new administration had come to power and benefited from the traditional honeymoon with Congress. More important, the party that controlled the Congress had been returned to power in the White House, creating an unusual era of good feelings between the two branches. In 1977 many Democrats believed that the fading New Deal coalition had been reassembled and that it was incumbent upon them to follow the leadership of their new President and a new Speaker of the House. The Speaker, Thomas P. O'Neill, recognized that these events were quite extraordinary and that the time frame for action, before strains in the Democratic coalition could develop, was limited. He thus pushed for quick action and insisted on

an omnibus bill as the only way to secure most of the President's proposals. "The only way we can write a national bill is if [the interest
groups] don't team up. If they logroll, you're in trouble" (quoted in
Malbin, 1983, p. 223).

The House passed an energy bill just two months after the President sent it to Capitol Hill, acting so quickly that outside actors barely
had time to mobilize. With a popular President and an issue that had
faded in salience, there were fewer obstacles to decisive action than
usual. A policy window had opened, but it would not stay open for
long (Kingdon, 1984, chs. 7–8). Interest groups began to mobilize
after the bill passed the House, and the legislation barely survived the
committee process in the Senate. The bill was emasculated in that
chamber, and only splitting it up into six separate bills saved it from
being killed altogether. The particular confluence of events that led
to House passage of Carter's comprehensive energy bill is not likely to
be repeated. The sagas of later attempts at energy policy formation
(see Chapters 4, 5, and 6) attest to this. Are there other proposals
for improving upon the record of energy policy decision-making in
Congress?

Can Reform Change Congress?

The lesson of the attempt to establish an Energy Committee in the
House of Representatives and of why Canada was able to enact energy legislation in 1980 is that institutional structures are not the key
to the puzzle. Congress established a budget process in 1974 with the
goal of providing some coordination in the authorizations and appropriations processes, yet a decade later it appeared that the House and
Senate Budget Committees had failed to keep spending under control and had merely added another layer to the expenditure process
(Sundquist, 1981, ch. 8; Ellwood, 1985). If we believe that conflict has
to be socialized into political party positions, we must find some way of
changing preferences so that cleavages on issues overlap rather than
cut across issues. The state of the party attachments in the electorate
makes institutional reform unattainable without such a transformation (cf. Fiorina, 1980, p. 44). Are there more modest ways of transforming the conflict within the halls of Congress so that some modi-
cum of agreement can be reached?

Two solutions have been offered, one focusing on expanding the
scope of conflict and the other on restricting it. The first proposes
bringing more actors into the fray so that each interested participant
will gain a stake in the outcome and become more predisposed toward
cooperation. The theoretical underpinning for this thesis comes from

a variant of democratic theory that views participation as heightening one's sense of community. The inclusion of more actors in energy policy decision-making would increase societal capacity "to withstand disturbances" and would lead to a more active "search" for solutions that might have eluded a smaller group (Orr, 1979, p. 1055; Lindberg, 1977b, p. 337).

Sinclair (1983, pp. 138ff) argues that it was precisely a strategy of inclusion that led to the passage of Carter's 1977 energy bill. The Speaker appointed an ad hoc Task Force to coordinate the activities of committees charged with handling the bill. The logic behind this and other task forces is that the members serving on them will develop stakes in the bill and will put aside their particular policy preferences to fight for the adoption of their own legislative creation. Sinclair (1983, pp. 144, 173) claims that members who had served on such bodies were considerably more loyal to leadership positions on key roll calls than members who did not have such positions, and that this "strategy of inclusion" has a significant impact on the probability that the bill will pass.

While the strategy of delegating some power to task forces may have built some goodwill, it is far from clear that it plays a crucial role in determining what the outcome will be. Examining roll-call behavior may not be sufficient, for the leadership may appoint loyalist members to the task forces. Furthermore, this strategy may indicate weak rather than strong leadership. During the 95th Congress (1977–78), 40 percent of all Democrats served on at least one task force (Sinclair, 1983, p. 143). If everyone is a leader, who is a follower? Might such an inclusive strategy indicate just how desperate for support the leadership was? If preferences are diverse and cross-cutting over a series of issues, there is little reason to believe that the legislators will be more willing to cooperate just because they have obtained a position, temporary at that, of leadership. Expanding the scope of conflict might be a useful strategy if a popular option is precluded from consideration by powerful committee leaders or by restrictive rules. In a decentralized Congress with an open agenda, it is more likely that task forces will mimic the Budget Committees as further institutional obstacles to policy adoption. Social-choice-theory literature informs us that preferences are more likely to cycle when the range of admissible preferences is large.

The second proposal emphasizes restriction of the scope of conflict. It does not propose limiting the number of actors, but rather changing the focus of discourse. If we begin with a commitment to achieving cooperation rather than winning benefits for oneself, agreement might be possible. Mansbridge (1980) calls such an approach "non-adversarial" democracy. A similar idea has been popularized by Fisher and Ury (1981) in their discussion of decision-making through negotiations. An application to energy policy is the National Coal Policy Project (1982) in which industry and environmental groups gathered together to seek what might be labeled a "prominent solution" to coal issues. The two sides met under pledges of comity and a commitment to seeking agreement; they reached accords on a variety of positions, stressing the increased use of the market for pricing and greater voluntary efforts by industry to meet environmental standards.

The example of the National Coal Policy Project should not lead us to be too optimistic. First, agreement could be reached only by excluding the more extremist members of both sides, as well as labor unions, farmers, Indian tribes, railroads, and consumers (Murray and Curran, 1982, pp. 12–13). Since the two major actors did use their unilateral vetoes often (Murray and Curran, 1982, p. 7), inclusion of other points of view would have dramatically increased the probability of stalemate. Without the participation of these groups, industry and environmentalists could (and did) impose many of the costs of energy policy upon the unrepresented. Second, agreement could be reached largely because the two major participants had promised in advance to seek an accord, be bound by it, and seek its adoption by Congress. Congress was far from overwhelmed by this proposal, not only because its view of coal policy was partial, but also because the process of decision-making involved was so radically different from its own.[1] One can argue that the adversarial approach taken by Congress makes successful policy formation improbable. However, it is intricately connected to democratic government through elections. Elections are inherently adversarial processes.

[1] Similar to the National Coal Policy Project (NCCP) have been recent attempts at dispute resolution between environmental and industry groups being fostered by the Environmental Protection Agency (EPA). While these efforts have sometimes reached successful resolutions to disputes, they have been plagued by many of the same charges as the NCCP: there must be an initial reservoir of good faith. Environmental groups believe that they need conflict to gather contributions from their constituents, so they are often reluctant to compromise. Issues that are fundamental to group identity are not likely to result in cooperation. Often groups excluded from the process, especially consumers, will fight whatever agreements are reached by environmentalists and industry representatives. The EPA has some institutional leverage: it can threaten to impose a policy alternative if the sides cannot agree on a solution, but some groups may well decide that even no rule is better than a bad compromise and prefer the adversarial process in Congress and the courts. Finally, and hardly surprisingly, the dispute resolution process works best on narrow technical issues. See Stanfield, 1986; for more details on the process, see Bingham, 1986.

While one approach focuses on expansion of the scope of conflict and the other on restriction of that scope, they are not polar opposites. Indeed, the theoretical underpinnings of these two proposed solutions, expansion of the number of actors with a direct stake in policy-making and the formation of small groups to make decision-making less complex, are not dissimilar. Both have been proposed by Lijphart (1977) as methods of reaching decisions in societies with deep cross-cutting cleavages. Certainly the energy issue in the United States shares the types of divisions, if not the severity, found in his "plural" societies. The only effective way to govern such nations, Lijphart argues persuasively, is to foster cooperation through power-sharing. The responsible-parties model highlights majoritarianism and the exclusion of the policy preferences of the party or parties that lose an election. In a society marked by multiple cross-cutting cleavages, it may not be possible to form a majority government. Should a coalition be formed, its actions might only serve to alienate the groups in the minority to the point of challenging the legitimacy of the system. Thus cooperative arrangements must be sought.

The most important is the grand coalition. Another (Lijphart, 1977, p. 40) is to restrict the scope of conflict by taking the bargaining game out of the legislature and moving it to a smaller group of leaders who will attempt to resolve the contested issues through "intimate and secret negotiations." This is the way conflicts are often resolved in Canada—through regularized meetings of the Prime Minister and provincial First Ministers. Furthermore, Lijphart (1977, pp. 29–31) argues that widespread participation in government through grand coalitions of all affected interests will lead players who do not trust each other to realize that they all must cooperate if they are all not to fail. This is the traditional argument for cooperative behavior in the Prisoners' Dilemma game. Why, if these solutions work elsewhere, will they not provide the answer to the coordination problem on energy or related issues in the United States Congress? The answer, I believe, lies in the nature of cleavages affecting each society. In Canada and the consociational democracies of Europe (Austria, Belgium, the Netherlands, and Switzerland), the cleavages dividing the populations (linguistic, cultural, religious, and regional) underlie the political conflicts that have been dominant for decades or even centuries. East versus West is a fact of Canadian life, as is Anglophone versus Francophone. These societies must find some mechanism for conflict resolution if they are to survive as nations. Thus the stakes are higher than in the United States, where the national motto remains *E pluribus unum,* one out of many, and we are moving toward even greater cultural homogenization. Issues such as energy are out of the ordinary in our politics.

While politicians feel considerable pressure to do something about energy, they do not believe that the situation demands sacrifices by their constituents. Indeed, their own risk-averse strategy suggests that they will be far better off defending their constituents against the costs of an energy policy than making the compromises such decision-making would entail. While the energy issue has a wide scope of conflict, it is unlikely to become as all-consuming as any of the cleavages affecting consociational democracies. Few legislators expect to face electoral defeat because of *failure* to address the energy issue, and none anticipates such severe repercussions of shortages as to tear the entire country apart. Thus the scope of conflict and the perception of costs are great enough to lead to disrupt the routine of universalistic decision-making in the Congress. However, neither is pushed to such an extreme that the entire fabric of the nation is endangered. There is just sufficient conflict to disrupt the norm of cooperative behavior, but not enough to scare decision-makers back to it. The lesson for Congressional leaders is not a happy one: when individual members have the greatest incentives to cooperate—on the pork barrel—leaders look strongest even though they may not have had to push their "followers." On the other hand, when leaders must try very hard—on shale barrel issues—they are unlikely to be successful. Similarly, when institutions appear to induce outcomes, cooperation is likely to obtain anyway. When there is institutional anarchy, this reflects the lack of a coherent preference structure. It is thus hardly surprising that entrepreneurs cannot redesign institutions to produce cooperation. If leadership were possible, wily entrepreneurs could produce agreement without large-scale shifts in institutional design.

No subgroup of decision-makers will be viewed as representative enough of the many interests involved in energy politics, nor will any collection of legislators interested in energy be small enough to resolve the issue in a manner likely to be acceptable to the full chambers. Only when the energy crisis becomes so severe that the very fabric of the society begins to come apart might cooperative solutions be sought. Even then the number of cleavages will determine whether a successful resolution can be obtained. Consociational societies are marked by a relatively small number of cleavages that polarize their political systems; the United States, in contrast, is more pluralistic and, under normal decision-making, more tolerant of differences. When multiple cleavages are combined with very high levels of conflict, the potential for conflict resolution is likely to be decreased rather than increased. Only if an energy crisis translates the debate into more straightforward redistributional arguments will there be strong incentives for politicians to seek cooperation.

Why Prominent Solutions Won't Work

The difficulty in energy policy formation is *not* the lack of prominent solutions. We saw in the natural gas (Chapter 5) and jurisdictional realignment (Chapter 6) examples that there often are such focal points. The catch is that they are based on economic rather than political rationality. Schelling (1979), who is in as good a position as anyone to suggest a prominent solution to energy policy, has in fact done so. He has suggested that such a policy should work through the market rather than price controls and that the government, rather than the price system, should compensate those who cannot afford increased energy prices. The producers gain further rents from their nonrenewable resources, the consumers an assured supply, the environmentalists cleaner air (since price increases reduce consumption, which in turn leads to less pollution), and the poor break even.

Even when there might be a prominent solution acceptable to more than just a few actors (in contrast to the National Coal Policy Project example), there are still few grounds for hoping that it will be enacted. If economic rents are to be shifted from some consumers to some producers, there is little guarantee that the rank and file will perceive the longer-term benefits of an assured supply. First, people pay attention to immediate problems such as price spikes rather than to distant events. Reelection-seeking legislators are thus also driven to myopia, especially when they confront the prospect that *costs* might be imposed on their constituents. A program of compensating the poor for energy price increases will appear to have redistributional consequences for most other citizens. Price controls, on the other hand, largely *benefit* the middle class and thus are politically popular.

Second, assured supply may hardly be reassuring to people who hear cries that the world is running out of cheap energy. Given the uncertainties involved in energy geology, the most anyone can claim is that we don't know what future resources are. There will always be pessimists who gain notoriety by predicting imminent disaster. All interpretations are subject to political coloration in a world of uncertainty. The issues are highly technical and thus easier for each interest group to manipulate since few legislators have the expertise to judge competing claims. Faced with uncertainty, members of Congress attempt to reduce the risks associated with imperfect information. This is what happens in the pork barrel Prisoners' Dilemma: since legislators cannot be sure which party will have the majority in future Congresses, they adopt the risk-minimizing strategy of universalism. In contrast, on shale barrel issues the information can readily be manipulated and there is no ready method of reducing uncertainty. Indeed, the inability to forecast the future raises the stakes. The actors do not know whether a particular course of action will succeed in improving energy security. The potential future benefits of a policy proposal will thus be discounted, and greater weight will be given to the more immediate and readily determined costs that constituents might have to bear. This exaggerated fear of clearly perceived costs and the lesser attention paid to future benefits make cooperation even less likely.

Uncertainty also increases the scope of conflict. Without accurate information, it is difficult to determine where the boundaries of a policy community lie. Which actors have legitimate arguments and which do not? When the potential scope of consequences is not readily determined, everyone who claims to have an interest must be considered to be a legitimate player. Further, the fact that information cannot be readily checked means that new purveyors of data or theories will appear on the scene promising more straightforward interpretations or methodological innovations. As technology changes, so does the data base. A new group of policy entrepreneurs will thus enter the fray. Each new technological development adds new terms to the language and each new term carries with it the potential for political exploitation. The language of energy politics becomes richer, but communication becomes more difficult. In the face of uncertainty, there is need for greater clarity in language. Instead, multiple interpretations abound, particularly as the size of the policy community increases. As Kitschelt (1984, p. 25) argues, experts claiming technological knowledge insist that their positions are the only correct ones. This insistence makes the policy process less subject to negotiation and compromise. Each side becomes more and more rigid in its refusal to accept others' interpretations of data. In this sense, the experiment of the National Coal Policy Project was doomed to failure. The grounds for compromise are narrow when participants in the policy process do not share the same fundamental assumptions.

Any leader trying to make some sense of the resulting conflict is bound to fail. Few things are as incomprehensible as highly technical language imbued with ideological interpretations. The combatants on each side realize that in periods of shortages their constituencies feel very deeply about energy issues. Thus they simplify their complex arguments into extreme claims and slogans, often with little correspondence to economic realities. Areas of agreement fade into battle cries. Since the many sides often do not agree on fundamental assumptions, there is little room for accommodation. Each side talks past the others.

The fundamental difficulty with "solutions" such as the National Coal Policy Project or Speakers' Task Forces is that they are institutional solutions to political problems. Both examples are of very malleable institutions, which can easily be overwhelmed by preference patterns. Because they are so malleable, actors may be willing to try them as possible solutions. This is the very source of their weakness. When less pliable structures such as committee systems are proposed as monopoly agenda-setters, institutions with real power, they will be roundly rejected from the outset. The very large-scale changes in institutional design that might have the potential to resolve policy stalemates will face even more difficult battles, because constitutional reform confronts the largest scope of conflict of all. Actors with even the most peripheral interests become involved in constitutional issues. Thus the constitutional issues most amenable to change are those with narrow scopes of conflict (such as Presidential succession) or on which consensus has been reached, as in the eighteen-year-old vote (Sundquist, 1986, ch. 1). As conflict becomes more widespread on a policy issue, the staying power of the status quo against alternative proposals increases—unless the cleavages have been socialized into two-party disputes in a majoritarian system.

When Prominent Solutions Can Work

The perspective I have offered might make one despair of any non-incremental policy change being enacted by the Congress. If this were the case, then energy would not be any different from other policy areas. Yet Congress has enacted major innovations in public policy. It is worthwhile to consider briefly some of the conditions under which such non-incremental decision-making occurs.

The condition under which large-scale policy change is most likely to occur is an electoral realignment. Shifts in voter attachments to political parties result in clear-cut policy differences between the parties. One party wins a mandate to govern and to enact its platform. For brief periods U.S. parties behave like those in Westminster systems (Brady, 1978). With public support for large-scale changes, majoritarian government is possible. Yet these events occur quite rarely in U.S. politics. They arise from stalemates in the political system stemming from macroeconomic crises (Dodd, 1986). The "triggering mechanisms" have historically been far more severe than the energy crises of the 1970's. Moreover, for a realignment to occur, there must be a "prominent" solution that voters find electorally attractive. In the absence of such a solution, there will be no ready mechanism for a new dominant electoral coalition to form. This is precisely the problem that arose on the energy issue in the 1970's.

Realignments are not the only circumstances under which majoritarian government can occur in the United States. Large-scale electoral victories, such as occurred in 1964 and to a lesser extent 1980, lead to widespread non-incremental policy change by Presidents who act very much like Prime Ministers (on 1964, see Sundquist, 1967; on 1980, see Uslaner, 1987). Like realignments, these mandates depend on the perception of public support for a particular bundle of policies and the existence of alternatives around which at least a majority of the electorate can be rallied. Unlike realignments, mandated Congresses have a very short life span, generally limited to less than two years. Even during Reagan's enormously successful 97th Congress (1981–82), the President was unable to secure passage of natural gas deregulation. In contrast to the budgetary and safety net issues that had historically divided the two parties, gas pricing coalitions crossed party and ideological lines.

Non-incremental policy change can occur even in the absence of majoritarian, or party, government. The 1960's saw major civil rights legislation enacted even before the Democratic landslide of 1964. The Clean Air Act of 1970 transformed environmental policy-making. In the late 1970's and early 1980's a wave of deregulation (airlines, communications, and trucking) swept Washington. The mid-1980's produced immigration and tax reform. These are but some of the policy successes that have occurred in the Congress. How were these innovations enacted?

Each case is distinct, but there are commonalities. Perhaps no issue of the 1950's or 1960's (with the possible exception of the war in Vietnam) generated as much sharp debate as did civil rights. The issue had clear redistributive overtones and was marked by relatively narrow majorities supporting government action to redress black grievances during the 1960's (Miller, Miller, and Schneider, 1980, pp. 174–76). What made the enactment of civil rights legislation possible was, in part, Presidential leadership but, more critically, bipartisan support for the policy. While the civil rights legislation of the 1960's was the product of majoritarian government imposed on an unwilling minority (the South), the coalition that prevailed was, by the standards of those typically found in the Congress, unusually wide.

The environmental legislation of the 1970's was a response to an aroused public that, according to members of Congress, demanded action virtually regardless of the cost. There were, of course, opponents of the Clean Air Act of 1970, but these interest groups had little impact on the Congress. Everyone was in favor of clean air. The principle had been raised to the status of motherhood (Jones, 1975, ch. 7). Rarely in U.S. history has such an issue been so consensual. Indeed, the Reagan administration's most prominent early embarrassments were attempts by James Watt, Rita Lavelle, and Anne Gorsuch Burford to undo the environmental legislation of the 1970's.

The deregulation efforts of the late 1970's and early 1980's were also successful because industry opposition was very weak and poorly organized in the face of an elite consensus or because the opponents were able to obtain satisfactory compromises that effectively neutralized them (Derthick and Quirk, 1985, p. 238). The elite consensus had focused on what academic observers clearly viewed as prominent solutions to the policy problems. On deregulation, in contrast to the civil rights and environmental issues, public opinion was not aroused, which restricted the scope of conflict and the ability of the industries to argue that citizens would incur real costs from these policies.

In contrast to issues such as natural gas pricing, these other deregulation questions drew an elite consensus (Derthick and Quirk, 1985, pp. 238–39). The elites take their cues not only from the academic experts but also from the mass public. The absence of an aroused citizenry made large-scale policy change possible because the opposition was not well organized. Tax reform, on the other hand, was enacted in 1986 because legislators perceived that their constituents strongly supported the legislation, even though there was little firm basis to support that claim. The *perception* of a consensus was sufficient to convince members of Congress to overwhelm an emerging destructive coalition of minorities (Uslaner, 1987). The same year legislators salvaged immigration reform by fashioning a bill appealing to groups that had strongly opposed it in the past—including Hispanics and Western employers of migrant labor. These former opponents sought to fashion an acceptable bill when they became convinced that public opinion was rapidly moving toward even harsher proposals (Pear, 1986).

The commonalities of these diverse non-incremental changes are the bipartisan, sometimes even consensual, support for new legislative initiatives and the availability of prominent solutions to the policy problems. In the case of civil rights, the coalitional structure eventually narrowed to two groups, the supporters and the opponents. The very ability of the former to shut off multiple filibusters in the Senate indicates how widespread support for the legislation had become, at least outside the South. While only a modest national plurality supported federal action to ensure desegregation, the figures hide very large differences in opinions between the North and South in 1964 (Miller, Miller, and Schneider, 1980, p. 209). As the issue became more polarized among both elites (members of Congress) and the mass public in the late 1960's and 1970's (Carmines and Stimson, 1986), new legislative initiatives on civil rights slowed dramatically. Opponents of legislation on the environment, deregulation, and immigration reform were less vocal, if for no other reason than that they felt badly outnumbered. The adversaries of tax reform were overwhelmed as the two major parties each sought to outmaneuver each other for long-term political gain on the issue.

Non-incremental policy change requires more than the existence of a prominent solution. By the 1970's most economists, whether Democrats or Republicans, advocated deregulation of energy markets. Unlike the other deregulation issues, energy costs were intense matters of public concern. In contrast to the environmental questions, they were afforded no public consensus on what needed to be done. For that very reason, even minority voices among energy scholars played critical roles in the public debate, as academic analyses were charged with being politically motivated.

To enact major policy changes, then, it is necessary to have either an effective consensus or a perceived mandate to govern in a majoritarian manner. Both were absent in the energy politics of the 1970's and early 1980's. Indeed, the nature of the issue and the pattern of public responses it engendered seemed to preclude either possibility. One cannot wave away the difficulties that Congress has experienced in trying to enact a comprehensive energy policy by arguing that the legislature does not do very well on policy-making in general. Congress does enact non-incremental policy changes.

What is at least equally important is that the conditions for establishing a consensus or a mandate are behavioral rather than structural. Civil rights legislation was enacted by strategic responses to institutional roadblocks; Senators worked to circumvent the Judiciary Committee by having legislation referred to the more hospitable Commerce Committee, adding major legislation as riders to non-controversial bills, and ultimately having to defeat filibusters on the floor (Bendiner, 1964). Responsibility for the environment, as noted in Chapter 1, is spread among many committees.

While tax reform was considered by just one committee in each house, the key legislative arena was effectively the full Senate. In that body, legislators imposed upon themselves a requirement that any amendment granting exemptions from taxes must restore equivalent amounts of revenue. What is remarkable is that these non-enforceable agreements, which virtually every member had an incentive to violate—and which most members dearly wished would be abrogated—held firm (Uslaner, 1987). The power of a perceived mandate is far stronger than the hold of institutional structures. Without such a charge, legislators in an otherwise anti-majoritarian polity will resist major shifts in policy regardless of the institutional structure. Congress succeeded and failed in the pre-reform era of strong committees and in the post-reform era of institutional anarchy.

The high degree of malleability of the rules of legislative procedures and, to a lesser extent, the committee system itself point to how slack has been built into an anti-majoritarian system. When committee systems appear to "induce" particular desirable outcomes (such as universalism), we are making inference in reverse. We devise pliable institutions to attain the goals we deem worthy and seek to replace those structures when they prove sufficiently inflexible.

The low malleability of constitutional structures sets the limits of what people believe ought to be accomplished. The "separation of powers" in the U.S. system mirrors the welcoming of preference cycles of pluralism (Miller, 1983). We do not want terribly divisive issues to be "resolved" by majoritarian politics, just as many Canadians fear that a sense of national identity will reduce all of them to some lowest common denominator. It is hardly an accident that non-incremental policy change in the United States usually requires something close to bipartisan consensus. Trying to enact reforms where policy initiatives fail is likely to prove frustrating. At the higher levels of malleability, failure of the committee reform effort shows how loosely structured public and elite attitudes on energy are. At the lowest (constitutional) level, deadlock is a defense against majoritarian solutions in a nation without a tradition of consociational bargaining.

This perspective offers a counterpoint to what I call the "mirage of institutional omnipotence." Committees are perceived as controlling the agenda under "normal" decision-making such as pork barrel legislation and under exceptional policy successes such as the Tax Reform Act of 1986, when the Senate Finance Committee rescued a moribund bill from certain oblivion. To be sure, committees are powerful and play a major role in shepherding legislation through the Congress. However, they cannot ensure the enactment of any policy, no matter how uncontroversial. In the former instance, the bases for cooperation can be found in the pattern of legislators' preferences. Non-incremental policy changes are most likely to occur when environmental pressures mount for new legislative initiatives. Similarly, policy failures—such as civil rights in the 1950's and energy policy in the 1970's—cannot be attributed solely to institutional factors such as the filibuster or Congressional decentralization. The filibuster was still in place in the 1960's when wide-ranging civil rights legislation was enacted, and many other non-incremental initiatives succeeded in the 1970's as energy legislation was stymied. What is important is not whether institutions appear important, but the conditions under which policy success and failure occur. To understand this, we must go beyond institutional design.

Beyond the Energy Issue

With energy currently on the back burner of the Congressional agenda, we might put our worries aside. This would be wrong. The issue will reappear. We should also recognize that the types of conflict covered by the framework are not limited to energy. Resource constraint issues include budget deficits. When popular programs are threatened with funding cuts, tempers flare. The pork barrel is hardly immune. The one-for-all spirit of cooperation gives way to partisan politics over distributive issues (see Chapter 2), sometimes in a body with a weakened sense of partisanship to pure individualism. Reaching accords on what are ordinarily the least controversial issues becomes difficult. The traditional norms of comity and reciprocity are less frequently observed (Michel, 1984). Leadership becomes concerned with day-to-day management of the agenda rather than with policy initiatives. Congress is preoccupied with (self-)damage control.

In the 99th Congress Republicans in the House of Representatives staged a temporary boycott of committee meetings to protest what they considered to be unfair overrepresentation by Democrats on those chambers. They repeated the show, taking a reluctant Minority Leader Bob Michel with them, to protest the seating of Rep. Frank McCloskey (D-Ind.) in a contested election. The small number of protesters who voted against approving the journal of the previous day's proceedings grew dramatically in 1985. New York and New Jersey Democrats, generally among the most supportive of each other of all legislators from neighboring states, fought a war over a pork barrel project, the Westway highway, for New York City.

Congress has stood in striking contrast to the more partisan Parliamentary systems found in other democratic societies. The jeering and name-calling in Westminster systems is an outward manifestation of old-fashioned party fights. The lack of comity in the Congress does not reveal neat patterns of cleavage. Democrats and Republicans may challenge each other on procedural issues, but remain internally divided on key policy issues. Energy, then, may have been the forerunner of a new politics of nasty individualism where cooperation is the exception and conflict is the norm. Particularly in a period of shrinking resources, the politics of universalism will be difficult to achieve. Legislators fight fiercely over turf when they have to protect their constituencies against losses.

As issues such as agriculture, mining, smokestack industries, trade, and, in the light of record federal deficits, even the entire budget take on the characteristics of resource constraint politics, we come back to the question whether energy is distinctive. Much of my argument has focused on the ways energy politics differs from the pork barrel, the classical example of "politics as usual" in the United States. Yet the mid-1980's have shown that energy prices do respond to market forces, as Stockman (1978) argued when proclaiming that energy is *not* distinctive and therefore should not be the focus of a "national policy." In the debate over natural gas regulation, legislators speaking for the industry noted that only gas of all commodities remained under federal price controls.

Yet during the 1986 debate over tax reform, when prices for oil and gas were severely depressed, oil-state Senators sought to preserve tax deductions for the energy precisely on the ground that this industry *is* distinctive. First, the nation's security depends on reliable domestic supplies of energy; second, the depressed state of the oil patch economy threatens this security; and third, the economics of energy development is far riskier than that of virtually every other enterprise (see the remarks of Sen. David Boren, D-Okla., in *Congressional Record*, daily ed., 99th Cong., 2d sess., June 12, 1986, pp. S7371–73). An analysis of the effects of the oil glut showed precisely how wide the scope of conflict is on energy—in bad times in the producing areas as well as in good times (Blumenthal, 1986). Is energy special or is it just another commodity?

Energy is distinctive—or at least was extraordinary in the 1970's. The politics of energy in that decade and the early 1980's points to a pathology that threatens the entire body politic. It is a politics of noncooperation in which prominent solutions are rejected precisely because they call for spreading out the pain when each side has clearly identified a villain (albeit a different one for almost every actor). As more sectors of the U.S. economy faced resource constraint problems (including the issue of the entire budget), claims for exceptionalism multiplied. After the energy crisis there were government bailouts for defense contractors, for the nation's third largest automobile maker, and one of the country's largest banks. Spending on agriculture expanded almost geometrically as farm failures multiplied. All of this is nothing new. It is the hallmark of pluralist politics and the basis of the pork barrel (Lowi, 1979).

What is different is the claims of exceptionalism for so many different enterprises. Everything is now central to the proper functioning of the U.S. economy (and, of course, its polity). Being exceptional means having a special status, not only receiving aid from the government but also being exempt from one's responsibility as a "corporate" citizen. It is a politics of rampant rational egoism, in which the temptation payoff is everything and everything else is nothing. In the 1970's energy was special, in both its economic and its political pathologies. It was the harbinger of other shortages to come, not all of which have quite the range of interested participants that we find on energy or agriculture. Yet every actor has learned how to yell loudly and thus to command the attention of politicians. Interest group politics in the 1980's is the story of many exceptionalisms and the nonnegotiable demands associated with them. The irony of the politics of energy is that it has begun to reappear in our national consciousness just as it no longer fills the average American with passion. U.S. politics of the 1980's may very well derive from the pathology of the spreading cancer of energy politics of the 1970's.

Some scholars have posited cyclical theories of political and economic crises (Shefter, 1985, ch. 9; Dodd, 1986). In such accounts, the current crisis too shall pass. Although the analyses of cycles otherwise has little in common with the market views of Stockman, they share at least one common assumption: crises are ultimately self-correcting by something akin to a market (either in commodities or people's votes). If this scenario is correct, then prophets of doom are not to be heeded since we shall pull out of this political crisis as we did the previous ones. There is much to be said for such a view of the world. The case studies presented in Chapters 4, 5, and 6 all have a sense of, in Yogi Berra's words, "déjà vu all over again." Synthetic fuels were to be developed in the 1940's and 1950's. Natural gas pricing issues date back to the 1930's. Congressional committee reform is an issue almost as old as Congress itself; energy committee reform was scuttled in the House in 1974 and succeeded to a minor extent in the Senate in 1977.

Even as we are tempted to accept cyclical theories, we must recognize that even as the economy may defy record deficits and wide swings in inflation, unemployment, and the price of basic commodities, the polity is not likely to withstand the onslaught of participation by so many new groups. Much as some politicians try to do so, one can't put the genie back into the bottle. The expanded scope of conflict is only part of the story. People pay more attention to the costs of governmental policies; fiscal illusions are more difficult to maintain. And citizens, in claiming exceptionalism, are unwilling to pay the costs of collective action. The bases of cooperation that are the hallmark of pluralism are under attack by hyperpluralism. We thus become the captives of markets because we can do little to manipulate them on energy or virtually anything else. Yet we do not even know what a beneficent market is because the effects of high energy prices are good for some parts of the country while others derive advantages from low prices. The cyclical forces that have restored order to our politics in the past have been realignments of our political parties (Dodd, 1986), but a realignment based on cyclical theories of politics is long overdue (Burnham, 1970) and nowhere in sight. Without a realignment, we shall not have a common language. Claims of exceptionalism only serve to restrict the scope of a language community while multiplying the number of tongues. Without a common language, we shall not have the basis for a politics of cooperation.

References

References

Alford, Robert R. 1963. *Party and Society: The Anglo-American Democracies*. Chicago: Rand McNally.

Anderson, Jack. 1983. "Synfuels Corp. Projects Offer Little Promise," Washington *Post*, May 24, p. B15.

Arieff, Irwin B. 1979. "House Committee Revisions Move Slowly: Key Tests Ahead," *Congressional Quarterly Weekly Report*, 37 (Nov. 3), pp. 2485–86.

Arrow, Kenneth J. 1951. *Social Choice and Individual Values*. New York: John Wiley.

Arrow, Kenneth J., and Joseph P. Kalt. 1979. *Petroleum Price Regulation: Should We Decontrol?* Washington, D.C.: American Enterprise Institute.

Asher, Herbert B. 1973. "The Learning of Legislative Norms," *American Political Science Review*, 67 (June), pp. 499–513.

Associated Press. 1986. "FERC Adopts New Natural Gas Regulation, Ending Price Controls," Washington *Post*, June 10, p. E2.

Axelrod, Robert J. 1986. "An Evolutionary Approach to Norms," *American Political Science Review*, 80 (Dec.), pp. 1095–1111.

——. 1984. *The Evolution of Cooperation*. New York: Basic.

——. 1970. *Conflict of Interest*. Chicago: Markham.

Banfield, Edward R. 1961. *Political Influence*. Glencoe, Ill.: Free Press.

Banking, Housing, and Urban Affairs Committee. 1979. *Energy Financing Legislation: Hearings Before the Committee on Banking, Housing, and Urban Affairs, United States Senate*. 96th Congress, 1st session. Washington, D.C.: Government Printing Office.

Barone, Michael, and Grant Ujifusa. 1984. *The Almanac of American Politics 1984*. Washington, D.C.: National Journal.

Barry, Brian. 1965. *Political Argument*. London: Routledge and Kegan Paul.

Baumol, William J., and Edward N. Wolff. 1981. "Subsidies to New Energy Sources: Do They Add to Energy Stocks?," *Journal of Political Economy*, 89 (Oct.), pp. 891–913.

Bendiner, Robert. 1964. *Obstacle Course on Capitol Hill*. New York: McGraw-Hill.

Benjamin, Milton R. 1983a. "Natural Gas: Decontrol Would Benefit Big Firms with Old Stock," Washington *Post* (Mar. 7), pp. A1, 24.

———. 1983b. "Decontrolling 'Old Gas' Seen as Inventive to Production," Washington *Post*, Apr. 7, p. A14.

———. 1983c. "GAO Questions Synfuel Firm's Need for Aid," Washington *Post*, May 24, p. A1, 4.

———. 1983d. "New Subsidy for Coal-Gas Plant Asked," Washington *Post*, Nov. 20, pp. A1, 8.

Benjamin, Milton R., and David Hoffman. 1983. "Natural Gas Decontrol Urged By '85," Washington *Post*, Feb. 9, p. A4.

Bernholz, Peter. 1977. "Prisoner's Dilemma, Logrolling and Cyclical Group Preferences," *Public Choice*, 29 (Spring), pp. 73–84.

Bernstein, Robert A., and Stephen R. Horn. 1981. "Explaining House Voting on Energy Policy: Ideology and the Conditional Effects of Party and District Economic Interests," *Western Political Quarterly*, 34 (June), pp. 235–45.

Berry, Glyn R. 1974. "The Oil Lobby and the Energy Crisis," *Canadian Public Administration*, 17 (Winter), pp. 600–635.

Berry, John M. 1983. "The Turmoil over Natural Gas," Washington *Post*, May 8, pp. L1, 3.

Bingham, Gail. 1986. *Resolving Environmental Disputes*. Washington, D.C.: The Conservation Foundation.

Blumenthal, Karen. 1986. "To Firms Sideswiped by Oil Slump, OPEC Is Moving Too Late," *Wall Street Journal*, Aug. 14, pp. 1, 10.

Bolling, Richard. 1965. *House Out of Order*. New York: E. P. Dutton.

Brady, David W. 1978. "Critical Elections, Congressional Parties and Clusters of Policy Changes," *British Journal of Political Science*, 8 (Jan.), pp. 79–100.

Buchanan, James M., and Gordon Tullock. 1962. *The Calculus of Consent*. Ann Arbor: University of Michigan Press.

Burnham, Walter Dean. 1974. "Theory and Voting Research," *American Political Science Review*, 68 (Sept.), pp. 1002–23.

———. 1970. *Critical Elections and the Mainsprings of American Politics*. New York: W. W. Norton.

Burns, John F. 1987. "Quebec Accepting a Role in Canada in a Constitution," New York *Times*, national ed., May 2 , pp. 1, 4.

Butterworth, Robert L. 1971. "A Research Note on the Size of Winning Coalitions," *American Political Science Review*, 65 (Sept.), pp. 741–45.

Byers, Edward, and Thomas B. Fitzpatrick. 1986. "Americans and the Oil Companies: Tentative Tolerance in a Time of Plenty," *Public Opinion*, Dec./Jan., pp. 43–46.

Cairns, Alan C. 1968. "The Electoral System and the Party System in Canada," *Canadian Journal of Political Science*, 1 (Mar.), pp. 55–80.

Carmines, Edward G., and James A. Stimson. 1986. "On the Structure and Sequence of Issue Evolution," *American Political Science Review*, 80 (Sept.), pp. 901–20.

Cavala, William. 1974. "Changing the Rules Changes the Game: Party Reform and the 1972 California Delegation to the Democratic National Convention," *American Political Science Review*, 68 (Mar.), pp. 27–42.

Chandler, Marsha A., and William M. Chandler. 1979. *Public Policy and Provincial Politics*. Toronto: McGraw-Hill Ryerson.

Chubb, John E. 1983. *Interest Groups and the Bureaucracy*. Stanford, Calif.: Stanford University Press.

Clarke, Harold D., Jane Jenson, Lawrence LeDuc, and Jon H. Pammett. 1984. *Absent Mandate: The Politics of Discontent in Canada*. Toronto: Gage.

———. 1980. *Political Choice in Canada*, abridged ed. Toronto: McGraw-Hill Ryerson.

Clausen, Aage R. 1973, *How Congressmen Decide: A Policy Focus*. New York: St. Martin's Press.

Clausen, Aage R., and Richard B. Cheney. 1970. "A Comparative Analysis of Senate-House Voting on Economic and Welfare Policy, 1953–1964," *American Political Science Review*, 64 (Mar.), pp. 138–52.

Cochrane, J. L. 1981. "Carter Energy Policy and the Ninety-Fifth Congress," pp. 547–600 in C. D. Goodwin, ed., *Energy Policy in Perspective*. Washington, D.C.: Brookings Institution.

Cohen, Linda, and Roger G. Noll. 1983. "The Political Economy of Government Programs to Promote New Technology." California Institute of Technology Working Paper 489.

Cohen, Richard E. 1983. "Regionalism Playing an Increasing Role in Shaping Congress's Policy Debates," *National Journal*, May 21, pp. 1053–57.

———. 1982. "One Big Roll of the Dice," *National Journal*, Mar. 6, p. 429.

Cohodas, Nadine. 1983. "Omnibus Social Legislation: Why It Fails," *Congressional Quarterly Weekly Report*, Oct. 15, p. 2154.

Committee on the Constitutional System. 1987. *A Bicentennial Analysis of the American Political Structure*. Washington, D.C.

Congressional Quarterly. 1980. *Congressional Quarterly Almanac 1980*. Washington, D.C.: Congressional Quarterly.

———. 1979a. *Congressional Quarterly Almanac 1979*. Washington, D.C.: Congressional Quarterly.

———. 1979b. *Energy Policy*. Washington, D.C.: Congressional Quarterly.

———. 1978. *Congressional Quarterly Almanac 1978*. Washington, D.C.: Congressional Quarterly.

———. 1977. *Congressional Quarterly Almanac 1977*. Washington, D.C.: Congressional Quarterly.

Converse, Philip E. 1972. "Change in the American Electorate," pp. 263–337 in Angus Campbell and Philip E. Converse, eds., *The Human Meaning of Social Change*. New York: Russell Sage Foundation.

Coombs, Clyde H. 1964. *A Theory of Data*. New York: John Wiley.

Corrigan, Richard. 1981. "Soaring Prices for Gas from Deep Wells May Force Early Rewriting of 1978 Law," *National Journal*, Nov. 21, pp. 2063–67.

Costain, R. Douglas. 1981. "Political Determinants of Synthetic Fuel Development: Oil Shale and Oil Sands." Prepared for the Conference on Canada and Mexico: The Comparative and Joint Politics of Energy, Cambridge, Mass., Apr.

Council on Environmental Quality. 1980. *Public Opinion on Environmental Issues: Results of a National Public Opinion Survey.* Washington, D.C.: Government Printing Office.

Dahl, Robert A. 1971. *Polyarchy.* New Haven: Yale University Press.

———. 1961. *Who Governs?* New Haven: Yale University Press.

Darmstadter, Joel, Hans H. Landsberg, and Robert C. Morton. 1983. *Energy Today and Tomorrow.* Englewood Cliffs, N.J.: Prentice-Hall.

Davidson, Roger H., and Walter J. Oleszek. 1977. *Congress Against Itself.* Bloomington: Indiana University Press.

Davidson, Roger H., Walter J. Oleszek, and Thomas Kephart. 1986. "One Bill, Many Committees: Multiple Referrals in the House of Representatives." Washington, D.C.: Library of Congress, Congressional Research Service.

Davis, David Howard. 1982. *Energy Politics.* 3d ed. New York: St. Martin's.

Davis, Joseph A. 1987. "House and Senate Vote to Repeal Fuel Use Act," *Congressional Quarterly Weekly Report,* May 9, p. 930.

———. 1985. "Synthetic Fuels Program Killed in Interior Appropriations Bill," *Congressional Quarterly Weekly Report,* Dec. 28, p. 2751.

———. 1984a. "House Demands Floor Vote on Synfuels Funding Cuts," *Congressional Quarterly Weekly Report,* July 28 , p. 1816.

———. 1984b. "House Energy Committee Approves Natural Gas Bill," *Congressional Quarterly Weekly Report,* Apr. 14, pp. 888–89.

DeParle, Jason. 1983. "Old Gas, New Gas," *The New Republic,* Apr. 11, pp. 14–16.

Department of Energy. 1984. *The First Report Required by Section 123 of the Natural Gas Policy Act of 1978.* Washington, D.C.: Department of Energy.

Derthick, Martha, and Paul J. Quirk. 1985. *The Politics of Deregulation.* Washington, D.C.: Brookings Institution.

Dewar, Helen. 1983. "Tight Fist Doesn't Disguise Domenici's Helping Hand," Washington *Post,* Oct. 9, p. A9.

Dobson, Wendy. 1981. *Canada's Energy Policy Debate.* Montreal: C. D. Howe Institute.

Dodd, Lawrence C. 1986. "The Cycles of Legislative Change: Building a Dynamic Theory," pp. 82–104 in Herbert F. Weisberg, ed., *Political Science: The Science of Politics.* New York: Agathon.

———. 1982. "The Logic of Institutional Inquiry: Understanding Legislative-Executive Relations." Presented at the Legislative Research Conference, University of Iowa, Iowa City, Oct.

———. 1981. "Congress, the Constitution, and the Crisis of Legitimization," pp. 390–420 in L. C. Dodd and B. I. Oppenheimer, eds., *Congress Reconsidered,* 2d ed. Washington, D.C.: Congressional Quarterly.

———. 1980. "Congress, the President, and the Cycles of Power," pp. 71–99 in Vincent David, ed., *The Post-Imperial Presidency.* New Brunswick, N.J.: Transaction Books.

———. 1977. "Congress and the Quest for Power," pp. 269–307 in L. C.

Dodd and B. I. Oppenheimer, eds., *Congress Reconsidered*. New York: Praeger.

———. 1976. *Coalitions in Parliamentary Government*. Princeton: Princeton University Press.

Doern, G. Bruce. 1983. "The Mega-project Episode and the Formulation of Canadian Economic Development Policy," *Canadian Public Administration*, 26 (Summer), pp. 219–38.

———. 1982. "Energy Policy and the Megaprojects as an Instrument of Economic Development." Presented at the Conference on the Limits of Government Intervention, Carleton University School of Public Administration, Ottawa, Ont., Oct. 6.

Doern, G. Bruce, and Glen Toner. 1985. *The Politics of Energy: The Development and Implementation of the NEP*. Toronto: Methuen.

Doran, Charles F. 1984. *Forgotten Partnership: U.S.-Canada Relations Today*. Baltimore: Johns Hopkins University Press.

Downs, Anthony. 1957. *An Economic Theory of Democracy*. New York: Harper and Row.

Drew, Elizabeth. 1975. "A Reporter at Large: The Energy Bazaar," *The New Yorker*, July 21, pp. 35–72.

The Economist. 1983. "American Survey: Water in the West," May 14, pp. 41–50.

Ellwood, John W. 1985. "The Great Exception: The Congressional Budget Process in an Age of Decentralization," pp. 315–42 in L. C. Dodd and B. I. Oppenheimer, eds., *Congress Reconsidered*, 3d ed. Washington, D.C.: Congressional Quarterly.

Energy and Commerce Committee. 1983a,b,c,d,e. *Proposed Changes to Natural Gas Laws: Hearings Before the Subcommittee on Fossil and Synthetic Fuels of the Committee on Energy and Commerce*, Parts I, II, III, IV, and V. United States House of Representatives, 98th Congress, 1st session. Washington, D.C.: Government Printing Office.

———. 1983f. *Natural Gas Contract Renegotiations and FERC Authorities: Hearing Before the Subcommittee on Fossil and Synthetic Fuels of the Committee on Energy and Commerce*. United States House of Representatives, 98th Congress, 1st session. Washington, D.C.: Government Printing Office.

Energy Information Agency. 1983. *Natural Gas Annual, 1982*. Washington, D.C.: Government Printing Office.

Energy, Mines, and Resources Canada. 1982. *The National Energy Program: Update 1982*. Ottawa: Energy, Mines, and Resources Canada.

———. 1980. *The National Energy Program*. Ottawa.

Energy and Natural Resources Committee. 1983a,b,c. *Natural Gas Legislation: Hearings Before the Committee on Energy and Natural Resources*, Parts I, II, and III. United States Senate, 98th Congress, 1st session. Washington, D.C.: Government Printing Office.

———. 1981. *Comprehensive Oil Shale Legislation: Hearing Before the Subcommittee of Energy and Mineral Resources of the Committee on Energy and Natural Resources*. United States Senate, 97th Congress, 1st session. Washington, D.C.: Government Printing Office.

Esman, Milton J. 1984. "Federalism and Modernization: Canada and the United States," *Publius*, 14 (Winter), pp. 21–38.

Farhar, Barbara C., Charles T. Unseld, Rebecca Vories, and Robin Crewes. 1980. "Public Opinion About Energy," *Annual Review of Energy*, 5, pp. 141–72.

Farhar, Barbara C., Patricia Weis, Charles T. Unseld, and Barbara A. Burns. 1979. *Public Opinion About Energy: A Literature Review*. Golden, Colo.: Solar Energy Research Institute. Reprinted by the U.S. Department of Commerce, National Technical Information Service, SERI/TR-53-155. Washington, D.C.

Fenno, Richard F., Jr. 1978. *Home Style*. Boston: Little, Brown.

———. 1975. "If, as Ralph Nader Says, Congress Is 'the Broken Branch,' How Come We Love Our Congressmen So Much," pp. 277–86 in N. Ornstein, ed., *Congress in Change*. New York: Praeger.

———. 1973. *Congressmen in Committees*. Boston: Little, Brown.

———. 1966. *The Power of the Purse*. Boston: Little, Brown.

Ferejohn, John A. 1974. *Pork Barrel Politics: Rivers and Harbor Legislation, 1947–1968*. Stanford, Calif.: Stanford University Press.

Ferejohn, John A., Morris P. Fiorina, and Richard D. McKelvey. 1984. "Sophisticated Voting and Agenda Independence in the Distributive Politics Setting." Hoover Institution Working Paper P-84-3.

Fiorina, Morris P. 1981a. *Retrospective Voting in American National Elections*. New Haven: Yale University Press.

———. 1981b. "Universalism, Reciprocity, and Distributive Policy-Making in Majority Rule Institutions," pp. 197–221 in J. P. Crecine, ed., *Research in Public Policy Analysis and Management*, vol. 1. New York: JAI Press.

———. 1980. "The Decline of Collective Responsibility in American Politics," *Daedalus*, 109 (Summer), pp. 25–45.

Fiorina, Morris P., and Roger Noll. 1978. "A Theory of the Congressional Incumbency Advantage and Its Implications for Public Policy." Presented at the Conference on Political Science and the Study of Public Policy, Hickory Corners, Mich., May.

Fischer, David W., and Robert F. Keith. 1977. "Canadian Energy Development: A Case Study of Policy Processes in Northern Petroleum Development," pp. 63–117 in Lindberg, 1977a.

Fisher, Roger, and William Ury. 1981. *Getting to Yes*. Boston: Houghton Mifflin.

Foster, L. T., and A. H. Jacobs. 1980. "Dimensions of Energy Attitudes in Ontario," pp. 59–72 in Edgar L. Jackson and Leslie T. Foster, eds., *Energy Attitudes and Policies*. Cornett Occasional Papers, no. 2. Victoria, B.C.: Department of Geography, University of Victoria.

Foster, Peter. 1982. *The Sorcerer's Apprentices: Canada's Super-Bureaucrats and the Energy Mess*. Toronto: Collins.

Freeman, J. Leiper. 1965. *The Political Process*, rev. ed. New York: Random House.

Fried, Edward. 1982. "Energy Security and the Common Interest," *Brookings Review*, Winter, pp. 10–13.

Fry, Earl H., ed. 1981. *Energy Development in Canada: The Political, Economic, and Continental Dimensions*. Provo, Utah: Brigham Young University, Canadian Studies Program.

Gais, Thomas L., Mark A. Peterson, and Jack L. Walker. 1984. "Interest Groups, Iron Triangles, and Representative Institutions in American National Government," *British Journal of Political Science*, 14 Apr., pp. 161–85.

Gettinger, Stephen. 1984a. "Divisive Natural Gas Bill Scrapped in House," *Congressional Quarterly Weekly Report*, Sept. 29, p. 2409.

———. 1984b. "Synfuels Program Survives: Funding Reduced," *Congressional Quarterly Weekly Report*, Oct. 13, p. 2640.

Gibbins, Roger. 1988. "Conservation in Canada: The Ideological Impact of the 1984 Election," pp. 332–50 in Barry Cooper, Allan Kornberg, and William Mishler, eds., *The Resurgence of Conservationism in Anglo-American Democracies*. Durham, N.C.: Duke University Press.

Giniger, Henry. 1981. "Canada's Advances on Energy Control," New York *Times*, Sept. 9, pp. D1, 10.

Goodwin, Crawford D. 1981a. "Truman Administration Policies Toward Particular Energy Sources," pp. 63–204 in C. D. Goodwin, ed., *Energy Policy in Perspective*. Washington, D.C.: Brookings Institution.

———. 1981b. "The Lessons of History," pp. 665–84 in C. D. Goodwin, ed., *Energy Policy in Perspective*. Washington, D.C.: Brookings Institution.

Governmental Affairs Committee. 1979. *Synthetic Fuels: Hearings Before the Committee on Governmental Affairs, United States Senate*. 96th Congress, 1st session. Washington, D.C.: Government Printing Office.

Hamlett, Patrick W. 1982. "Technological Policymaking in Congress: The Creation of the United States Synthetic Fuels Corporation." Presented at the 1982 Annual Meeting of the American Political Science Association, Denver, Sept.

Hardin, Russell. 1982. *Collective Action*. Baltimore: Johns Hopkins University Press for Resources for the Future.

———. 1971. "Collective Action as an Agreeable n-Prisoners' Dilemma," *Behavioral Science*, 16 (Sept.), pp. 472–81.

Harrison, Rowland J. 1981. "The Constitutional Context of Canada's National Energy Program," pp. 65–75 in Fry, 1981.

Hartz, Louis. 1955. *The Liberal Tradition in America*. New York: Harcourt, Brace, and World.

Hayes, Thomas C. 1986. "Oil's Plunge Drags Gas Down," New York *Times*, May 23, pp. D1, 3.

Heclo, Hugh. 1978. "Issue Networks and the Executive Establishment," pp. 87–124 in A. King, ed., *The New American Political System*. Washington, D.C.: American Enterprise Institute.

Helliwell, John F. 1979. "Canadian Energy Policy," *Annual Review of Energy*, 4, pp. 175–229.

Helliwell, John F., and Robert N. McRae. 1981. "The National Energy Conflict," *Canadian Public Policy*, 7 (Winter), pp. 15–23.

Helliwell, John F., Mary E. MacGregor, Robert N. McRae, and Andre Plourde. 1986. "The Western Accord and Lower World Oil Prices," *Canadian Public Policy*, 12 (June), pp. 341–55.

Hershey, Robert D., Jr. 1984a. "Synthetic Fuels Agency Faces a Funds Cutback," New York *Times*, May 15, pp. D1, 4.

———. 1984b. "Synthetic Fuel Funds Debated," New York *Times*, Oct., pp. D1, 6.

———. 1983. "Natural Gas: A Winter of Discontent," New York *Times*, Feb. 6. pp. F1, 29.

———. 1982a. "Reagan Ends Push on Gas Decontrol," New York *Times*, Mar. 2, pp. D6, 14.

———. 1982b. "U.S. Blocks Rise in Natural Gas Rate," New York *Times*, Oct. 29, pp. D1, 16.

———. 1982c. "The Struggle to Spend Billions on Synthetic Fuels," New York *Times*, Nov. 9, p. A26.

———. 1981a. "Gas Price Decontrol is Hinted," New York *Times*, Feb. 6, pp. D1, 11.

———. 1981b. "Synthetic Fuels: Program Lags," New York *Times*, May 12, pp. D1, 13.

———. 1981c. "Cabinet Group Urges an End to Price Controls on All Gas," New York *Times*, Aug. 10, pp. A1, D6.

———. 1981d. "The New Battle over Natural Gas," New York *Times*, Sept. 6, pp. F1, 18.

———. 1981e. "Oil Shale: A $3.4-Billion Gamble," *International Herald Tribune*, Nov. 10, pp. 9, 11.

———. 1981f. "Gas Price's 'Category Creep,'" New York *Times*, Dec. 17, pp. D1, 15.

———. 1980. "Blessing or Boondoggle? The $88 Billion Quest for Synthetic Fuels," New York *Times*, Sept. 21, pp. 3F, 8–9F.

Hofstadter, Richard. 1955. *The Age of Reform*. New York: Random House.

Inglehart, Ronald. 1977. *The Silent Revolution*. Princeton: Princeton University Press.

International Energy Agency. 1982. *World Energy Outlook*. Paris: Organization for Economic Cooperation and Development.

Interstate and Foreign Commerce Committee. 1979a. *Synthetic Fuels Commercialization: Hearings Before the Subcommittee on Energy and Power of the Committee on Interstate and Foreign Commerce, United States House of Representatives.* United States House of Representatives, 96th Congress, 1st session. Washington, D.C.: Government Printing Office.

———. 1979b. *Natural Gas Issues, 1979: Hearings Before the Subcommittee on Energy and Power of the Committee on Interstate and Foreign Commerce.* United States House of Representatives, 96th Congress, 1st session. Washington, D.C.: Government Printing Office.

Interstate Natural Gas Association of America. 1984a. "Analysis of Price Fly-

Up Under the Natural Gas Policy Act." Washington, D.C.: Interstate Natural Gas Association of America.

————. 1984b. "Voluntary Carriage in 1983." Washington, D.C.: Interstate Natural Gas Association of America.

Inter-University Consortium for Political and Social Research. 1982. *Codebook for Federal Energy Administration, Energy Crisis Behavior and Attitudes in the United States, February, 1977.* Ann Arbor, Mich.: ICPSR.

Irvine, William. 1981. "Epilogue: The 1980 Election," pp. 337–398 in Howard R. Penniman, ed., *Canada at the Polls, 1979 and 1980.* Washington, D.C.: American Enterprise Institute.

Isikoff, Michael. 1985. "Firms Will Abandon Synfuels Facility," Washington *Post*, Aug. 2, p. A17.

————. 1984. "Energy Firms Spurning Subsidies from Embattled Synfuels Corp.," Washington *Post*, Feb. 17, pp. D9–10.

Jacoby, Henry D., and Arthur W. Wright. 1983. "The Gordian Knot of Natural Gas Prices," pp. 125–28 in Mitchell, 1983.

Jones, Charles O. 1979a. "Congress and the Making of Energy Policy," pp. 161–78 in Robert Lawrence, ed., *New Dimensions to Energy Policy.* Lexington, Mass.: Lexington Books.

————. 1979b. "American Politics and the Organization of Energy Decision Making," *Annual Review of Energy*, 4, pp. 99–121.

————. 1975. *Clean Air.* Pittsburgh: University of Pittsburgh Press.

Jones, Charles O., and Randall Strahan. 1985. "Crisis Response in Washington: The Case of Oil Shocks," *Legislative Studies Quarterly*, 10 (May), pp. 151–79.

Jonson, Ben. 1981. *Everyman Out of His Humour*, pp. 275–411 in G. A. Wilkes, ed., *The Complete Plays of Ben Jonson*, vol. 1. Oxford: Clarendon Press. Originally published in 1599.

————. 1961. *Everyman in His Humour*, pp. 1–98 in B. Jonson, *Three Plays*, vol. 2. New York: Hill and Wang. Originally published in 1598.

Kadane, Joseph B. 1972. "On Division of the Question," *Public Choice*, 13 (Fall), pp. 47–55.

Kalt, Joseph P. 1981. *The Economics and Politics of Oil Price Regulation.* Cambridge, Mass.: MIT Press.

Kalt, Joseph P., and Mark A. Zupan. 1984. "The Ideological Behavior of Legislators: Rational On-the-Job Consumption or Just a Residual?" Presented at the Conference on the Political Economic of Public Policy, Center for Economy Policy Research, Stanford University, Mar.

Kash, Don E., and Robert W. Rycroft. 1984. *U.S. Energy Policy.* Norman: University of Oklahoma Press.

Katz, James Everett. 1984. *Congress and National Energy Policy.* New Brunswick, N.J.: Transaction Books.

Keeter, Scott. 1984. "The Cross-Cutting Nature of the Environmental Cleavage." Presented at the Annual Meeting of the Midwest Political Science Association, Chicago, Apr.

Key, V. O., Jr. 1964. *Politics, Parties and Pressure Groups.* 5th ed. New York: Thomas Y. Crowell.

Kingdon, John W. 1984. *Agendas, Alternatives, and Public Policies.* Boston: Little Brown.

———. 1973. *Congressmen's Voting Decisions.* New York: Harper and Row.

Kitschelt, Herbert. 1984. "Resolving Policy Conflict Through Expert Advice." Presented at the Annual Meeting of the American Political Science Association, Washington, D.C.: Aug. 30–Sept. 2.

Klose, Kevin. 1983. "After '82 Scare, Michel Again the Man to Beat in Peoria," Washington *Post*, Nov. 25, p. A2.

Knoke, David, and Edward O. Lauman. 1983. "Issue Publics in National Policy Domains." Presented at the 1983 Annual Meetings of the American Sociological Association, Detroit, Sept.

Koford, Kenneth. 1985. "Different Preferences, Different Politics: A Reinterpretation of Lowi's Thesis." Presented at the 1985 Annual Meeting of the Midwest Political Science Association, Chicago, Apr.

Krehbiehl, Keith. 1987. "Why Are Congressional Committees Powerful?," *American Political Science Review*, 81 (Sept.), pp. 929–35.

———. 1986. "Unanimous Consent Agreements: Going Along in the Senate," *Journal of Politics*, 48 (Aug.), pp. 541–64.

Kumins, Lawrence C. 1983. "Natural Gas Policy Act." Issue Brief IB81020, Library of Congress, Congressional Research Service. Washington, D.C.: Library of Congress.

Kumins, Lawrence C., Donald Dulchinos, and Alvin Kaufman. 1984. "Natural Gas Supply and Demand Under Selected Legislative Options: A Regional Analysis." Congressional Research Service, Library of Congress. Washington, D.C.: Library of Congress.

Kurtz, Howard. 1983. "Congress' EPA Investigation Is a Story of Overlapping Fiefdoms," Washington *Post*, Feb. 20, p. A10.

Landsberg, Hans H. 1980. "Let's All Play Energy Policy!," *Daedalus*, 109 (Summer), pp. 71–84.

Landsberg, Hans H., et al. 1979. *Energy: The Next Twenty Years.* Cambridge, Mass.: Ballinger.

Lanouette, William J. 1982. "Canadian Electricity May Be Cheaper, But It Doesn't Come Free of Problems," *National Journal*, May 22, pp. 910–12.

Lash, Jonathan, and Laura King, eds. 1983. *The Synfuels Manual.* New York: Natural Resources Defense Council.

Laumann, Edward O., John P. Heinz, Robert Nelson, and Robert Salisbury. 1986. "Organizations in Political Action: Representing Interests in National Policy-Making." Presented to the Annual Meeting of the American Sociological Association, New York, Aug./Sept.

Lebus, Margaret M. 1981. "The Synthetic Fuels Industry in Kentucky: An Assessment of Socioeconomic Issues," reprinted in Science and Technology Committee, 1982, pp. 270–328.

LeDuc, Lawrence. 1984. "Canada: The Politics of Stable Dealignment," pp. 402–24 in Russell J. Dalton et al., eds., *Electoral Change in Advanced Industrial Democracies*. Princeton: Princeton University Press.

LeDuc, Lawrence, and J. Alex Murray. 1983. "A Resurgence of Canadian Nationalism: Attitudes and Policy in the 1980s," pp. 270-290 in Allan Kornberg and Harold D. Clarke, eds., *Political Support in Canada: The Crisis Years*. Durham: Duke University Press.

Lemco, Jonathan, and Peter Regenstrief. 1984. "The Fusion of Powers and the Crisis of Canadian Federalism," *Publius*, 14 (Winter), pp. 109–20.

Levy, Walter J. 1981. "Oil: An Agenda for the 1980s," *Foreign Affairs*, Spring, pp. 1079–1101.

Lewington, Jennifer. 1981. "Consumer Oil Cost More than Triples over Next 5 Years," *Globe and Mail* (Toronto), Sept. 2, p. 1.

Lewis, David K. 1969. *Convention*. Cambridge: Harvard University Press.

Lijphart, Arend. 1977. *Democracy in Plural Societies*. New Haven: Yale University Press.

Lindberg, Leon N., ed. 1977a. *The Energy Syndrome*. Lexington, Mass.: Lexington.

———. 1977b. "Comparing Energy Policies: Political Constraints and the Energy Syndrome," pp. 325–56 in Lindberg, 1977a.

Lopreato, Sally Cook, and Fred Snoller. 1978. "Explaining Energy Votes in the Ninety-Fourth Congress," Center for Energy Studies, University of Texas at Austin, mimeo.

Lowi, Theodore J. 1979. *The End of Liberalism*. 2d ed. New York: W. W. Norton.

Luce, R. Duncan, and Howard Raiffa. 1957. *Games and Decisions*. New York: John Wiley.

Lueck, Thomas J. 1983a. "More Gas Pipeline Units Move to Trim Supplies," New York *Times*, Apr. 6, pp. D1, 7.

———. 1983b. "Pipelines Act to Cut Gas Costs," New York *Times*, May 16, pp. D1, 7.

———. 1983c. "Tenneco Told to Honor High-Priced Gas Pacts," New York *Times*, June 28, pp. D1, 4.

Lyons, Richard L. 1980a. "On Capitol Hill," Washington *Post*, Mar. 25, p. A7.

———. 1980b. "The Left and Right United Against Energy Board," New York *Times*, June 25, pp. D1, 5.

Maass, Arthur. 1951. *Muddy Waters*. Cambridge: Harvard University Press.

Malbin, Michael J. 1983. "Rhetoric and Leadership: A Look Backward at the Carter National Energy Plan," pp. 212–45 in Anthony King, ed., *Both Ends of the Avenue*. Washington, D.C.: American Enterprise Institution.

Malcolm, Andrew H. 1982a. "Calgary Corrals the Bankers," New York *Times*, Jan. 11, pp. D1, 3.

———. 1982b. "Canadian Energy in Flux," New York *Times* International Economic Survey, Feb. 14, p. 48.

———. 1982c. "Canada Tar Sands: Hope and Challenge," New York *Times*, Feb. 15, pp. D1, 2.

———. 1982d. "Energy Revisions Proposed in Canada," New York *Times*, Apr. 9, p. D3.

————. 1981. "Pleasing Both Sides, Court Just Sharpens Canada Crisis," New York *Times*, Oct. 4, p. F4.

Mansbridge, Jane J. 1980. *Beyond Adversary Democracy*. New York: Basic.

Maraniss, David. 1983a. "The Committee: Competing Interests Snarl Gas Debate," Washington *Post*, June 26, pp. A1, 14.

————. 1983b. "Power Play: Chairman's Gavel Crushes Gas Decontrol Vote," Washington *Post*, Nov. 20, pp. A1, 9.

Markus, Gregory B. 1982. "Political Attitudes in an Election Year," *American Political Science Review*, 76 (Sept.), pp. 538–60.

Marmorek, Jan. 1981. *Over a Barrel: A Guide to the Canadian Energy Crisis*. Toronto: Doubleday Canada Ltd.

Martin, Douglas. 1985. "Developing Canadian Oil Sands," New York *Times*, Aug. 27, pp. D1, 7.

————. 1984 "New Interest Found in Canada for Oil Sands Project," New York *Times*, May 28, pp. 33, 35.

————. 1983 "Canada Freezes Prices of Natural Gas and Oil," New York *Times*, July 1, pp. D1, 2.

————. 1981. "Decontrolling Natural Gas," New York *Times*, Aug. 4, p. D2.

Masselli, David Charles, and Norman L. Dean, Jr. 1981. *The Impacts of Synthetic Fuels Development*. Washington, D.C.: National Wildlife Federation.

Matthews, Donald R. 1960. *U.S. Senators and Their World*. Chapel Hill: University of North Carolina Press.

Mayhew, David R. 1974. *Congress: The Electoral Connection*. New Haven: Yale University Press.

————. 1966. *Party Loyalty Among Congressmen*. Cambridge: Harvard University Press.

Mazmanian, Daniel, and Jeanne Nienaber. 1978. *Environmentalism, Participation, and the Corps of Engineers*. Washington, D.C.: Brookings Institution.

McDougall, Gordon H. G., and Gerald Keller. 1981. *Energy: Canadians' Attitudes and Reactions (1975–1980)*. Ottawa: Consumer and Corporate Affairs Canada.

McKelvey, Richard D., and Peter C. Ordeshook. 1984. "An Experimental Study of the Effect of the Procedural Rules on Committee Behavior," *Journal of Politics* 46 (Feb.), pp. 182–205.

McKelvey, Richard D., and William Zavoina. 1975. "A Statistical Model for the Analysis of Ordinal Level Dependent Variables," *Journal of Mathematical Sociology*, 4, pp. 103–30.

McKinsey, Lauren. 1981. "Canada's National Energy Program: The Politics of Federalism." Presented at the Conference on Canada and Mexico: The Comparative and Joint Politics of Energy, Harvard University, Apr. 9–10.

Means, Robert C. 1983. "The Intrastate Pipelines and the Natural Gas Policy Act," pp. 71–107 in Mitchell, 1983.

Michel, Bob. 1984. "Politics in the Age of Television," Washington *Post*, May 20, p. B7.

Miller, Nicholas R. 1983. "Pluralism and Social Choice," *American Political Science Review*, 77 (Sept.), pp. 734–47.

————. 1975. "Logrolling and the Arrow Paradox: A Note," *Public Choice*, 21 (Spring), pp. 107–10.

Miller, Warren E., Arthur H. Miller, and Edward J. Schneider. 1980. *American National Election Studies Data Sourcebook, 1952–1978*. Cambridge: Harvard University Press.

Miller, Warren E., and J. Merrill Shanks. 1981. "Policy Directions and Presidential Leadership: Alternative Interpretations of the 1980 Presidential Election," *British Journal of Political Science*, 12 (July), pp. 299–356.

Miller, Warren E., and Donald E. Stokes. n.d. *Representation in the American Congress*. Ann Arbor: University of Michigan, mimeo, ch. 2.

Milstein, Jeffrey S. 1978. "How Consumers Feel About Energy: Attitudes and Behavior During the Winter and Spring 1976–77," pp. 79–90 in S. Warkov, ed., *Energy Policy in the United States*. New York: Praeger.

————. n.d. "Energy Consumers' Attitudes, Awareness, and Behavior." Unpublished mimeo, U.S. Department of Energy, Office of Conservation and Solar Energy.

Mitchell, Edward J., ed. 1983. *The Deregulation of Natural Gas*. Washington, D.C.: American Enterprise Institute.

Mitchell, Edward J. 1979. "The Basis of Congressional Energy Policy," *Texas Law Review*, 57 (Mar.), pp. 591–613.

Morgenthaler, Eric. 1981. "Shale Oil Has a Future, But It's Still Too Early to Tell How Big a One," *Wall Street Journal*, Aug. 31, pp. 1, 9.

Mosher, Lawrence. 1981. "Reagan and the GOP Are Riding the Sagebrush Rebellion—But for How Long?," *National Journal*, Mar. 21, pp. 476–81.

Murphy, James T. 1974. "Political Parties and the Porkbarrel: Party Conflict and Cooperation in House Public Works Committee Decision-Making," *American Political Science Review*, 68 (Mar.), pp. 169–85.

Murray, Alan. 1983a. "Pressure from Consumers Pushes Congress into Action on Pricing of Natural Gas," *Congressional Quarterly Weekly Report*, Mar. 5, pp. 443–47.

————. 1983b. "Reagan Gas Decontrol Plan Victorious in Test Showdown," *Congressional Quarterly Weekly Report*, Apr. 23, pp. 779–80.

————. 1983c. "Tie Vote in Committee Kills Natural Gas Compromise," *Congressional Quarterly Weekly Report*, May 14, p. 941.

Murray, Francis X., and J. Charles Curran. 1982. *Why They Agreed: A Critique and Analysis of The National Coal Policy Project*. Washington, D.C.: Georgetown University Center for Strategic and International Studies.

National Coal Policy Project. 1982. *The National Coal Policy Project: Final Report*. Washington, D.C.: Georgetown University Center for Strategic and International Studies.

Newsweek. 1982. "The Death of Synfuels." International edition, May 17, pp. 43–44.

New York *Times*. 1984. "Newfoundland Is Denied Hibernia Oilfield Control." Mar. 9, pp. D1, 13.

————. 1983. "House Panel Defeats Natural Gas Rollback." Nov. 18, p. D2.

————. 1982a. "Pullout By Exxon Jolts a Boomtown" Oct. 10, p. 33.

————. 1982b. "BP Canada Plans Sale to Ottawa." Nov. 1, pp. D1, 4.

————. 1974. "Consumers in U.S. Face Competition." Mar. 11, pp. 1, 46.

Niemi, Richard G., and John R. Wright. 1987. "Voting Cycles and the Structure of Individual Preferences," *Social Choice and Welfare*, 4, no. 3, pp. 173–83.

Nivola, Pietro S. 1980. "Energy Policy and the Congress: The Politics of the Natural Gas Policy Act of 1978," *Public Policy*, 28 (Fall), pp. 491–543.

Norrie, Kenneth. 1984. "Energy, Canadian Federalism, and the West,"*Publius*, 14 (Winter), pp. 79–93.

————. 1981. "Canada's National Energy Program: A Call for Perspective," pp. 143–55 in Fry, 1981.

Nutting, Brian. 1983a. "Natural Gas Decontrol Bill Starts Moving in Senate Panel," *Congressional Quarterly Weekly Report*, July 23, p. 1524.

————. 1983b. "Energy Panel Sends Senate Natural Gas Decontrol Bill," *Congressional Quarterly Weekly Report*, July 30, pp. 1549–50.

————. 1983c. "House Natural Gas Measure Faces Fight in Energy Panel," *Congressional Quarterly Weekly Report*, Aug. 6, pp. 1617–18.

————. 1983d. "Natural Gas Pricing Measure Sparks Senate Floor Debate," *Congressional Quarterly Weekly Report*, Nov. 5, pp. 2335, 2338.

————. 1983e. "Senate Rejects Competing Natural Gas Plans," *Congressional Quarterly Weekly Report*, Nov. 19, p. 2460.

Oil and Gas Journal. 1982a. "Division of AAPG Urges Faster Gas Price Deregulation." Jan. 25, p. 90.

————. 1982b. "U.S. Shale Oil Project Delayed; Others Advance." Feb. 4, pp. 171–72.

————. 1982c. "Canadianization Seen Threat to Self-Sufficiency." Feb. 22, p. 68.

Olsen, Marvin E. 1981. "Consumers' Attitudes Toward Energy Conservation," *Journal of Social Issues*, 37, no. 2, pp. 108–31.

Olson, I. M., and Associates. 1984. "Policy Analysis of Current and Future Natural Gas Prices Under the NGPA," reprinted in *Congressional Record* (Daily edition), 98th Congress, 2d session (Oct. 10), pp. H11851–H11854.

Olson, Mancur, Jr. 1969. "The Principle of 'Fiscal Equivalence': The Division of Responsibilities Among Different Levels of Government," *American Economic Review Papers and Proceedings*, 59 (May), pp. 479–87.

————. 1965. *The Logic of Collective Action*. Cambridge: Harvard University Press.

Omang, Joanne. 1982. "The Synthetic Fuels Party Has Gone Flat," Washington *Post*, Feb. 7, p. A16.

————. 1980. "An Uneasy Utah Is Awaiting Massive Energy, MX Projects," Washington *Post* (May 17), pp. A1, 18.

Opinion Research Corporation. 1976a. "Private Individuals' Willingness to Make Energy-Saving Efforts and Their Perception of the Likelihood of Others Doing the Same." Highlight Report, Volume 19. Prepared for the Federal Energy Administration. Washington, D.C.: U.S. Department of Commerce, National Technical Information Service.

————. 1976b. "Public Knowledge, Attitudes and Behavior Relating to Natural Gas Issues." Highlight Report: Volume 20. Prepared for the Federal Energy Administration. Washington, D.C.: U.S. Department of Commerce, National Technical Information Service.

Oppenheimer, Bruce I. 1981. "Congress and the New Obstructionism: Developing an Energy Program," pp. 275–305 in L. C. Dodd and B. I. Oppenheimer, eds., *Congress Reconsidered*, 2d ed. Washington, D.C.: Congressional Quarterly Press.

————. 1980. "Policy Effects of U.S. House Reforms: Decentralization and the Capacity to Resolve Energy Issues," *Legislative Studies Quarterly*, 5 (Feb.), pp. 5–30.

Oppenheimer, Joe A. 1973. "Relating Coalitions of Minorities to the Voters' Paradox." University of Texas, mimeo.

Orr, David W. 1979. "U.S. Energy Policy and the Political Economy of Participation," *Journal of Politics*, 41 (Nov.), pp. 1027–56.

Osterlund, Peter. 1985. "New Rules for Natural Gas: Customer Savings vs. Industry Losses," *Christian Science Monitor*, Nov. 27, pp. 3, 4.

Palmer, Jerald D. 1981. "An Overview of Canada's National Energy Program," pp. 77–95 in Fry, 1981.

Pammett, Jon H. 1986. "Social Class and Vote in Canada." Presented at the Annual Meeting of the Canadian Political Science Association, Winnipeg, Saskatchewan, June.

————. 1984. "Elections," pp. 271–86 in Michael S. Whittington and Glen Williams, eds., *Canadian Politics in the 1980s*, 2d ed. Toronto: Methuen.

Parris, Judith. 1979. "The Senate Reorganizes Its Committees, 1977," *Political Science Quarterly*, 94 (Summer), pp. 319–38.

Pasztor, Andy. 1983. "Synfuels Plant Sees $770 Million Losses by 1995," *Wall Street Journal*, Apr. 11, p. A3.

Pear, Robert. 1986. "Immigration Bill: How 'Corpse' Came Back to Life," New York *Times*, Oct. 13, p. A16.

Pelham, Ann. 1980. "Synthetic Fuels Bill Nearly Ready for Carter," *Congressional Quarterly Weekly Report*, 38 (June 21), pp. 963–66.

Perry, Harry, and Hans H. Landsberg. 1981. "Factors in the Development of a Major U.S. Synthetic Fuels Industry," *Annual Review of Energy*, 6, pp. 233–66.

Peterson, Cass. 1986. "Interior Dept. Seeks to Give Public Land to Energy Firms," Washington *Post*, Aug. 4, p. A3.

Peterson, Iver. 1984. "Cities, Baling at Prices, May Seize Gas Utilities," New York *Times*, Mar. 29, p. A16.

Plattner, Andy. 1983. "Scrappy House Energy Panel Provides High Pressure Arena for Wrangling over Regulation," *Congressional Quarterly Weekly Report*, Mar. 12, pp. 501–8.

Pratt, Larry. 1982. "Energy: The Roots of National Policy," *Studies in Political Economy*, 7 (Winter), pp. 27–59.

————. 1976. *The Tar Sands: Syncrude and the Politics of Oil*. Edmonton, Alberta: Hurtig.

Pressman, Steven. 1983. "Lobbying Free-for-All Opens As Congress Begins Markup of Natural Gas Pricing Bills," *Congressional Quarterly Weekly Report*, Apr. 23, pp. 793–97.

Presthus, Robert. 1973. *Elite Accommodation in Canadian Politics*. Cambridge: Cambridge University Press.

Price, David E. 1972. *Who Makes the Laws?* New York: Schenkman.

Prindle, David E. 1981. *Petroleum Politics and the Texas Railroad Commission*. Austin: University of Texas Press.

Rae, Douglas W. 1967. *The Political Consequences of Electoral Laws*. New Haven: Yale University Press.

Ranney, Austin. 1962. *The Doctrine of Responsible Party Government*. Urbana: University of Illinois Press.

Rapoport, Anatol, and Albert M. Chammah. 1965. *Prisoner's Dilemma*. Ann Arbor: University of Michigan Press.

Rapoport, Anatol, Melvin J. Guyer, and David G. Gordon. 1976. *The 2 x 2 Game*. Ann Arbor: University of Michigan Press.

Rapoport, Anatol, and Carol Orwant. 1962. "Experimental Games: A Review," *Behavioral Science*, 7 (Jan.), pp. 1–37.

Rawls, John. 1971. *A Theory of Justice*. Cambridge: Harvard University Press.

Reistrup, John. 1980. "Trudeau's Unity Effort Faces Showdown in West," *Washington Post*, July 24, p. A14.

Reiter, Howard L. 1985. *Selecting the President*. Philadelphia: University of Pennsylvania Press.

Richards, John, and Larry Pratt. 1979. *Prairie Capitalism: Power and Influence in the New West*. Toronto: McClelland and Stewart.

Riddlesperger, James W., Jr., and James D. King. 1982. "Energy Votes in the United States Senate, 1973–1980," *Journal of Politics*, 44 (Aug.), pp. 822–37.

Riker, William H. 1980. "Implications from the Disequilibrium of Majority Rule for the Study of Institutions," *American Political Science Review*, 74 (June), pp. 432–46.

———. 1958. "The Paradox of Voting and Congressional Rules for Voting on Amendments," *American Political Science Review*, 52 (June), pp. 349–66.

Riker, William H., and Steven J. Brams. 1973. "The Paradox of Vote Trading," *American Political Science Review*, 67 (Dec.), pp. 1235–47.

Rosenbaum, Walter A. 1981. *Energy, Politics and Public Policy*. Washington, D.C.: Congressional Quarterly.

Rosten, Leo. 1970. *The Joys of Yiddish*. New York: Washington Square Press.

Rudolph, Joseph R., Jr. 1983. "Perspectives on the Synfuel Industry: Coal Liquefaction in the United States, the United Kingdom, and the Federal Republic of Germany." Presented at the 1983 Annual Meeting of the American Political Science Association, Chicago, Sept.

Rusk, James. 1981. "Oil Pact Gives Alberta Almost What It Wanted," *Globe and Mail* (Toronto), Sept. 2, p. 5.

Rusk, Jerrold G. 1970. "The Effect of the Australian Ballot Reform on Split Ticket Voting: 1876–1908," *American Political Science Review*, 64 (Dec.), pp. 1220–38.

Rycroft, Robert W., and James E. Monaghan. 1982. "National Security Policy: Synfuels and the MX System," pp. 69–100 in J. W. Regens, R. W. Rycroft, and G. A. Daneke, eds., *Energy and the Western United States*. New York: Praeger.

Salant, Stephen W., and Eban Goodstein. 1987. "Committee Voting Under Alternative Procedures: An Experimental Analysis." Presented at the Carnegie-Mellon Conference on Political Economy, Carnegie-Mellon University, Pittsburgh, Pa., May 1–2.

Salisbury, Robert H., John P. Heinz, Edward O. Laumann, and Robert L. Nelson. 1986. "Who Works with Whom? Patterns of Interest Group Alliance and Opposition." Presented at the Annual Meeting of the American Political Science Association, Washington, D.C., Aug.

Sanders, M. Elizabeth. 1981. *The Regulation of Natural Gas*. Philadelphia: Temple University Press.

Schattschneider, E. E. 1960. *The Semisovereign People*. New York: Holt, Rinehart and Winston.

Schelling, Thomas C. 1979. *Thinking Through the Energy Problem*. New York: Committee for Economic Development.

———. 1978. *Macromotives and Microbehavior*. New York: W. W. Norton.

———. 1960. *The Strategy of Conflict*. Cambridge: Harvard University Press.

Schneider, Judy. 1980. "Multiple Referrals and Jurisdictional Overlaps, House of Representatives, 94th and 95th Congresses," pp. 441–62 in Select Committee on Committees, *Final Report of the Select Committee on Committees*, United States House of Representatives, 96th Congress, 2d session. Washington, D.C.: Government Printing Office.

Schuller, Frank Clayton. 1982. "The Dual Market of NGPA-78: Problems, Prices, and Prospects." Presented at the 1982 Annual Meetings of the American Political Science Association, Denver, Sept.

Schurr, Sam, et al. 1979. *Energy in America's Future*. Baltimore: Johns Hopkins University Press.

Schwartz, Thomas. 1981. "The Universal-Instability Theorem," *Public Choice*, 37, no. 3, pp. 487–501.

———. 1977. "Collective Choice, Separation of Issues and Vote Trading," *American Political Science Review*, 71 (Sept.), pp. 999–1010.

Science and Technology Committee. 1982. *The Socioeconomic Impacts of Synthetic Fuels: Hearing Before the Subcommittee on Energy Development and Applications of the Committee on Science and Technology, U.S. House of Representatives*. 97th Congress, 2d session. Washington, D.C.: Government Printing Office.

Sears, David R., Tom Tyler, Jack Citrin, and Donald R. Kinder. 1978. "Political System Support and Public Response to the Energy Crisis," *American Journal of Political Science*, 22 (Feb.), pp. 56–82.

Select Committee on Committees. 1980a. *Energy Jurisdictions of House Committees: Hearings Before the Select Committee on Committees, United States House of Representatives*. 96th Congress, 1st session. Washington, D.C.: Government Printing Office.

———. 1980b. *Final Report of the Select Committee on Committees*. United States

House of Representatives, 96th Congress, 2d session. Washington, D.C.: Government Printing Office.

―――. 1980c. *Report of the Select Committee on Committees to Establish a Standing Committee on Energy.* 96th Congress, 2d session. Washington, D.C.: Government Printing Office.

Sen, A. K. 1971. "The Impossibility of a Paretian Liberal," *Journal of Political Economy,* Jan./Feb., pp. 152–57.

―――. 1967. "Isolation, Assurance, and the Social Rate of Discount," *Quarterly Journal of Economics,* 81 (Feb.), pp. 112–24.

Shaffer, William R. 1980. *Party and Ideology in the United States Congress.* Lanham, Md.: University Press of America.

Shapiro, Margaret. 1984. "House Slashes Funding for Synfuels Program," Washington *Post,* Aug. 3, p. A2.

Shefter, Martin. 1985. *Political Crisis/Fiscal Crisis.* New York: Basic.

Shepsle, Kenneth A. 1986. "Institutional Equilibrium and Equilibrium Institutions," pp. 51–81 in Herbert F. Weisberg, ed., *Political Science: The Science of Politics.* New York: Agathon.

―――. 1984. "The Congressional Budget Process: Diagnosis, Prescription, Prognosis," pp. 190–237 in W. Thomas Wander, F. Ted Hebert, and Gary W. Copeland, eds., *Congressional Budgeting.* Baltimore: Johns Hopkins University Press.

Shepsle, Kenneth A., and Barry Weingast. 1987. "The Institutional Foundations of Committee Power," *American Political Science Review,* 81 (Mar.), pp. 85–104.

―――. 1984. "When Do Rules of Procedure Matter?," *Journal of Politics,* 46 (Feb.), pp. 206–221.

―――. 1981. "Political Preferences for the Pork Barrel: A Generalization," *American Journal of Political Science,* 25 (Feb.), pp. 96–111.

Simeon, Richard. 1980. "Natural Resource Revenues and Canadian Federalism: A Survey of the Issues," *Canadian Public Policy,* 6 (Feb.), Supplement, pp. 182–91.

Sinclair, Barbara. 1987. "The Transformation of the U.S. Senate—Institutional Consequences of Behavioral Change." Presented at the 1987 Annual Meeting of the Midwest Political Science Association, Chicago, Apr.

―――. 1986. "Senate Styles and Senate Decision-Making," *Journal of Politics,* 48 (Nov.), pp. 877–908.

―――. 1983. *Majority Leadership in the U.S. House.* Baltimore: Johns Hopkins University Press.

―――. 1981. "The Speaker's Task Force in the Post-Reform House of Representatives," *American Political Science Review,* 75 (June), pp. 397–410.

Sinclair, Ward. 1983. "Peppermint Farmers Ask Uncle for a Sweet Deal," Washington *Post,* Mar. 10, p. A17.

Smiley, Donald V. 1984. "Public Sector Politics, Modernization, and Federalism: The Canadian and American Experiences," *Publius,* 14 (Winter), pp. 39–59.

————. 1980. *Canada in Question: Federalism in the Eighties*, 3d ed. Toronto: McGraw-Hill Ryerson.

Smith, David E. 1981. *The Regional Decline of a National Party: Liberals on the Prairies*. Toronto: University of Toronto Press.

————. 1975. *Prairie Liberalism: The Liberal Party in Saskatchewan 1905–71*. Toronto: University of Toronto Press.

Smith, Steven S. 1986a. "Decision-Making on the House Floor." Presented at the Annual Meeting of the American Political Science Association, Washington, Aug.

————. 1986b. "Revolution in the House: Why Don't We Do It on the Floor?" Brookings Institution Discussion Paper in Governmental Studies, no. 5.

Sniderman, Paul M., with Michael Gray Hagen. 1985. *Race and Equality: A Study in American Values*. Chatham, N.J.: Chatham House.

Stanfield, Rochelle L. 1986. "Resolving Disputes," *National Journal*, Nov. 15, pp. 2764–68.

Stevenson, Garth. 1979. *Unfulfilled Union: Canadian Federalism and National Unit*. Toronto: Macmillan of Canada.

————. 1977. "Federalism and the Political Economy of the Canadian State," pp. 71–100 in Leo Panitch, ed., *The Canadian State*. Toronto: University of Toronto Press.

Stewart-Patterson, David. 1985a. "Ottawa Cuts Aid to Firms Drilling for Oil," *Globe and Mail* (Toronto), Oct. 31, pp. A1, 2.

————. 1985b. "Tory Energy Plan Puts End to NEP," *Globe and Mail* (Toronto), Oct. 31, p. B1.

Stobaugh, Robert, and Daniel Yergin, eds. 1983. *Energy Future: Report of the Energy Project of the Harvard Business School*, 3d ed. New York: Vintage.

Stockman, David A. 1978. "The Wrong War? The Case Against a National Energy Policy," *The Public Interest*, 53 (Fall), pp. 3–44.

————. 1975. "The Social Pork Barrel," *The Public Interest*, 39 (Spring), pp. 3–30.

Stokes, Donald E., and Warren E. Miller. 1962. "Party Government and the Saliency of Congress," *Public Opinion Quarterly*, 26 (Winter), pp. 531–46.

Sundquist, James L. 1986. *Constitutional Reform and Effective Government*. Washington, D.C.: Brookings Institution.

————. 1981. *The Decline and Resurgence of Congress*. Washington, D.C.: Brookings Institution.

————. 1967. *Politics and Policy*. Washington, D.C.: Brookings Institution.

Sussman, Barry. 1979. "Poll Finds House Believes Energy Shortage Is Real," Washington *Post*, Nov. 5, pp. A1, 8.

Taylor, Paul. 1982. "In the Pipeline: The Fight over Faster Natural Gas Price Decontrol," Washington *Post*, Jan. 19, p. A4.

Thurow, Lester C. 1979. *The Zero-Sum Society*. New York: Basic.

Tocqueville, Alexis de. 1945. *Democracy in America*, vol. 2. Translated by Henry Reeve; originally published in 1840. New York: Alfred A. Knopf.

Toner, Glen. 1984. "Oil, Gas, and Integration: A Review of Five Major Federal Energy Decisions," pp. 226–47 in Jon H. Pammett and Brian W. Tomlin, eds., *The Integration Question.* Toronto: Addison-Wesley Ltd.

Toner, Glen, and François Bregha. 1984. "The Political Economy of Energy," pp. 105–36 in Michael S. Whittington and Glen Williams, eds., *Canadian Politics in the 1980s.* 2d ed. Toronto: Methuen.

———. 1981. "The Political Economy of Energy," pp. 1–26 in Michael S. Whittington and Glen Williams, eds., *Canadian Politics in the 1980s.* Toronto: Methuen.

Toner, Glen, and G. Bruce Doern. 1986. "The Two Energy Crises and Canadian Oil and Gas Interest Groups: A Re-examination of Berry's Propositions," *Canadian Journal of Political Science,* 19 (Sept.), pp. 467–93.

Tussing, Arlon R., and Connie C. Barlow. 1984. *The Natural Gas Industry.* Cambridge, Mass.: Ballinger.

United Nations. 1984. *Energy Statistics Yearbook 1982.* New York: United Nations Department of International Economic and Social Affairs, Statistical Office.

Uslaner, Eric M. 1989. "Looking Forward and Looking Backward: Prospective and Retrospective Voting in the 1980 Federal Elections in Canada," *British Journal of Political Science,* 19 (Apr.).

———. 1987. "The Decline of Comity in Congress." Presented at the Annual Meetings of the American Politics Group of the Political Studies Association of the United Kingdom (London, Jan.) and the Midwest Political Science Association (Chicago, Apr.).

———. 1981. "Ain't Misbehavin': The Logic of Defensive Issue Voting Strategies in Congressional Elections," *American Politics Quarterly,* 9 (Jan.), pp. 3–22.

———. 1978a. "Procedural Reforms and Policy Incentives in the Contemporary House of Representatives: A Framework for Examining Some Seeming Paradoxes Towards Parties and Leaders." Paper presented at the Annual Meeting of the Midwest Political Science Association, Chicago, Apr.

———. 1978b. "Policy Entrepreneurs and Amateur Democrats in the House of Representatives: Toward a More Party-Oriented Congress?," pp. 105–16 in L. N. Rieselbach, ed., *Legislative Reform.* Lexington, Mass.: Lexington Books.

Uslaner, Eric M., and M. Margaret Conway. 1985. "The Responsible Congressional Electorate: Watergate, the Economy, and Vote Choice in 1974," *American Political Science Review,* 79 (Sept.), pp. 788–803.

Uslaner, Eric M., and J. Ronnie Davis. 1975. "The Paradox of Vote Trading: Effects of Decision Rules and Voting Strategies on Externalities," *American Political Science Review,* 69 (Sept.), pp. 929–42.

Walker, Jack L. 1983. "The Origins and Maintenance of Interest Groups in America," *American Political Science Review,* 77 (June), pp. 390–406.

Washington Post. 1984. "House Moves to Gut Synfuels Corp." July 26, p. A6.

———. 1983. "Gas Decontrol Will Boost Cost, U.S. Study Says." May 21, p. A7.

Weaver, R. Kent. 1984. "Are Parliamentary Systems Better? The Policy Consequences of Political Institutions." Presented at the Annual Meeting of the Association for Public Policy Analysis and Management, New Orleans, Oct. 18–20.

Weaver, Warren. 1979. "Little-Known Mechanics of Energy Nuts-and-Bolts," New York *Times*, Oct. 28, p. 4E.

Weingast, Barry. 1979. "A Rational Choice Perspective on Congressional Norms," *American Journal of Political Science*, 23 (May), pp. 245–62.

Whittington, Les. 1985. "Despite Mulroney's Pledge, Canada's Business Ownership Thrives," Washington *Post*, Aug. 30, p. F4.

Wildavsky, Aaron, and Ellen Tenenbaum. 1981. *The Politics of Mistrust*. Beverly Hills: Sage.

Williams, Robert J. 1981. "Candidate Selection," pp. 86–120 in Howard R. Penniman, ed., *Canada at the Polls, 1979 and 1980*. Washington: American Enterprise Institute.

Wilson, Ernest. 1985. "The Petro-Political Cycle." Ann Arbor: University of Michigan, mimeo.

Wilson, James Q. 1980. "What Can Be Done?" Presented at the Fourth Annual Public Policy Week Conference, American Enterprise Institute, Washington, D.C., Dec.

———. 1973. *Political Organization*. New York: Basic.

Wilson, John. 1983. "On the Dangers of Bickering in a Federal State: Some Reflections on the Failure of the National Party System," pp. 171–222 in Allan Kornberg and Harold D. Clarke, eds., *Political Support in Canada: The Crisis Years*. Durham: Duke University Press.

Wilson, Rick. 1986. "Forward and Backward Agenda Procedures: Committee Experiments on Structurally Induced Equilibrium," *Journal of Politics*, 48 (May), pp. 390–409.

Wilson, Woodrow. 1967. *Congressional Government*. Cleveland: Meridian. Originally published in 1885.

Wolfinger, Raymond E., and Steven J. Rosenstone. 1981. *Who Votes?* New Haven: Yale University Press.

Wren, Christopher H. 1985. "Canada Constitution Looms as Quebec Issue," New York *Times*, Feb. 19, p. A8.

Index